A House
in Sicily

 This Large Print Book carries the
Seal of Approval of N.A.V.H.

A House in Sicily

Daphne Phelps

Thorndike Press • Thorndike, Maine

Published in 2000 by arrangement with Carroll & Graf
Publishing, Inc.

Thorndike Large Print ® Basic Series.

The tree indicium is a trademark of Thorndike Press.

The text of this Large Print edition is unabridged.
Other aspects of the book may vary from the original edition.

Set in 16 pt. Plantin.

Printed in the United States on permanent paper.

Library of Congress Cataloging-in-Publication Data

Phelps, Daphne.
    A house in Sicily / Daphne Phelps.
      p. (large print) cm.
    ISBN 0-7862-2383-9 (lg. print : hc : alk. paper)
    1. Sicily (Italy) — Description and travel. 2. Sicily (Italy)
— Social life and customs. 3. Phelps, Daphne — Homes
and haunts — Italy — Sicily. 4. Large type books. I. Title.
DG864.3 .P53   2000
  945′.8—dc21   99-058235

To Concetta Genio without whose manifold skills, generosity of spirit and steadfast friendship over the years, I would never have been able to save Casa Cuseni.

Acknowlegements

My most appreciative thanks go to Euan Cameron my agent and editor, for his energy and patience, to Jessica Spencer who, with her training in history and her word processor, helped me to get some chronological order into my manuscript; also to Professor Thomas Kilroy of Dublin who long ago gave me invaluable advice in the only lesson on writing I had before I plunged into authorship.

Contents

Acknowledgements. 6

Foreword by Denis Mack Smith . . . 11

Introduction 14

The First Months. 35

The Decision to Stay 61

The Baronessa, Giuliano
and the Rat 67

Problems/I Become a Locandiera. . . 80

A Very Marriageable House 89

Vincenzino. 98

Beppe 110

Concetta 141

Mrs Dylan Thomas 153

The Godfather 158

Social Work in Sicily. 207

Archaeology. 228

Puppets' Godmother. 239

Policemen. 254

Bertrand Russell. 269

Siciliana: A GENEROUS HEART . . . 290

THE ENGLISH WAY 296

THE CRUCIFIX 302

OUR LOCAL VENUS 304

A Generous Aunt 307

Angelo and his Women 312
Henry Faulkner 331
Dogs and Ducks 383
Roald Dahl 402
In Somma 408

Picture acknowlegements

Photographs of Roald Dahl, Tennessee Williams and Caitlin Thomas reproduced by permission of Camera Press Ltd.

The s*alotto, salone* and Brangwyn dining room at Casa Cuseni reproduced by permission of The World of Interiors/Richard Davies. All other photographs reproduced by permission of Daphne Phelps.

The house and garden that he [Robert Kitson] made in Taormina are witness to an engineer's sense of proportion, an artist's love of colour and an architect's instinct for dramatic angularity.

Charles Quest-Ritson in
The English Garden Abroad, 1992

Foreword

Anyone reading this book will quickly realise that the author is a remarkable person with an unusual story to tell. Daphne Phelps has enough curiosity and literary skill to have become a successful novelist had she been so inclined, but instead has chosen to describe real life as seen by a privileged observer in provincial Sicily. At the end of the Second World War, after training as a psychiatric social worker in England, she inherited by chance one of the most beautiful houses in Taormina and has lived there ever since. These few autobiographical sketches will show that in fifty years she has found the key to many arcane secrets of this fascinating island. Hers has been a difficult but wonderful life in a hospitable but often baffling and sometimes frightening part of the world. Every imaginable problem had to be overcome by an inexperienced householder, not only financial difficulties but suspicious local authorities and anonymous denunciations, not to mention incessant and importunate suitors. She

11

nevertheless acquired a deep affection for the country and its people. Always sympathetic, often admiring, sometimes sceptical but never cynical, she also had the fortunate advantage of enjoying the unexpected and finding humour in almost everything.

Much of the humour was provided by a constant stream of foreign visitors when, to make ends meet, she registered Casa Cuseni as a *locanda* or lowly lodging house. Students, professors, artists and directors of national art galleries, all were attracted to Casa Cuseni when they found that, under the shadow of Mount Etna, they could broaden their experience and find answers to many sociological or academic problems. In several short vignettes we are given unconventional portraits of Bertrand Russell, Tennessee Williams, Caitlin Thomas and Roald Dahl. Among many unnamed but important visitors was someone I take to be the writer Jocelyn Brooke, and there are off-stage appearances by Gaylord Hauser and even Greta Garbo. But quite as memorable as these names from the past are individual present-day Sicilians who have left no other memorial and with whose lives the author became casually involved. Few readers will be able to forget her protector, Don Ciccio the local Mafia leader, who was a long way from the stereotype representative of Cosa Nostra.

The inspiration behind this book is a fascination with the whimsicalities of human nature. It will give pleasure to any tourist who knows this magical country, and not only to them.

Denis Mack Smith

Introduction

My strange Sicilian life had its roots at the turn of the century, but I was only born eleven years later. In 1900 Robert Hawthorn Kitson, my mother's brother, arrived in Sicily. He had travelled down through Italy looking for the perfect place to build his house, and when he came to Taormina on the east coast of the island, he was enchanted by its magical beauty and by the overwhelming view of Etna — the highest and most active volcano in Europe. In those days it was still unspoiled and much like the place that Goethe had described ecstatically, over a hundred years previously as 'a stupendous work of Art and Nature'. Robert was twenty-seven years old, strikingly handsome, tall, with piercing blue eyes, high cheekbones and a skin that with southern sun had shed its Yorkshire pallor and taken on a warm bronze colour; his moustache was Edwardian and bushy. He was aware of his good looks and he enjoyed them without being tiresomely vain. His doctors had warned him that, after a second attack of acute rheumatic fever, he should never risk another English winter. His father had recently died leaving him comfortably, but not excessively, well-off. For years his fervent and frustrated ambition had been to devote himself to becoming a painter in watercolours, but after Cambridge, where he had rowed and played tennis for his college as well as obtaining a first-class degree in the Natural Science Tripos (with Geology as a special subject), he had dutifully, as an only son, gone into the Kitson family locomotive engineering business in Leeds. He had actually started to learn the business from the bottom up, rising at 5 a.m. with the labourers. It had been one of the outstanding successes of the English industrial revolution and the family had produced inventors as well as businessmen and politicians. The men of Robert's generation, however, were historians, painters, architects and dons. They felt distaste for industry. Robert's second severe attack of rheumatic fever — the first attack had happened when he fell through the ice as an undergraduate while skating on the Cam to Ely — rescued him from a fate that would have been, for him, worse than death.

Rejoicing in his new-found liberty, Robert cautiously waited to build until he was certain of his choice, and then he bought a 12,000-square-metre site on the hillside that rose precipitously above the small town of Taormina at the top of which the Greeks in the 4th century BC had built their acropolis and later Arabs and Normans their castles. A ridiculously small sum was asked for the site: it lay outside the medieval fortifications on land uncultivated except for a few almond and olive trees. The locals preferred to live within the walls of the town in easy reach of the cafés and shops on the main street. They were astonished that the 'mad Englishman' was prepared to *walk* such a distance to his house — it took less than fifteen minutes from the centre — and was preparing to build, as one of them disdainfully put it, where 'there are nothing but pigs and peasants'.

He was not so mad. For my uncle, the view compensated for any disadvantages such as the relative distance, the precipitous hillside and the absence of water — except for the Greek wells sunk over 2,000 years before to collect the often scarce rain. This would do, he calculated, for irrigation and washing purposes, but for drinking and building water would have to be brought up on the back of a mule or a donkey.

On one side his boundary was a Roman aqueduct. Towering above it was a magnificent limestone rock, rising sheer beside the castle and above the grey-green olive trees and yellow broom bushes. Below lay the compact little town, with its ancient terracotta tiled roofs and houses grouped around churches of different centuries, and every now and then medieval and baroque 'palaces' and fountains. The main street, the Corso, stretched along the line of an old Roman road from the Porta di Messina to the Porta di Catania. Both towns were about fifty kilometres away and had only recently been joined by a railway. The Corso was the nightly setting for the *passeggiata,* when all social classes would walk slowly up and down to meet their friends and to drink, gossip and gamble. At least the men of the working classes did — they kept their women at home.

The view from the chosen site was breathtaking. It stretched down and across to the majestic, isolated, triangular peak of Etna rising straight from the sea; snow-capped for over half the year and at other times riven by streams of red-hot lava, or with great billowing clouds of steam and gases bursting out of its central crater nearly 11,000 feet high. It was a safe distance away and there were several protecting ranges of low hills between it and Taormina. To the south, the view stretched on clear days a hundred kilometres down the east coast of the island, over the Ionian Sea 800 feet below. The climate, if one avoided the scorching suns of July and August, was near perfection with just enough grey cloud to relieve the boredom of perpetual sun and blue. There was never frost, although some snow was said to fall every forty years or so. Rain fell almost entirely in the late autumn and early winter months and in most years was sufficient to keep the valleys green with citrus and other trees and bright with bougainvillaea and wild, subtropical flowers.

Only a few foreigners had discovered this paradise; mass tourism was still years away. Edward VII and the Kaiser had not yet arrived to make Taormina fashionable.

The house which Don Roberto, as he soon became known, designed and built on this stupendous site was of simple classical proportions. It took over three years to build as there was no mechanical aid available of any kind. Photographs show women in skirts almost to the ground with kerchiefs on their heads, apparently doing most of the work along with the mules who brought up water from a fountain below. The men appear mostly to be measuring walls, managing plumb lines, keeping accounts or helping to load huge baskets of earth and rubble on to their women's heads. It seems that only when it came to levering vast rocks out of the hillside with iron bars, which they wielded with great skill, had the men to leave their lighter jobs. But it was also they who, unimpeded by skirts, went up the rickety ladders as slowly the house grew upwards.

Full use was made of local materials: out of the boulders prised from the hill my uncle built the massive outside walls of the house over half a metre thick covered with a golden-yellow stucco; he used local stone, marble, wood and terracotta, delighting in the skills of local artisans handed down from father to son for centuries. There seem to have been no building safety regulations and, *alla Siciliana*, risks were ignored without apparently any major disaster. The rooms were based on cubes and double cubes, with high ceilings designed for coolness, and oak floors for warmth; the walls of the five main bedrooms were whitewashed, as were those of the entrance hall and stairs which were of Carrara marble. On the ground floor was a large *salone* with three French windows, with frames and shutters painted a warm blue, opening on to the terrace and the Etna view seen between columns carved out of the golden stone of Syracuse. The *salotto,* or library, was on one side of it and on the other was the dining room, the only exception to the general simplicity of the structure. It was the creation of Sir Frank Brangwyn, RA: he designed the panelled walls, the round table, the high-backed chairs and the sideboard all in *noce americano* — the lovely rich brown wood of the pecan tree; and he painted frescos above the panelling, of figures in blue, on a warm, light brown wood background with flowers and fruits. The room has been described as the only surviving complete interior designed by Brangwyn at the height of his powers and as a major achievement of the Arts and Crafts movement.

Years later my old friend Jocelyn Brooke was to describe Casa Cuseni and its setting in his book *The Dog at Clambercrown,* thoughtfully disguising both our names:

Taormina may or may not be the most beautiful place in the world: what is certain is that the Villa Aurora is the most delightful house in Taormina. Set on the hillside, high above the town, it was built in the early nineteen-hundreds by Ariadne's uncle, a painter: a plain, unpretentious but roomy house with a broad verandah and a garden ascending in terraces, at the back, nearly as far as the Madonna della Rocca . . . The view from the terrace is stupendous: the town with its jumble of red roofs lies beneath, and below the town, the sea and the narrow peninsula of Naxos; beyond stretches the plain of Catania, and beyond that again, towering above the vast wide-flung landscape, the enormous mass of Mt. Etna.

Don Roberto, with his humanity, generosity, impish sense of humour, his ability to learn Italian rapidly — and also the far more difficult Sicilian dialect that few foreigners attempted — endeared himself to and forged a link with the 'little people', as he referred to them, that was to endure to the end of his life, through peace and two wars, and even during the Fascist period, when he became 'the Enemy'. He detested the constant round of cocktail parties, preferring to meet Sicilians in the evening *passeggiata*, or in the Dopo Lavoro Club.

He was always drawing and painting the people around him, and he was never without a sketchbook in his pocket or hand. He was appointed President of the Hostel for the Aged Poor in the town, the only refuge for impoverished elderly citizens with no devoted families who could take them in, as was the custom in those days when people were willing to make great sacrifices for their parents.

Before the house was finished, he started designing a multi-terraced garden. As far as possible he left the original olive and almond trees, planting orange, lemon and grapefruit trees with flowering shrubs and creepers nearby. Underneath the terrace, in front of the house, he made a vast water storage tank which collected rain water, making it possible to irrigate all the garden below, while the garden above the house was fed by stone tanks above ground linked, one to the other, down the hill and by the deep pool in which he also swam. It was mathematically calculated that, when both pool and moon were full, snow-capped Etna could be seen, reflected in the water between pink columns covered with wisteria. As in the house, he made full use of the local craftsmen's skills; they were still experts in the art of *ciottolato* pebble mosaics and they could still make terracotta jars larger than any potter would manage today. Don Roberto used these pots, decorating many corners of the garden with them and filling them with flowers of all kinds. Not only was his design beautiful, it was also, as befitted one of a family of engineers, very functional.

By 1908 he had established a pattern of life: with Casa Cuseni as his base he would usually spend September to December in Sicily; January to February in North Africa, mainly in Tunisia and Egypt, and, on one occasion, in India; February to June were spent in Sicily, after which he visited England and France. He never missed staying in Venice and Rome on his way back to Sicily, and he managed productive sketching and painting trips to Spain and the Middle East where he collected Persian rugs and pottery. Often he was accompanied by painter friends: Brangwyn, Cecil Hunt and others. This pattern was only interrupted by three wars: that of 1914–18 when he, a very unmilitary figure in uniform, worked for the Italian Red Cross helping troops in Naples; Mussolini's Abyssinian war of 1935 when, for a time, he thought it wise to leave because of sanctions pressed largely by Britain; and the third, in 1940, when to his deep distress he became 'the Enemy'.

That year he stayed dangerously late, hoping to the last that Italy would stay out of Hitler's war. Mussolini was sitting on the fence to see which way things went. Then, with the fall of France the Fascist press changed to attacking the Allies and it was clear that the 'Jackal', as Churchill called him, had decided to join the German conquerors. Heartbroken, Don Roberto knew he must leave. But he found that his passport was missing; he never knew who had stolen it. It meant that he could not fly to Malta as he had intended in a crisis, but had to go to Rome to obtain documents from the British embassy. All trains were being commandeered for troops and, with difficulty, a seat was found for him. He reached Calais just as all traffic on the Channel had stopped and he was sent back to Paris. He came out, he said, on the last plane (but he was given to exaggeration) and was to face his first English winter for forty years.

Immediately he left, his beloved Sicilians, the cook, the gardener and neighbours, organised by Don Carlo Siligato, his old friend, began hiding his treasures.

They could not understand how Don Roberto prized the worn Middle Eastern prayer rugs, the cracked old Persian pottery, his pictures, the 2,000-year-old Hellenistic pieces, and the Foggini bust of a saint, more highly than essential everyday objects such as mattresses, blankets and saucepans. But they saved what they knew was important to him. They were none of them young and the hill to the various hiding places was steep.

After a few days the head of the Fascist police sent for the faithful organiser, Don Carlo: 'You have been denounced anonymously for hiding the enemy's possessions,' he said. It was a terrible moment.

Then, *sotto voce:* 'Can you get everything away before four o'clock tomorrow when I shall *have* to put two men on the gate?'

He, too, was devoted to Don Roberto.

At the end of the war, travel for civilians was strictly limited, and it was only in January 1946 that Don Roberto was able to become the first foreign resident to return to Taormina. The local Mayor had declared to the British authorities that the presence of Signor Kitson was *'indispensabile per la ricostruzione di Taormina'*.

After a journey, of great difficulty, by boat to Naples and then alternately by

25

train and bus — a thousand bridges were said to have been destroyed between Rome and Taormina — he received a triumphal welcome as, one by one, his treasures were produced. At times his Sicilian friends had been near to starvation as their meagre rations had not always been available. They could have sold his treasures to Italians, British, German or American troops and bought food on the black market — he would have understood — but they had remained faithful and were much more certain than he that one day Don Roberto would return to Casa Cuseni. He was then honoured by being made President of the Commission in charge of restoring bombed Taormina — he, who had been an 'enemy' a few months previously. And, once more, he took the Hostel for the Aged Poor under his wing. He presided over it for twenty-five years.

Casa Cuseni had seen three occupations, one Italian and two military — first by the Germans and then by the British. It was damaged, though not seriously, but both money and means to repair it were in short supply owing to government controls, so Robert made just two rooms fit for himself to live in. For the next seventeen months he never left Taormina except to go down to the sea to bathe. He had to walk as the Germans had taken his car. Amazingly, his health resisted his first ever Sicilian summer. He had survived an operation for cancer seventeen years before and a third attack of rheumatic fever in 1909 when doing relief work in appalling conditions after the Messina earthquake in which 80,000 people died. But, now in his seventies, he knew his heart was damaged, and in June 1947 he left to consult a London cardiologist. He stayed in England for three months seeing family and friends as well as his doctor, and visiting art exhibitions.

It was during this period that I came to know him more intimately and I promised to give up whatever I was doing and go out to Sicily as his chief executor. When younger I had always been a trifle scared of him: he was quick and impatient and did not suffer fools gladly. I understood little of his passionate feeling for art and was afraid to show my ignorance. He had often invited me to Casa Cuseni to learn about the problems that I would have to face without his help but, apart from an early visit in 1935, I had been working and was only free each August when he was in England.

The last time I saw him we had a very happy weekend in Sussex in perfect weather. It was then that he suddenly said: 'I've decided to leave Casa Cuseni to you.'

I was speechless. We were both very English and frightened of emotion, so we changed the subject! On thinking it over that night I was sure that 'you' must have meant 'you four' — I had two sisters and a brother.

Less than three weeks later a cable arrived at the Child Guidance Clinic where I was working in Sussex, informing me that my uncle had died the day after his return to Taormina. Shocked, I exclaimed, 'This means that I've got to go to Sicily!'

The unsympathetic psychiatrist with whom I was working said at once, 'I warn you Daphne, people who settle in those out of the way places become very eccentric.'

I had no intention of settling in Taormina; in fact my uncle had told me that it would be impossible. After Italian and British taxes had been paid and legacies to others of the family, my share would be inadequate to run a house like Casa Cuseni and it would have to be sold. His sudden death in September 1947 meant that I had to face the problems on my own. My Italian was almost non-existent; I had never dealt with property before or had any experience of coping with Sicilians.

However, I had had a fairly eventful existence. After Oxford, I had qualified as a psychiatric social worker and then specialised in Child Guidance. I had sailed for the United States during the summer of 1939, intending to visit American clinics. I had hesitated a bit before going but my job was not developing as I had hoped — we were all pioneers in the profession in those days. Besides, the threat of war had hung over us for so long that I suddenly thought: If I lead my life as if war is going to break out next month, I'll be white-haired and never have been anywhere. So I sailed on the *Empress of Britian* on 19 August. Two days later the Russo-German pact was signed. Soon after my voyage the ship, with its first-class dining room decorated by Brangwyn, was at the bottom of the sea. On 3 September war was declared.

I tried to go home, but the British Consul in Boston had never heard of either of my two 'reserved occupations'; these, I had been told, would mean that I would be wanted immediately in case of an emergency. He told me that no women were now being allowed to cross the Atlantic. Already the Germans had sunk the *Athenia* with many women and children on board. He told me that there was a much more important job to be done in the US putting the Allied point of view to the Americans. He never asked me how I was to support myself as a propagandist. All my small savings were immediately blocked in England. I had only a visitor's visa and therefore no right to work. I got around this restriction by going off adventuring for two exciting years, making myself useful to various people who gave me hospitality, and I visited forty-two of the then forty-eight US states. I chauffeured, I translated medical French, I was an au pair, I was a high-class parlourmaid (but much preferred being a 'char'). I saw America as few foreigners have, from many different angles.

Finally, I succeeded in returning home with the help of the American Red Cross. It took twenty-two days in convoy to reach Loch Ewe in Scotland in August 1941. For the next year I worked as part of a Ministry of Home Security team enquiring into the psychological effects of bombing, for offensive and defensive purposes, and the next three in the psychiatric department of the London Hospital in Stepney

dealing with breakdowns and nervous ill-
nesses in war conditions. Then followed
two years in a pioneer Child Guidance service in West Sussex. All this varied experience proved useful, in due course, for
having to deal with Sicilian problems.

After receiving the news of my uncle's
death, I worked on to the end of the year
— one cannot just abandon patients —
struggling in my limited leisure time to
brush up my almost non-existent Italian.
My plan was to go over there, deal with the
legal complexities, sell the house and
return to England. However, at that
period, soon after the war, no one was
allowed to take money abroad without special permission from the Bank of England
and they demanded a very sound reason
before giving consent. My brother and
fellow executor, who was unemployed after
he had left the Indian Civil Service with
the ending of the Empire, had promised to
obtain an allowance for me. Unlike me, he
was used to dealing with administrators
and national banks. Suddenly he phoned:
'I've got a new job and I'm off to Jamaica
in half an hour. You'll have to tackle the
Bank yourself. Phone them! Goodbye!'

Phone the Bank of England? It would
never have entered my head. Surprisingly

there it was in the directory, in small print, just beneath the Bank of China — in heavy important black. Daringly I dialled, not knowing what to expect. I put my request at once, only to be met with: 'No, of course the Bank cannot countenance any such thing. We'd all enjoy a holiday in Sicily.' (Everyone was suffering from post-war gloom and weary of being cooped up in England under austerity conditions.)

With yet more daring, I protested, to be met with: 'It's quite out of the question. We can't have questions asked in the House about why we allowed Miss Phelps a holiday in Sicily.'

Nervously I persisted: 'I very much doubt if it'll be much of a holiday. It would be the fulfilment of a solemn promise given to my uncle years ago. He knew that a member of the family after his death would *have* to go out to deal with the many problems that would arise.'

Again, 'No.'

'But I've given up my job to be free to go.'

'It's no use.' But the voice did not ring off.

Almost defeated, I asked the Bank what it suggested I should do.

It replied: 'Leave it to your lawyer.'

With all due respect, I asked, had the Bank ever met a Sicilian lawyer? It admitted that it hadn't. 'Well neither have I, but I rather think you *don't* leave them to do things on their own.'

There was a moment's silence, then the Bank actually laughed — and gave me the right to a businessman's allowance for a fortnight. The first hurdle was cleared. £140! Fortunately, businessmen do themselves well, and I and a friend were to live for four months on this sum.

The next problem was that we never found a will referring to Casa Cuseni, which had been my uncle's largest asset. There was an English will in the hands of his solicitor in which the *residue* was left to his sister, my aunt. Probably he had intended to make one, leaving the house to me, once back in Sicily, but his death was so sudden that he had no time. So Casa Cuseni became part of the residue and due to my aunt.

Aunt Beatrice was a remarkable woman. Comfortably off, she had lived in my grandmother's huge house while devoting herself to voluntary work. She was one of the first women magistrates in England and was appointed the first woman Lord Mayor of Leeds, our fifth city, in 1943. For years she confronted Yorkshire criminals without blanching, but she would have been at a loss if she had had to face one hand-kissing Sicilian flatterer, and she was thankful that I was prepared to undertake the whole business for her. In time I was to be thankful that she was in the background, and had she not existed I would have had to invent her. I would find myself saying, when I had to get an unpopular decision accepted, 'The Signorina Padrone is a very strong-minded woman and we all have to do what she commands.' In fact she never interfered and loyally backed me up.

And so I was launched on my Sicilian adventure which up till now has lasted not a fortnight but over half a century.

The First Months

We left Victoria in a cold grey drizzle in the first week of February 1948. My companion was Eve Gibbs and I could not have been more fortunate. She was convalescent after an illness and had been advised to have a complete break. To Sicilian men who had not met professional women she would seem a dark-eyed beauty and little more. In fact she had been the only woman on a business efficiency team sent to the US after the war to get up to date with staff management and other business affairs. She had also been head of training in the huge John Lewis Partnership. The only disadvantage was that she had no Italian, and I little more.

At Calais it was still pouring. It never stopped raining until we left Switzerland and found blue sky and dazzling sun as we emerged from the tunnel under the Alps. Italians looked shabby, hungry and pale; they had had a hard war. Not so the sleeper attendant who said that he'd left us to the last 'because with your beautiful smiles you would not be angry'. He regaled us with risque stories of other passengers and showed every sign of wishing to spend the night with us. But we were firm: it was our first encounter with the Italian *pappagallo*. On the next train after Rome we each received the first of many proposals of marriage. Foreign women were all considered rich and they were then few and far between. It was always worth trying.

I slept with my precious documents, prepared by the Italian legal attaché in London, under my pillow. Without them I could not even have entered Casa Cuseni. The train divided at the Straits and one by one the pieces were shunted on to the ferry for Messina in Sicily. At Messina I changed into my deepest black. It was only five months since my uncle's death and I had never worn mourning. But I was thankful I had changed in time. To have appeared in ordinary clothes would have led to disaster at the very beginning. I would have shocked everyone profoundly. Five years was considered by most to be the correct mourning for an uncle, ten for a parent and the rest of one's life for a spouse. Few women after their twenties were out of black.

Never shall I forget the sensation of our arrival in Sicily. The sky was the bluest of blues; on one side of the train the sea was sparkling, to the other were mountains, and orange and lemon groves. The sun was dazzling. It was *hot*. Nowadays, it must be difficult for people who have always been free to travel to realise the sheer exhilaration and sense of liberation we felt after so many years of being boxed up in England, in war conditions, with the phrase 'Is your journey really necessary?' constantly ringing in our ears. We dashed in amazement from one side of the carriage to the other, it was almost too much after the years of war and drabness.

At Taormina we were met by Don Carlo, my uncle's old and faithful friend, who gave us lunch in his family's hotel. After the meal, which was lavish compared with what was legally permitted in England, we went to the magistrate's office with my documents. He stamped them and sent an official to Casa Cuseni with us to help me break the seals which had been placed on all doors by the British Consul and the town council immediately after my uncle's funeral. They were not a defence against burglars, simply bits of tape (stamped with a seal at either end) stretched across the openings and were meant to show the family that no one had passed through since my uncle's death. Only I had the right to break them.

At the gate was a small crowd of retainers and their families all in deepest black. One by one they kissed my hand. Buneri, the gardener, with over thirty-five years of service, was silent and sad. Clearly he had worked steadily before my arrival; the garden was overflowing with freesias, cinerarias, roses, stocks, star of the Veldt, even petunias, and above it all were almond trees in full bloom. The scent was overwhelming under the warm spring sunshine. Turiddu, manservant and chauffeur, with only thirty years, was as ebullient and self-important as I had remembered him, repeatedly stressing his (questionable) devotion to my family. Don Carlo had mercifully brought an English-speaking nephew with him, who had once been a liaison officer with the RAF. Turiddu was distressingly graphic in his description of how he had found my uncle dead in bed. He looked fat and prosperous, but his wife and children had clearly suffered hunger during the war.

Maria, the cook, who had worked for my uncle for forty-seven years, ever since she was sixteen, was not to be seen. She had watched the house and garden being slowly created and had become a legend in our family. I found her waiting with dignity, tears streaming down her face, on the terrace in front of the house. Her welcome was cool as she kissed my hand. She had expected me, she said, to be my elder sister; I had only been there once before, whereas my sister had been a guest more often, more recently. Many women will work happily for a man, but hate being 'under' a woman. I was to bless my psychiatric training; while I became nominally mistress of the house, I left her in undisputed charge of the kitchen quarters. I never crossed their threshold until one day, after three months, she invited me in; the next day she spoke Sicilian to me as she had always with Don Roberto. I knew the battle was won.

Maria was an illiterate peasant, a stout, elephantine figure with alarmingly swollen legs supporting her huge body. Her wits were very much about her and, had she wanted to, she could have made my Cuseni life a burden. She had worshipped Don Roberto. He had been by far the most important man in her life. One day when she had worked for him a mere thirty years, breakfast, usually at 8 a.m., was a few minutes late and Maria, surprisingly, was in her best clothes. 'Maria, why the finery?' Nervously she replied, 'Signore, I was married this morning.' Then hastily, 'But I arranged it at a time least inconvenient for you.' My uncle was furious: it was not at all convenient — he should have been consulted. But the wily Maria knew that, had she consulted him, she would never have been married; consent would never have been given. It turned out that her husband was her cousin who, in need of a housekeeper after his mother had died, had married to settle a boundary dispute. Maria continued in Casa Cuseni while Don Leo, her husband, was sent to the country to guard and tend her mountain property; he lived with her only when Don Roberto was away and the two were invaluable caretakers at Casa Cuseni — a splendid arrangement for all.

Buneri, the gardener, was as thin as Maria was bulky. He too was illiterate. He was a gentle, undemanding soul; a peasant deeply attached to his family, his small mountain property and his beloved garden. Sadly, he was slowly going blind. The contrast with Maria was great: during the war, unlike her, he had worked steadily for the

Italians, and then for the Germans and finally the British, occupying Casa Cuseni, while Maria — who had made no secret of her feeling for Don Roberto — was suspected as an enemy sympathising with the Allies. Thus the Germans had turned her out for three long years. Buneri had no difficulty in transferring his devotion to me.

Turiddu was very different from the other two. He had been one of the first Fascists in Taormina — attracted, childlike, to the bands and flags — but the bottom of his world had fallen out when it looked as if he might have to go and fight in Abyssinia. He hastily obtained a medical certificate: not a difficult feat if you knew the right people. One of our problems with him was that he knew so much more about Sicilian life than we did and he mistook this for general male superiority. My Italian was only fractionally better than Eve's. He, who had never tackled a foreign language, was quite ignorant of the difficulties of learning one when we were so preoccupied with other problems. Like most Sicilians he had never met professional women — they barely existed in Sicily in 1948 — and he did not expect us to have minds of our own. Alas, he was not suited to being a woman's servant. Don

Roberto had put up with him because he was amused by his histrionic outrageousness, and touched by his dog-like devotion until he gradually absorbed Mussolini's denunciations of the English. 'If you feel like that about the English,' my exasperated uncle would exclaim, 'you shouldn't be working for an Englishman. You're fired!' This after twenty-five years' service. Shaken and absent for a day or two, Turiddu would return contrite, and almost apologetic, until the next outburst and dismissal. It was a kind of game they played, but not one that I could manage.

It was owing to everyone's devotion to Don Roberto that I got into the house my very first day — a feat declared impossible by a leading English resident who had suggested that we would have to spend a night in the luxury hotel, the San Domenico. This would have cost half our exiguous allowance!

That evening a recovered Maria turned out the unused kitchen and served a five-course dinner, while Turiddu and his wife prepared the bedrooms that had once been my grandmother's and her lady's maid's. Meanwhile I had to sign many documents to take personal responsibility for the house and its contents. Several people whom I didn't recognise told me that Don Roberto had always considered their son, daughter or other relation as his adopted niece or nephew. Their eye was clearly on the main chance as they hoped to ingratiate themselves with me by kissing me on both cheeks. They didn't.

As I had guessed, and told the Bank of England, the next few months were far from a holiday: they were filled with weariness and confusion and involved long hours of exhausting concentration while dealing with complicated legal problems with my feeble Italian. I struggled to understand what my lawyer and the notary said (the latter, a rather worn old man, had to be addressed as *Magnifico*), striving not to say 'Yes' when I meant 'No', and above all trying to avoid signing my name in the wrong place.

'You may trust people if you like — it is better not to,' said Don Carlo ominously. By now he was calling himself my uncle.

Later I was to be proffered blank pages and asked to sign. I told them that my father was a lawyer and that, from earliest years, he had warned me *never* to sign anything before reading it. My lawyer was chosen by Don Carlo who told me he was very rich, the most eligible bachelor in Taormina, and certain to be the next judge. He was in deepest, blackest mourning for an uncle who had died about the same time as mine, but I was dressed in colours again, having, we hoped, persuaded them that we thought that mourning was felt inside and not shown by clothes. The general gloom of the lawyer's appearance was accentuated by coal black hair, eyes and moustache.

He bowed to me, kissed my hand and announced, 'Signorina, were I not like this,' with a wide gesture of his hands, 'I would ask you to come out with me.'

It was a lucky escape, I felt.

Five witnesses came to the house, gave their names, those of their fathers and their dates of birth, and were then prepared, it seemed, to swear that black was white — or to anything that they felt would be in my interest — which was fortunate. I asked Eve to disguise her presence as far as possible (she was far too attractive for that, especially among a group of Sicilian men) and just sit watching their faces and gestures, whilst I would try to concentrate on the language and avoid taking any drastic decision until she and I had had time to compare notes.

A serious difficulty was that the manager of the Bank of Sicily refused to accept my documents. These should have given access to the money my uncle had thoughtfully left in his account, assuming that I would be able to draw on it at once. First the manager insisted that a special stamp was missing; then a signature from Rome had to be procured; then a seal from London, and so on and on. It was some time before I discovered that the rogue wanted to buy the front garden to build himself a house on a site by now considered almost central. He calculated that if he kept me short of cash I would have to sell at a bargain price. He also tried to buy some of my uncle's pictures at rock bottom prices. I let him have one as a sweetener, but it was of little use. The blocking continued.

Slowly we proved the validity of my uncle's English will and the power of attorney my aunt had given me to act in her name. Curiously enough I then became her *procuratrice*. I had thought that a simple thing to start with would have been to get house and contents valued; my English lawyer had asked for this as soon as possible. I was told that there was no such thing as a valuer, honest or no. This seemed odd, but I couldn't shake them. What then should I do?

'You could ask the cabinet-maker to do it.'

I didn't think that the English probate authorities would accept his valuation of pictures, ceramics and other antiques. But they *had* to.

The cabinet-maker's estimate came, in all, to a derisory £500. But when the lawyer looked at it he exclaimed, 'You *can't* send that, you'll be ruined!' And he reduced the figure to £250.

I found myself in the absurd position of trying to push the figure up against him: 'Don't you see, *Avvocato,* that if we want to take things to England the Customs officials there will be strict. We *must* state a reasonable sum.' I knew that valuations for probate were kept low, but even so, £250 could hardly have been accepted. In the end when, months later, I decided that I *might* be able to stay and so keep possessions here, the problem disappeared, but not before I had succeeded in getting the figure raised once more to £500!

The possibility that Don Roberto's insurance policies might have run out was an alarming one, and if they had, I couldn't imagine how I could pay the premiums in view of the present lack of cash. I asked Don Carlo where they were.

'There aren't any,' he answered.

'It can't be true. Don Roberto was English, a Yorkshireman at that. Of *course* he was insured. Everyone is insured.'

'He never was.'

It hardly seemed possible, but I had to accept his word. However, on going through papers I found three large insurance policies covering everything.

I produced them triumphantly: 'There, I knew it!'

'Look at the dates, Signorina.'

I did. It was incredible. They were for 1941, 1942 and 1943, the time when the Germans were in occupation. With teutonic thoroughness they had overlooked nothing. They didn't know what the Englishman had discovered many years before: that one could pay as many instalments as one liked but that getting a claim paid by an Italian company was lengthy, expensive and very uncertain. So he had decided to shoulder the risk himself, like most Sicilians. Despite my original amazement I have followed Don Roberto's example and so far — I touch wood as *we* do and iron as *Italians* do — I have not regretted it. A friend suggested that when the Germans took out the policies they were so sure of winning the war that they thought they were protecting what they already regarded as their own property.

The struggle to learn the language was wearing, when study necessarily took place after long days of dealing with endless kind visitors who felt it their duty to welcome my uncle's niece. Brief visits, they evidently felt, would hardly have been polite, so they would stay and stay until my head was reeling.

At last they would say 'Signorina, it is time for me to *togliere il disturbo* and leave.' To which I was instructed that it was up to me to reply: 'No disturbance, I assure you, Signore, but a great pleasure.'

This invariably had the effect of making them remain. I wilted.

In addition to making an inventory of all the possessions and cataloguing the books, I had to learn how to manage property (war-damaged at that), something completely new to me; and to control a full-time staff of three. They were paid what seemed to me a pittance, but my uncle had given each of them a house.

I was soon to learn the strength of Sicilian jealousy. My aunt had generously said that her brother's clothes should be distributed among the staff, although with rationing in England still severe, my brother and brother-in-law would have been glad if some had come their way. I had thought that my carefully considered division would have been accepted. Not a bit!

Each one eyed the pile given to the others, then: 'Signorina, I wanted a raincoat for my husband, you've given me a suit.'

Or, 'I wanted the long johns he always gave me.'

'What about warm pyjamas?'

It was a shock after English reticence.

At least there was one major problem I thought I should not have to tackle: finding a buyer for the house. Within a day or two of the news of my uncle's death reaching England, Viscount Bridport, who was also the Duca di Bronte (the bilateral descendant of Lord Nelson through his sister), was on my doorstep in London. The title of Duca had been given to Nelson, together with a vast estate on the foothills of Etna, in return for his nefarious work propping up reactionary Bourbons.

'We've always wanted that house, it's the most beautiful in Taormina. Please will you promise to give me the first refusal?'

If we *had* to sell, as my uncle had declared, then the blow would be slightly softened if a member of the Nelson family bought it, one who appreciated the house's beauty and who had known my uncle.

In 1947 the future of Italy was uncertain. The whole world was watching, hoping or fearing, according to the observer's political views, that she might become Communist. Togliatti, the leftist leader, was apparently close to Stalin and was often in Moscow. The Communist world then seemed a monolithic organisation and the Cold War was raging. Rumour had it that if the extreme left came to power then the US and its allies would try to hold the north as far as Rome and let the south go. Whether true or not, such theories did not encourage foreigners to invest in property in Sicily. It was therefore reasonable for the Duca to ask me to wait for a final decision until after the elections to be held in April 1948, and I agreed.

When, a few months later, I arrived back in Taormina from London, it seemed as if the whole town knew that the Duca was to be the next owner. He had a cousin staying in the town who, it appeared, had been asked to keep an eye on me. If there were any rumours that I had entertained pos-

50

sible buyers, she would be up at once assuring me that the Duca was serious about the deal.

Had the Communists won in April the only possible buyers would have been appalling *nouveau riche* types: vulgar, fat men of dubious origin, but almost certainly connected with the Mafia, then increasing its hold on Sicily. Two or three of these came up to the house with the manager of the San Domenico hotel where the Kaiser and Edward VII had stayed in the early years of the century, though *not* at the same time. This was one of the very few hotels then open and the Duca, a rich man in Sicily (but a poor one in England), always stayed there — a fact that was going to acquire considerable significance for me later. The manager clearly wished to claim a commission due by law to the person who introduced seller to buyer in property deals. I was delighted that I was able to tell him and his friends that the house was not for sale.

One looked disappointed: 'We would like to see over it.'

'Signore, I hoped you had understood that it is not for sale.'

'Then you are throwing us out?'

'Yes, if you put it like that, I am! And

now Signor Direttore, I have an appointment. Please leave.'

I may have made unpleasant enemies like this, so I was grateful to the Duca for the protection afforded by his intention to buy.

When the time came, the Catholic Church exerted all its power, particularly over the women who were then to vote for the first time, and after a violent election the result was a landslide for the Christian Democrats (and indirectly the Mafia). The party and its allies were to govern Italy for the next forty years or so.

The Duca had discussed with my brother in London the matter of price and, equally important, as we both wanted sterling, the amount to be paid in either currency. It had been agreed that the Duca should give me his decision before midnight on 23 April. He arrived at Casa Cuseni at five o'clock and insisted on seeing over the whole house, insensitive to my feelings of imminent loss as he decided that he would add an extra bathroom here, and a washbasin there, and change the colours of the walls.

If it was painful for me, it was far worse for poor Maria who had known and loved the house from the laying of the first stone;

the whole place was bound up with the memory of her adored Don Roberto. Hoping to spare her, I suggested that the Duca needn't inspect her kitchen. But he insisted that he wished to see everything. She was dignified; she kissed the Duca's hand and called him *Eccellenza*. Then she stood, arms akimbo, with her back to her larder — at least one bit should be kept from him for the present.

Buneri had tears in his eyes but he too kissed hands.

Suddenly in rushed Turiddu. Entirely out of character he had somehow got left behind. '*Eccellenza,* welcome, welcome!' There was no doubt about *his* intention to get in with the new lot . . .

The Duca, saying he had an appointment at six, suggested that there was no need for him to look over the garden — he knew it so well. On the contrary, I replied, it was important that we should discuss the boundary. My aunt, now the owner, had agreed that we should keep some of the land above Casa Cuseni and, with the money that we could not take out of Italy, build a small house for the family to visit from time to time. The Duca said he must leave: would I agree to him postponing his final decision until the next morning when he would come up at ten o'clock? Of course I agreed.

The 23rd of April is the day sacred to San Giorgio, the patron saint of England and of Castelmola, the small hilltop village above Taormina where the saint is deeply revered. My uncle never missed a *festa*. He was admired as much in the village as he was in Taormina. When the saint on a magnificent white stallion had had to be repainted, the townsfolk wouldn't pay the painter until Don Roberto had inspected the work and declared, 'It is well done — he merits.'

When, after the war, the village had received a small grant from the government and they were asked what they would like to spend it on — either a water supply or the restoration of the twelfth-century church of San Giorgio — they voted and San Giorgio won. I rather think that the women who had to carry all the water up on their heads were not allowed to vote . . .

After leaving us that evening, the Duca drove up to Castelmola in his Rolls Bentley and we, with scarves on our heads, walked up the steep, rough mountain path with Buneri and Turiddu. The evening before, the saint had been moved in procession from his church to the modern

Duomo which left more room for the devotion of the people. There he was, on his horse, with little Santa Margherita praying on her knees by the horse's feet while the ferocious dragon threatened her. (We saw with amusement that the stone commemorating the Emperor Constantine's visit in the fourth century had been translated from the Greek and the date of the great converter to Christianity changed to three hundred years before the birth of Christ — BC instead of AD.)

The ducal party, dressed in Scottish tweeds as for a point-to-point, were sitting on the only fair-sized balcony overlooking the Piazza. The Duca spotted us and graciously invited Eve and me to sit with them. I declined, saying that I had promised to go round with the procession as Don Roberto had always done (though he would have been sketching the wonderful figures and faces).

I was glad that I had done so because suddenly a man detached himself from the crowd and shouted: 'Don Roberto is dead, but we have his representative still with us!' I had thought that no one knew who I was.

After midnight we walked back down the rugged path to Casa Cuseni.

The next morning the Duca arrived punctually at ten. We shook hands and then he said briefly and abruptly, 'I'm not buying. I hope I haven't upset you too much?'

It was an appalling blow: one moment I was going to have millions of lire and the next none. I would not be able to pay the staff, nor my uncle's legacies, nor even be able to stay on while I searched for another buyer. Had he struck me twice in the face he could not have shaken me more, but I amazed myself: my public school training had so conditioned me that I never blinked an eyelid until he left us alone. I was shattered. He had taken seven months to come to this decision, when we could have been seeking other buyers. Yesterday he was buying, we both felt certain. Whatever had happened to change his mind?

Don Carlo was equally amazed. We searched for reasons: was it that I had refused to sit with him at the *festa*, or that I had not congratulated the Duchess on the recent birth of a son and heir?

'The Duca,' I said, 'is a British naval officer, *not* a Sicilian. He would certainly not have allowed these minor slights, if slights they were, to interfere with a wish to own Casa Cuseni, which had been in his mind for so long.' It seemed to me that his lack of any explanation was neither British nor naval.

It was Don Carlo's nephew who produced a possible solution. This deal had been fixed in England where no commission would have been paid to the fixer. In Taormina for years property sales had been few and far between. People wanted money; this deal did not please them and they stopped it.

'But who and when? I know exactly where the Duca was last night — at Castelmola and he stayed late. Who could have changed his mind, and how?'

'They would have threatened to destroy his fruit orchard from which he derives his wealth, or they would have told him that Casa Cuseni was not a good buy, its foundations had been damaged by bombs — they would have found any reason to put him off.'

It sounded very *mafioso*, but the nephew was probably right. It would also have explained the Duca's silence and failure to give a reason for this extraordinary behaviour. Perhaps the insulted San Domenico manager had played his part?

We were now right back to the beginning. I desperately hoped that we could avoid selling that much-loved house to one of the vulgarians who had wanted it. The immediate and more pressing problem was that we could not stay on with no money. Eve and I rapidly divided the furniture into three groups, putting sticky labels on to each piece: the first lot was to be sold; the second to be sent, when possible, to England; and the third, labelled *Casetta,* to be kept for the little house we *might* some day build above. At that time I had not the slightest idea of the great value of much of the furniture, but I was determined that it should not be sold for the pittance offered by the local antique dealers.

We could not possibly keep on three full-time staff. It was essential that the house should be occupied to guard against burglars, and we couldn't, if we were going to sell, neglect the garden. Growth and decay are rapid in Sicily, and watering a necessity. Besides, both Maria and Buneri had had longer periods of service and shown their steady devotion — in contrast to Turiddu's rather chequered career. It was clear that he would have to be the one to go, especially as we should need neither a *cameriere* (general manservant) nor a chauffeur. I consulted my lawyer who said he thought a man should do the dismissal, but I felt that I, as a member of the family and as my aunt's *procuratrice,* should do it.

I sat on the splendid baroque throne, that had once belonged to a bishop, and summoned Turiddu to the *salone.* I broke the bad news as kindly as I could.

At once he began shouting and screaming, flailing his arms around: 'Thrown to the door like a dog after thirty years of devoted service! I shall sue!'

I wish I had followed my lawyer's advice. The next days were horrible. Turiddu insisted on waiting at table, but instead of his usual garrulity, he placed himself silently right behind my chair; I seemed to feel his blazing eyes boring through my back. He had been lent a gun by Don Carlo, 'to protect the Signorina with', but I feared he might turn it on me. I assured him that in due course he would be paid all that the law prescribed, but he would have to wait like the others until I could get possession of the money — and I reminded him that my uncle had given him a house. I had to call the lawyer in. He, as a man and a Sicilian, would stand no nonsense and I almost felt sorry for the monstrous Turiddu.

Eve and I left for England in early May, thinking it quite possible that we might never see Casa Cuseni again.

'We haven't accomplished *anything* we came out to do,' I said, in despair.

'Yes, but we still stand possessed of everything we found,' said Eve, 'and that's no mean feat.'

She was wrong, but I only discovered it years later.

The Decision to Stay

We returned to a London still in the grip of post-war austerity. I decided that I would try to keep myself free from any but temporary work until I had dealt with the sale of Casa Cuseni. Almost immediately, I heard from the Ministry of Education that I had been recommended for a post organising social psychiatric help for British families, based in Germany with the army of occupation. Germany or Sicily? One could hardly imagine a greater contrast — the defeated, bitter sullenness of the one and the warmth and friendliness of the other. However, still feeling perhaps irrational guilt at having sat out the blitz in California, I felt I had a duty to learn more about what I would be expected to do before making up my mind.

I decided — I like to think on good grounds — that I would refuse, as I did not think that lecturing to audiences of anxious parents would be much help. They would tend to extract from what was said, whatever fitted with their own preconceived ideas. I would much have preferred contact with small discussion groups who could then, themselves, spread ideas to others. In a very small way this is what I have tried to do in Sicily: that is, to sow seeds.

The first World Congress on Mental Health, with over 2,000 members, was being held in London that summer. At it I met my old director of Child Guidance, Dr Kate Friedlander. She had promised earlier that, whenever I wished to return after my Sicilian absence, there would always be a post for me in her team. To my surprised concern, she scarcely seemed to remember me any longer. Months later I was to learn that lung cancer (she was a chain smoker, but in those days the link had not been recognised) had already spread to her brain. It caused her death soon after the Congress.

In retrospect, my decision to leave my profession was made that much easier by Kate's death. I could not imagine that anyone else could have been so exhilarating a director and so inspiring a teacher.

In 1949 the government had at last granted a tourist allowance of £35 a year. With my aunt's agreement, I suggested to various friends, mostly writers and painters who could work anywhere and who had the same allowance, that we might pool our £35 and go and live in the beautiful house until the money gave out, or it was sold. And that was how it all started. Soon I saw a glimmer of hope that Casa Cuseni *might* be saved for us. My brother, and fellow executor, was still advertising the house in London, New York and Paris, but no buyers appeared — the political situation in Italy was still too dicey. I had relinquished any idea of finding a suitable Italian buyer. So in the meantime, I decided that I would enjoy the house while it was still ours.

By good fortune, Julian Trevelyan, the painter, whose family had had long-standing links with Taormina where his parents had met at the house of his cousin Florence Trevelyan (the first English resident there in the late nineteenth century), had just heard of my tentative plans, on a rainy day in London, when he stopped to give a lift to two painter friends. He told them about Casa Cuseni. They immediately got in touch with me, and in the early spring of 1949 came to join me out there. Shortly afterwards Julian, Mary Fedden and her cousin Biddy Cook also arrived, in Julian's old Hillman.

The six of us lived very simply. On 8

March we awoke to find snow, several inches deep. The sun was already melting it. 'Quick!' I suggested. 'Paint it! They say this only happens once in forty years. You could sell and earn.' They did, and our possible stay in the house was prolonged. More currency arrived with other friends. Then, at long last, I was given access to my uncle's money from the bank.

Still wondering how I should do what my uncle had declared was an impossibility, since, as he had said, a house like Casa Cuseni eats money, I enquired about an endowment fund that might enable me to turn it into a centre for writers and painters, such as I had seen in the US. But with that first year's guests I found that this was happening spontaneously. I began to think that I could possibly make both ends meet with paying guests, and so keep the control of the house in my own hands instead of having to be responsible to a committee.

Nevertheless, this was rather a leap into the unknown and Sicily's reputation was not reassuring. My uncle had risked it in a very different world; he was well off, I wasn't. But I had always been a bit of a maverick, enjoying the unexpected, and Sicily was sure to provide that. A regular, steady life would have bored me. I carefully considered the pros and cons: I should miss London life, museums, theatres, concerts, the relative sanity of British democratic and legal systems. I might cut myself off from my large and growing family, my friends and my profession. But I would have all the varied richness of Sicily: history, archaeology, volcanology, folklore, botany and so on — and, above all, that superb climate and that magical house.

I began to consider principles to guide me on this uncharted adventure. First, never, under any circumstances, should I get into debt once the staff and legacies had been paid. I would make Sicilians realise that I was precise and accurate in financial dealings with them, unlike so many of the rich, and that I would keep my word. Secondly, I would never raise a mortgage on the property; I had ready seen how disastrous this could be. Conversely, I would never lend to anyone: it would be much wiser to give, if at all possible, although opportunities for that would probably not be great. A Phelps cousin, curiously enough also living in Taormina, had warned me: '*Everyone*, the Mayor, the archpriest, the neighbours have all touched me for a loan. I always say no. "But you are a very rich man," they say. "Yes, and do you know why? Because I have always said no to people like you!" ' Lastly, I must never marry an Italian. At that time — the law has since been changed — the whole of a woman's property, including her children, belonged to her husband. The modern Italian wife now enjoys all the advantages of the British one, and perhaps more.

Even then I felt glad that I was not abandoning my country because I disliked it, or disapproved of developments there. I still feel profoundly English, as did my uncle. Sun and idleness do not make for happiness in the long run: he had his painting and his deep interest in the welfare of the townspeople; I was to be, at various times, cook, gardener, upholsterer, typist, electrician, house painter, plumber, interpreter and guide, through sheer necessity and lack of cash. Above all I was hostess to very varied guests, many of whom helped me with their different expertises. I had a great deal to learn.

The Baronessa, Giuliano and the Rat

In order to pay death duties I had reluctantly to let the whole house for several months. This, in post-war conditions, was not easy. However, it happened that Gaylord Hauser, a self-made Californian millionaire, who had emigrated from Germany at the age of eighteen and had chosen the name of Gaylord to be impressive, adding it to the title of Doctor, had arrived in Taormina with his partner and wanted the house for some months. During this time he wrote *Look Younger, Live Longer*, which was a best-seller in both the United States and Britain over the next ten years. Perhaps he was inspired by the house and view.

He claimed that he was entitled to the 'Doctor' as 'It signifies a teacher, and who if not I is a teacher?' — he who had taught so many of the famous, the aristocratic and even royalty to eat healthily. I had never heard of him, but he had excellent references from his bank and I was assured that he would respect and care for my precious antiques. I had feared that the house would not be luxurious enough, but he was determined to come to Taormina and it was the only one large and grand enough for him.

A few years previously Dr Hauser had summoned Californian journalists one Tuesday, saying that on the next Saturday he was to marry Miss Greta Garbo. He swore them to secrecy until after the event. Alas, on Friday the diva decided that she 'wished to be alone . . .' One day, during his visit, I was surprised to see in the local paper a photo of the balcony and windows of *my* bedroom in Casa Cuseni, illustrating an article with imposing headlines to the effect that Miss Harriet Brown (Garbo's well-known alias) would shortly be occupying that room. I cheerfully foresaw financial possibilities if I could let the bed in which She had slept. But although the people of Taormina declare that she *did* come, I was never wholly convinced. She may well have chosen to 'be alone' once more.

I now had the problem of finding somewhere to stay as I had to remain in Taormina for business matters, mostly taxes. Again I was lucky: I was asked if I would take over the management of a small and very pleasant hotel. It had been bought by a Dutchwoman in her seventies, of great elegance and charm, who later became the friend and hostess of Queen Juliana. During the war she had married her Sicilian manager, a complacent husband twelve years younger than herself, so that she could remain in Sicily having acquired Italian nationality through her marriage. He devotedly managed the hotel, working as hard as any of the servants whose hours and conditions appalled me. The owners were hoping to have a much-needed holiday and a change from the cares and anxieties of carrying on a business in Taormina. However, until the very last moment they did not know whether American dollars owing to her would arrive in time for their holiday. These were the days of the strictest control in all European countries over the export of currency. To have dollars was to be really privileged; it meant a certain freedom to travel.

'If they come,' she said, 'and only if, we want you to manage the hotel. You will receive your keep and half any profits.'

'But I'm totally inexperienced. You're very trusting — and very generous. I really think that's a bit too much.'

But she insisted. It was only later that I realised that they had not expected any profits as all their previous Dutch and British clients found it difficult to come so far when they could only afford to pay for a very brief stay out of their very limited currency allowance. Even in Italy money was still scarce among the professional classes who formed their main clientele. Only very slowly was tourism beginning to recover from the devastation of the war.

The American money turned up, to my immense relief, and I moved into the hotel. I had innocently supposed that I should be left with some of the dollars to meet immediate expenses.

But: 'We are taking all the dollars with us,' she explained 'We can leave you no money as we shall need it all. I'm afraid the safe is empty, but I hope that you will soon have some paying people — but we can't be certain, can we? Now you must understand that everything hangs on one very important client — the Barone di ——. He is very rich. He comes from Palermo, but he has had to leave his *palazzo* there because of Giuliano, the Brigand. He and his wife are terrified of being his next kidnap victims. He's the captain of the yacht club and so a marked person. He has, thank goodness, been our guest for several months. I don't know what we should have done without his regular cheques. You will find one in the safe, but you won't be able to cash it for a week and the next one won't be due for a month. He always gives me the cheque a month in advance but is careful to postdate it. Once you can get that money you will be all right for a time.'

Giuliano, a bandit in the north-west part of the island, was the terror of the rich but the hero of less privileged Sicilians. I promised that I would treat the Barone and Baronessa with the utmost consideration and respect. If I couldn't cash the cheque I should have no means of keeping the hotel going or of providing myself with anywhere to stay while I waited for the next allowance of currency, not due for a long time.

I settled into my comfortable quarters and quickly made friends with the overworked and underpaid staff, as well as with the Barone. He was a genial little man with the usual paunch of the middle-aged Sicilian. His wife was austerely dignified, despite her plump body. Their manners were exquisite. Each night we dined in the beautiful subtropical garden among palms and the tall white poppies. The tables were placed by the patient staff just outside the french windows of the dining room. The servants were elderly, but seemingly willing to slave for hours. They waited on me endlessly, and I couldn't prevent it. I had come from wartime England where we had considered no work beneath us, but here in Sicily a lady was still a lady and should not be expected to soil her hands with any menial task.

My table was next to the huge french window leading to the garden from the dining room, and all but a few guests had to pass it on the way to theirs. The Barone and his wife would come out at a later, more fashionable hour — eating too early was not aristocratic — and as they passed my table they would silently make a slight inclination of their heads to me. I would bow back and say *'Buona sera'*. The same procedure took place after the meal was finished, except that this time I said *'Buena notte'*. They would graciously acknowledge my greetings and continue on their way to their comfortable quarters, the suite reserved for the most favoured guests.

One evening at six o'clock I arrived in my office to find the Barone pacing up and down the entrance hall in a state of great agitation.

'Ah, Signorina, thank goodness you're back at last. It's terrible, terrible, the servants won't take it seriously. But if nothing is done, I and the Baronessa will have to leave at once. We *can't* stay. We left Palermo because of her heart condition — it was too serious for her to face the continuous strain of the unending fear of Giuliano and his kidnapping. We came here for peace and a rest from our terrible fear. And we found it here kilometres away from that brute. We have been peaceful and happy, but this evening — you can scarcely believe it — I saw *two huge* grey *rats*, RATS!' The little man was shouting himself hoarse. 'Rats playing on the balcony outside our bedroom. At any moment they might have come inside. Had the Baronessa seen them, she would have had a heart attack at once. I rang for the *cameriere*, I called them all, but they didn't think anything of it. In fact they laughed. *Carissima* Signorina, I know you will know how serious the danger is, I know *you* won't laugh. Please, *please* do something about it at once. We don't want to leave.'

Still less did I want them to go. There were still three days before I could touch

73

that cheque. In general, clients only paid when they left. If they left, would the Barone claim the whole cheque in compensation for such a disastrous situation? Would he leave part of it? I put on my most concerned expression and assured him that every possible step should be taken at once. If he would keep the Baronessa away I would have the gardener put a ladder up outside to the balcony and *two* traps and *two* kinds of poison would be scattered at once on the offending balcony. In the dark she would of course see nothing — and, I hoped, hear nothing since during even the hottest days of summer Sicilians tend to sleep with their windows tight shut.

The Barone was somewhat calmed by my obvious determination.

'I promise you that before daylight the gardener will remove any resulting corpse and all traces of traps and poison.'

The little man clasped my hand in both of his: 'Thank you, thank you, Signorina, I knew that you would understand.'

'Signor Barone, you too must play your part and keep the Baronessa well away from that balcony until the dark will hide it all.'

'Yes, yes, indeed, Signorina. I know that

all will be well in your hands.'

I summoned all the staff, trying to guess whether any of them knew or guessed just how much was at stake.

'The battle against the rats must be pursued before any other duty. It doesn't matter if dinner is late — even *very* late. Traps and poison must be placed at once on the balcony from the *outside*. Traps — but not poison,' I hastily added, 'must be placed in the kitchen, in the pantries and in the larders and any room in the basement where rats are likely to look for food. If there aren't enough then Salvatore must go out and buy them. Where there is no poison, cats must be borrowed or found. All this must be done *at once!*'

Two hours later the Barone came once more bustling into my office. He had left the Baronessa deeply absorbed playing patience.

'Thank you, thank you, Signorina, I knew that you would act like all your countrymen with energy and understanding.' (He had recently known the countrymen as conquerors.) 'I shall be eternally grateful. You will have saved my poor wife's life. I will not forget.' And he hurried back to the lady.

Another three hours later, I was sitting at

my table outside the dining room, some- what relaxed and feeling that the danger had been averted. A calm and collected Baronessa, followed by the Barone, who actually winked, passed by me with their usual small bow and sat down at their table beneath a magnificent palm tree: the tree trunk rose at least five metres before it spread out in a fan of branches under which was a carefully shaded light directed on to the table. I continued my meal. The Baroni started theirs, appar- ently happy and relaxed. After a while I glanced in their direction and up at the palm tree's light. To my horror I saw a veritable king of rats right above them. I watched, frozen to my seat, as the crea- ture came slowly down over the heads of my all-important clients. Any moment now he will jump — perhaps right into the Baronessa's soup — she will have a heart attack — perhaps she will die — the Barone will leave — the cheque will be claimed. My imagination had no limits. I watched, appalled, as the wretched animal changed its mind and turned back — per- haps to the ripening dates? Slowly the per- formance was repeated. Up and down, round the tree out of sight. My heart was beating so fast, as if *I* might have the heart attack at any moment. I managed to continue eating, trying to appear unconcerned as the rat went up and down and round about, but seldom coming further than about a third of the way down the long trunk.

The Baroni had by now reached the meat course. I was terrified that the scent might decide the rat to make a final leap on to their table. But no, it stayed up above. They finished their course blissfully unaware of what I was watching. There was still the dessert to be got through . . . Then, all of a sudden, something that had never happened before: both husband and wife rose to their feet simultaneously. The waiters made way for them, making their usual obeisance, which was gracefully acknowledged by the couple.

And then, slightly inclining their heads to me: '*Buona notte,* Signorina.'

'*Buena notte,* Signori Baroni.'

They ascended the stair to what I hoped was now their firmly shuttered bedroom. Was the cheque secure?

I sat there in a daze, taking my fruit, drinking my coffee and hoping. As the light had been turned out, the rat, if there, was no longer visible. When I finally went upstairs, the Barone was waiting for me.

77

What could have happened? But he seemed friendly. I hoped I could relax.

He advanced, hand outstretched, smiling: 'Signorina, did you see what I saw?'

I nodded. After all, it could have been something else. I had never noticed him looking upwards.

But he continued, 'There on the palm, right above our heads was the largest rat I have ever seen. At any moment he would have leapt on to our table. I couldn't let the Baronessa suspect. We had to finish the course. But, before the fruit, I said I felt unwell — that it must be the heat. We left before disaster struck. She knows nothing. Never shall I be able to thank you enough for all your kind concern. I am sure that what you have caused to be done will mean that we can stay. That devil will not survive the night. Thank you, thank you, thank you.'

This time our four hands shook one another's with fervent relief.

Three days later I cashed the cheque and a beaming Barone handed me a new one. Silently I thanked San Giorgio, Sant'Alfio and all the miracle workers of Sicily for having — this time — been on my side.

On her return, the Dutchwoman said:

'Everyone loved you, but the Barone was head over heels with you.' I didn't tell her why. It would have seemed too unromantic. *Rats?*

Problems/I Become a Locandiera

While preparing Casa Cuseni for Gaylord's arrival, I had been on a stepladder, cleaning a splendid baroque carving over the *salone* fireplace, when a puffing messenger from the police arrived up the hill.

'Signorina,' he announced, with no preliminaries, 'you must leave the country within twenty-four hours. Your permit has expired.'

It was, of course, out of the question, I protested. I had urgent business to see to. Then, as I thought brilliantly, I asked how could I pay urgent taxes if I had to leave the country?

'You can go to Malta and come back the next day.'

'I have neither the time, the money, nor the inclination to go to Malta.'

'Then you must get a medical certificate saying you *must* stay here for your health.'

I realised now why my uncle's doctor had offered me one at any time. 'Of *course*

I can get one, but I prefer to stay here on honest grounds.'

'Signorina, please be reasonable!' I wasn't sure who was being *unreasonable*. 'You must come and see the Commissario at once.

The Commissario was an ex-Fascist like everyone, and used to being obeyed. There was no discussion; he simply dictated a letter for me to send to a high authority — could it have been the Minister of Health? I was suffering from rheumatoid arthritis of such severity that I was unable to travel. Nervously, I asked whether it couldn't be something less visible — muscular rheumatism perhaps? 'No, we must make it strong. A specialist will in due course come to see that the certificate is valid.'

'Won't that be awkward?' I asked, thinking my acting powers might not be adequate.

'Leave that to me.'

So I stayed and took up my duties at the hotel of the Baronessa and the rats.

Some time later in the summer, when I was back in Casa Cuseni, there appeared a stout man, mopping his brow after having climbed to the terrace where I was having tea. In his hand he had a number of very official-looking documents. I got up with alacrity and offered him a chair and a drink.

'Thank you, that is very kind but I have a little acid on the stomach, would you have any bicarbonate of soda?'

I had and he sat sipping while I strove to steal a look at the documents.

At last he said, 'I am the specialist come to see that your medical certificate is true. How long do you want to stay?'

I overcame my embarrassment at having shown no sign of arthritis, kept my head and said, with as solemn a face as I could muster, 'Signore Dottore, the sun of Sicily has done me so much good that I have been able to book my passage for London next week.'

We neither of us showed that we thought this a strange situation. Perhaps to him it wasn't . . . At any rate it had cost me nothing.

The tax assessments themselves were a nightmare. Inexperienced, I foolishly and innocently declared the actual figure as I had done in England. In Sicily one never does that, and, as a result, the tax authorities increase the figure considerably. One is then involved in long and exhausting arguments which one hopes, probably in vain, will end in a fair deal.

Another serious difficulty was my name. Unexpectedly everyone called me Signorina Kitsoni or variations of it. Because they were so devoted to my uncle they assumed my name must be his. Reluctant to lose Phelps, I would say over and over again: 'My mother was a Kitson, but I *did* have a father so my name is not the same as hers.' They would look at me amazed, then recovering after a brief pause would say: 'Ah *si, si,* Signorina Kitsoni.'

If the name was difficult, the spelling was even worse and three Christian names added to the confusion. Margaret was easy — there was a saint; Daphne was purely pagan; at Hawthorn all gave up. To this day I have some of the envelopes addressed to me: Miss Rapline Mitzen, Sign. Chizzen Dalfin, Signorina Dafen Plepisi, Jahne Pewelps and so on. On legal documents this mattered. Sicilians don't like to admit that they don't know, they just make a courageous effort, and they found it difficult to distinguish between first and surnames. Phelps could be treated as if it began with a P or an F, and Kitson, which they thought was my name, began with a K which in Italian barely exists. To get round this one they would begin it with a CH which is the K sound phonetically. Once they even managed Miss Daplin Felpis Esq.

It seemed that at school children were taught to memorise everything except the alphabet. This would lead to chaos in most offices as employees searched through piles of unfiled or badly filed documents. The crisis came when my lawyer lost all the essential documents without which I had no ability to act. They had been prepared in London and had cost the then huge sum of £90. He declared he hadn't got them — the *Magnifico* had. The latter denied it and I felt he was right. Knowing that the *avvocato* went to Messina each week, I got my good friend, his wife (I was fast learning the value of friends) to search his office — and there they were.

It did not take me long to realise that I had unknown enemies. Various petty and unnecessary difficulties arose. Gradually I was beginning to suspect that it had something to do with my being English and one of a nation which was the most recent conqueror of Sicily. I think it is fair to say that nearly all the well-off had, of necessity, been Fascists and they still resented their defeat. Several of the leading figures of the town including the ex-Mayor — a man who, years before, had courted my attractive young mother by filling her shoe with roses and violets — had been imprisoned by the British. Many of them had happily entertained top Nazis when Kesselring's headquarters were in the town. I made no secret of my detestation of Nazis and arrogant Fascists, and perhaps I was unwise in showing my preference for the simpler folk. They were so much warmer and more friendly and I deeply sympathised with them over their constant struggle with poverty and injustice. Then my enjoyment of their colourful *festas* and their puppets and processions was probably considered plebeian. I think the rich may even have felt that I was tainted by Communist ideas . . .

One of them went a bit too far when she accused me of having made off with some of the gate money when I organised a garden party in aid of the Hostel for the Aged Poor. She was the wife of the ex-Fascist Mayor. Her enmity I felt was an honour. The atmosphere was unpleasant, but such circles could generally be avoided. For twenty-five years I was to have no phone. Several of my guests declared it was one of the loveliest things about Casa Cuseni never to hear that 'blasted bell'. Anyone who really wanted to see me would take the trouble to walk up the hill. The hill also helped me to distinguish beggars in real need from those who often made more than men doing a hard day's work. At the first call I would offer bread and cheese. Only the hungry would come back and I would then give more.

When, in 1948, I came back from my first two-month break in England — I had already decided that I couldn't take the summer heat and it was good to be in England again — I found a summons to see the Commissario. I always found this alarming, it was an echo of a summons to see the Senior Prefect, although he had shown himself my friend in the matter of the certificate. But laws and regulations are so immensely complicated that it is virtually impossible to be on the right side all the time. If one has an enemy, and they are easy to acquire, anonymous denunciations, one of the less pleasant aspects of Sicilian life, are only too common. Something out of order can always be dug up.

He began severely, 'Signorina, you have been denounced for running a *pensione* without a licence.'

It had never entered my English head that I should have had one. At home if one has a house that is too big for one it is so easy to take paying guests and, if the rents are declared for income tax, that, I believe, is that.

The Commissario melted a little and said that it was all right for me to have guests — and they could even pay under the counter — but I had had too many and all the small *pensioni* nearby were envious, as they had had so few clients since the war.

I explained that these 'guests' were my friends who came to Taormina to see me and enjoy Casa Cuseni. Were I not here they were unlikely to come. I was in no way stealing other people's clients.

He was sorry, but declared that I must have a licence and suggested that I should become a *locandiera*, the lowest form of hotel-keeper. This would keep the cost modest. A *locanda* was usually pretty shabby and frequented by lower-class commercial travellers. But I liked the musical sound of the word and Goldoni, with his celebrated play *La Locandiera*, had made the character famous and attractive. In any case I preferred it to my other unexpected designation which I discovered when I consulted municipal records. There I was officially registered as a 'well-standing [i.e.

financially independent — untrue], nubile Protestant . . .'

And so in 1950 I became a *locandiera*. The great advantage was that because of the *locandas'* lowly state, taxes were modest.

A Very Marriageable House

A widespread dream among young Sicilian men, ever since foreigners began to arrive here, had been to marry a rich girl from abroad. Many were the girls who lost their hearts — and also their heads — as they fell for Adonises on the beach, or for musicians who serenaded them at full moon. They would know little about Sicilian attitudes to women, and did not realise that they would gain not only a husband but also an all-embracing family — and probably a highly critical mother-in-law.

Eve and I, in 1948, were a bit of a sensation: while she was attractive, I was clearly the better financial bet for marriage, or so they imagined, believing that the house was mine. Conversation with men young and old tended to go something like this:

'Are you married?'

'No.'

'When are you going to be married?'

'*Chi lo sa* — who knows?'

'Why aren't you married?'

The answer to that was easy in Sicily: 'It's better to be free.'

They recovered from this startling idea, then: 'Are you the heiress?'

Me, modestly: 'No.'

This clearly took them aback. I could see behind their faces the thoughts going round, then: 'Who *is* the heiress?'

'My aunt.'

More thought, then: 'How old is your aunt?'

'Seventy-five.'

Immediately, 'Will you marry me?'

I would giggle. I found this the easiest defence. Sicilian men do not like being refused or snubbed and it is wiser not to, especially if their help could one day be valuable.

Once I told a recently divorced English friend about local hopes: 'So many men want to marry my house. One or two of them wouldn't mind if I came along with it!'

'Well,' he said, 'it *is* a very marriageable house!' looking at it with admiration. (This later became the title of a BBC interview I did on the Home Service with James McNeish.)

There were other memorable and

strange conversations.

'Signorina, did you pass a discreet war?'

I hesitated, never having considered my war from this angle, and then answered, 'No, not very.'

'Why, what did you do?'

'I crossed the Atlantic in twenty-two days in convoy in 1941 and spent the rest of the war in the centre of London.'

The reaction appeared to be one of pity, and almost contempt, implying surely I could have done better than that — and this was from someone trying to impress me!

A little later I was told that when the RAF warned that they were going to bomb Taormina (a most legitimate objective since Kesselring's headquarters were there and the whole Malta campaign had been planned in it), the inhabitants, including the firemen, left for the mountains above. At this I laughed, thinking of the endless nights that we had fire-watched in London — men and women of all ages and abilities.

'Why do you laugh? It was very discreet.'

The opposite of a discreet war was obviously an indiscreet one, and could there be a better example of that than Britain in 1940 after Dunkirk and the fall of France?

I thought a lot about this. Here were two islands with mixed populations off the main continent of Europe. The one had been attacked throughout the centuries by all the martial races and had been conquered over and over again. They had never chosen war — or had a chance of winning when it came. They probably decided that the only hope was to be discreet, survive the fighting if possible and then, with their superior wits and cunning, outwit their probably more stupid conquerors. Britain and its peoples, on the other hand, mercifully defended by a wider stretch of sea, had not been conquered for a thousand years. They had always felt they had a chance of victory and had succeeded, ever since the Normans, in defeating every attacker. I was not in England in 1940, but amazed foreigners who were and who felt that they were caught like rats in a trap before the imminent arrival of Hitler from whom they had fled, told me that they were astounded by the calm reaction of the British to the extreme danger. All classes drew together, appeasers almost ceased to exist, and as so often when their backs were against the wall, the British indiscreetly heaved a sigh of relief that they were alone together with no more damn foreigners to let them down.

To return to the house that wasn't mine . . . In dealing with its many suitors I devised various strategies other than a giggle that would spare them feelings of outright rejection. To one I said that I was much too independent and would make a hopeless Sicilian wife; to another I showed myself to be flighty when I danced with several different men in one evening, and even allowed a light flirtation. In those days Sicilian men liked their women to stay at home while they went out and courted foreigners — that is, when there were any. Above all, I stressed that I was *not* an heiress.

I detached one ardent suitor in my second year by introducing him to a beautiful, blonde actress. He at once offered to give her Italian lessons. She insisted that I would be there as a chaperon and interpreter. He began: 'Let us start with the Hearticles,' breathing a mouthful of stale garlic at her. It was the only lesson! But he persisted, inviting her to go for a walk with him. He was proud of his English and it certainly was imaginative: 'Ham I not the 'appiest man in all the world? On my right harm I 'ave the kindest lady [me] and on my left the loveliest girl in Hall the world.'

She giggled with me and he decided to look elsewhere.

Another one I helped to emigrate to Canada, assuring him that there was no future for a man of his talents in Taormina. He went to Toronto and was most successful. A few years later he invited me to stay with him in Milan where he now worked as economic adviser to the Ontario government. As we got into his impressive car he said, 'Look where we are parked.' It was next to a large notice saying RISERVATO PER LE AUTORITÀ. I was suitably impressed.

Meanwhile Maria was enjoying herself, accepting at the back door gifts that I had refused at the front. Only two was I unable to turn away. The first was a huge chocolate Easter egg. We had both been severely rationed for years and our mouths watered at the sight. The second arrived carried by two men followed by the proud donor. It was a Roman amphora which had recently been fished up in the bay of Naxos, and it had been filled with thousand-year-old Byzantine coins in solid gold. When the donor casually announced that it still had sand in the bottom I couldn't resist getting a hose to clear it out. Alas, there was no coin left.

'I hadn't known you were so keen on the coins. I will get one — it would make a beautiful ring.'

I'm afraid I said that I was really thinking of earrings . . . Poor young man, he had taken the trouble to get a beautiful wrought-iron stand to hold it. It still graces the stairs.

After I had read a book called *Man about the House* (whose hero was an Italian man-servant who gradually insinuated himself into the affections, and then the bed, of his rich, unmarried employer and acquired her fortune) I realised that a curious interview, apparently with an applicant for a job, was in fact an attempt on his part to put his foot on the first rung of a ladder to fortune.

It was a cold, damp day but he found me, to his surprise, in the garden in apron and boots — and peasant ones at that — bending over with my hands in the earth planting stocks and cinerarias. In those days no Sicilian lady would have been, far less have been discovered, in such an ungainly position. He clearly fancied *his* appearance. Stovepipe trousers had just come in and so had long hair; he was sporting both. The hair was dark and greasy and caught up in his crimson polo-

95

necked jersey. A peaked cap, set at a rakish, *mafioso* angle, completed the picture.

After a moment's hesitation while he decided that, despite my appearance, I evidently was the *padrona*, he started on his prepared speech: 'Signorina, I have heard that you are a pearl and I would wish to be the diamond next that pearl.'

I looked him up and down with distaste. Could this creature have come for *work?* I was looking for a cook and general handyman but was determined to go slowly and had not advertised my need. Too many undesirables would have sought the post, in the hope of gaining control over the foreign woman with no obvious man around to protect her.

'I'm making no decision now,' I said briskly. 'Give me your name and address and, should I want you, I will in due course send for you.'

'But I cannot imagine, Signorina, that you could ever give *my* place to another! If the Albergo Grande Palazzo offered me 500,000, nay let us say 600,000, I would still choose to be your diamond. What devotion could be more than *that?*'

Taken aback by my calm lack of enthusiasm, he hesitated a moment and then repeated his ardent ambition to work for me and me alone. I turned back to my planting and he sadly backed away down the garden path, shaking his head the while at the unreasonableness of women. Now, when we meet on the street, he looks elsewhere. He has clearly decided that his hopes for a fortune do not lie in my direction.

Vincenzino

A replacement had to be found for the disgraced Turiddu who was now in his element as the Archpriest's right hand man, stage-managing the cathedral services. Vincenzino had the face of a saint — an intelligent, emaciated one — and the temper of a wasp. The former, allied to his general competence, had been largely responsible for his being able to find as many jobs as he wanted; the latter had led to his losing them, or rather his walking out on them, generally after less than a month. His varied talents were much sought after. He was quite firm about his conditions of employment: he was to live in and he was to be paid the ridiculously small sum of 5,000 lire a month, no more, no less. He came to me as a *cameriere*. We soon found that he could fill the roles of first-class chef, for which he produced a tall white cap; butler, in white gloves; hospital nurse, nanny, marketeer, account keeper, launderer, and last, but by no means least, cabaret star.

His repertoire consisted of stories of the

Sicilian saints, a curious and picturesque lot, and of incidents in his previous places of employment. He would pass the dishes with a professional flourish and then, while they were being enjoyed, he would walk round the table gesticulating, reciting and miming.

'St Pancras,' he would begin, 'to you he is a station, but to us he is the patron saint of the village. He was a bishop.' (Up went his hands to form a mitre and to describe his elegant little imperial beard.) 'He came from the East, so he was black. He lived at the time when the Turks — Arabs — were our conquerors here. He believed in making friends with the enemy so that he could live in peace. One day the Turkish governor invited him to a banquet. St Pancras accepted and found a magnificent hall with tables laden with food and drink. But there was a problem: St Pancras had to say grace without offending his hosts, who were heathen. He was a clever one — too clever. He thought carefully and then, pointing with his hands as if he were giving a blessing — but the Turks didn't know it was that — he said, "Ah, how interesting is the shape of this room. It is as far from here to there as it is from there to there." At the sign of the cross all the pagan glass and crockery cracked and split open letting all the good food and drink go to waste. The furious Turks set upon their guest and murdered him. He was a great martyr and saint, but he made a terrible mistake: he allowed his town — this town — to be bombed in the last war exactly on his own day. So we had to put him in *castigo* for nine years, Signorina, just to show him. Can you imagine it? The worst disaster in all our history and he allowed it to happen on his day.'

Vincenzino would then clear away the plates.

On subsequent days he would act, sparing us no gory detail, the garish stories of the Saints Agatha and Lucia. They also suffered under the Arabs when they refused the propositions of the alien governor, saying that they belonged body and soul to the One above. With rising excitement Vincenzino would become the enraged and lustful governor, the torturers, the wild oxen who refused to move when chained each to a limb and beaten so that they would tear the victims apart; he would even become the flames which were kindled but crept away from the pyre. Having withstood so much, the virgins, praying with clasped hands amidst the horror, became holy martyrs as the climax was reached and the eyes of Lucia were put out and the breasts of Agatha were cut off. Nothing was left to our imagination . . .

Later, tiring of such tales, he would take off the notables of the town. As he had been for brief periods in all their houses, observing their quirks and eccentricities. It was a rich collection. The wealthy, miserly old woman who only let him buy scrag-end of meat and was outraged when he borrowed their only umbrella — or rather piece of an umbrella — when it was raining, screeching at him, 'Put it back, put it back. How *dare* you; that's not for the likes of you, that's *mine*.'

Vincenzino went on: ' "Signora," I said with dignity, "if you can't afford to let me borrow that miserable bit of a thing, then you are not worthy for me to work for you." And off I went, but I took that piece with me, and if you don't believe me, Signorina, I'll show it to you. I kept it as a souvenir, just to serve her right! It was mostly holes and spokes, but she said that it wasn't for the likes of me. And I was going out in the rain for *her* miserable shopping. And then, Signorina, the Signora died. She was a great fat one, that one, although she only lived on scrag-end.

They had to make a special coffin, and even then that wasn't enough: they had to take the doors off to get it in and out. It was a beautiful sunny day for the funeral with blue skies and not a cloud in sight. There was a long procession through the Corso. Everyone was there as it was a rich family. I waited outside the Duomo until the coffin came out. Then, when the last mourners had joined the procession, I opened the piece of umbrella, and there was stuff only on half of it — and even that had holes — and then I walked behind with a long solemn face. People stared. They said, "But Vincenzino, it isn't raining, and even if it were that thing wouldn't keep you dry." I looked at them. They know me and my ways. Then I said, "*They* will understand." '

Apart from my uncle, for whom he had once worked for four months when Maria was in hospital, there had only been one employer of whom he approved. She had an only child, a daughter, whom she spoiled and worshipped. The family was not well off, and Vincenzino, who became devoted in his waspish way, felt that he should make face for them. So when the daughter was away at university he would send her postcards, read by all the people through whose hands they passed, as he very well knew they would be. He signed them 'From *one* of your devoted servants, Vincenzino'.

'It made her seem so important, Signorina, and she deserved it. So that was good. She had snob relations in that town. But really I only worked for them a few hours a week, and I was the only one.'

A rich friend of mine, enchanted with Vincenzino's innumerable skills, before leaving gave him a grey worsted suit of superb quality, telling him that the other half of the material had been bought for the Duke of Windsor. Vincenzino had certainly never seen, let alone possessed, such a wonderful garment. We expected him to be deeply impressed by the ducal connection. But he merely uttered a dignified 'Thank you', bowed and left the room. Embarrassed, I explained that I thought he was overwhelmed by the grandeur of the gift which had made him, for once, speechless. That was all until that evening. Work finished, the double doors of the drawing room were flung open without warning, and there was Vincenzino resplendent in the suit — except that he was rather too small to fill it.

Silently he advanced upon the donor,

dropped on one knee, kissed his hand, paused dramatically and announced, '*You* have given me this suit. *I* will now act *Giulio Cesare* for you.'

And without further ado he swelled to the size of Caesar with a great booming voice; he shrank to become the pleading Calpurnia with a high falsetto; he became the whole Roman army marching away with trumpets and all. Somehow he managed to be both Brutus and Antony. The room was alive with characters. It ended. He bowed, taking our applause with professional aplomb. Then he left the room at once. He had, as he would have said, 'disobligated' himself for the present.

Next day I congratulated him, 'Vicenzino, it was wonderful. But how did you know all that?'

'Signorina, I notice everything, everywhere. One of my posts was with the chief actress when they were doing *Giulio Cesare* in the ancient theatre. I managed to see all the rehearsals, over and over again. I did my work quickly and then I escaped and rushed to the theatre. How could I ever forget it? But I only do it myself on special occasions. It is too tiring being so many people. That lady, Signorina, was the one with the telephone.'

'The telephone?'

'Haven't I done that? No? You shall have it tomorrow.'

The next day at dinner: 'This is a story about when telephones first came to Sicily, a long time ago. This lady had the first one I had ever seen. I was very ignorant then. Well, one day the Signora told me that her husband might ring at any time from Rome, and that I must answer it if she wasn't there. Of course it would happen when she was in her bath. Actresses, Signorina, take baths at funny times. That thing began going TRRRR- Trrrr- Trrrr. So I go up to it and look at it making that horrible noise, and I ask, "Is that the *Ingegnere?*" He doesn't answer. It just goes on more and more, Trrrr- Trrrr. I say, "*Ingegnere,* please be patient and wait a bit. The Signora is in her bath. Just you wait and she'll come all right." But it goes on and on whatever I say. "*Ingegnere,* can I get you a coffee to pass the time?" He doesn't answer even then — only Trrrr- Trrrr- Trrrr.'

By this time Vicenzino was on his knees, wringing his hands before the imagined instrument that I was beginning to see too.

' "*Please,* please" ' — imploring and by now almost in tears — ' "please be quiet and wait. She's well. She'll come all in good time. It's only the bath. I'll go and get some coffee." I thought that that might calm him, and that somehow I could pour it down the mouth of that thing. I was very ignorant. I thought there must be a tube from him to me. And all he went on doing was Trrrr- Trrrr- Trrrr. I ran and banged on the bathroom door shouting, "Come quickly, Signora, quickly. The *Ingegnere* wants you and he won't speak to me. I don't know why, but all he does is Trrrr, Trrrr." At last she came and picked it up.' (Vincenzino then imitated his mistress burbling kisses into the phone.) ' "*Carissimo* — no one answered? It's that *cretino* Vincenzino." But how was I to know, Signorina, that you had to pick up that thing to speak and hear?'

Vicenzino stayed with me for two years, which was a record in his turbulent life. It meant hard work on my part in dealing with his tantrums. About every month — his usual time for leaving a job — he would get up late, do no work, then throw himself into a chair with his legs flung to one side of it and whine, 'The blood is coming out of my feet. I can't stay in this place a moment longer.' We could see no sign of blood, but we would gather round praising and flattering him and telling him we couldn't do without him. Many a crisis was overcome in this way. But one month he refused to sleep in the house. He arrived later and later. There was no miming and very little work.

One day he suddenly blurted out, 'Signorina, it breaks my heart but I must leave your service.'

'But why, Vincenzino?'

'I am ill.'

'I'm sorry. What's the matter?'

'I don't know, but I must go.'

'But don't you think that as this is the only place you've ever wanted to stay in, it would be a mistake to go? Let me call a doctor and get you put right. You could have an X-ray.' I knew that in those days this was what they all wanted.

'Signorina, you are very kind, but it is no good. I am like the birds in the air — here I feel I'm in a cage. I must fly away.'

'But why don't you take a holiday? Fly away and come back when you feel like it. You must think of your old age. When you are here with me you have insurance stamps which will get you a pension. Don't throw it all away for nothing. Whatever will you do when you are no longer able to work?'

'I shall go into the Hostel for the Aged Poor.'

'But Vicenzino, you really will feel in a cage there. There are rules that you have to obey. And in any case we don't yet know whether it will keep going. Suppose it shuts down, then what will you do?'

It was useless, the wasp side was uppermost. I am sure that in his next post he entertained his employers by carefully reproducing caricatures of me. It came to my knowledge later that he was going about saying that I had stolen a parcel of woollen underclothes sent to him by my friends . . . Perhaps he showed me wearing 'his' combinations?

The years passed. I heard that Vicenzino worked sporadically — a few days here and there. He had established his speciality as wedding cakes. He would sculpt three tiers and more. At the reception the doors would be thrown dramatically open, and Vicenzino, in his tall chef's cap, his black eyes beaming with the joy of creation, would advance bearing his masterpiece. He would place it on the table in front of the newly-weds, take three steps backward, then bow and, when once more erect, would declaim an original poem in pure dialect that he had specially composed for the occasion. But no one can live just on wedding cakes and poems — not even an emaciated wasp of a man. We kept the hostel going, old age pensions were raised, and in due course Vincenzino was accepted as a resident. Two cataract operations had put an end to his wanderings. The nuns recognised his restlessness and gave him many exceptional privileges. He was allowed to go out as much as he liked and to break many rules. But he was in another cage. One morning he was found hanging over the stairwell of the hostel. This time there had been no other escape.

Beppe

After Vincenzino's desertion I had once again to look for a *cameriere*. The applicant was introduced to me as an 'orphan'. It was my first attempt to find a servant on my own, and my difficulties with the language — and still more with the dialect — added to our joint embarrassment at the interview. Beppe was tiny: less than five feet tall. He was dressed in a bright orange, striped suit, and was so dark that he might well have come from Africa, as doubtless his ancestors had. Twenty-four years old, he had been driven by the miserable poverty and unemployment in his 'country' — a tiny village on the north coast of Sicily — to seek work in the much larger, southern centre, where, rumour said, there were wealthy foreigners and tourists who paid fabulous wages and gave enormous tips, and even — in the past — had been known to marry local inhabitants of quite poor families, whom they had then wafted off to their own countries to live in riches and comfort for the rest of their idle lives.

Beppe had never worked indoors, but he was sure he could learn if only I would give him the chance. The bargain was struck. For 10,000 lire a month, and his keep, he would show me what he could do and how quickly he could learn.

With astonishing speed and dexterity he mastered his new job, working with willingness and pleasure at all the routine tasks, and showing an honesty in his shopping accounts most unusual in that part of the world where the fruits of cheating the *padrone* were regarded as a legitimate subsidiary wage. When his indoor work was done, he would dash out to the garden to prune or graft trees or to unblock the antique drains, or to repair a damaged wall. There was always something needing to be done, and nothing was too much trouble. After a fourteen-hour day he would retire to his room, where, in complete silence, he would occupy himself until the light went out an hour later. Maria, the old cook, told me that he was writing letters to his girl, and indeed envelopes with curious, scratchy writing (he had managed to scrape together a few hours' schooling during the war, and only his exceptionally quick intelligence had enabled him to write at all) would be taken out to post.

After ten days, Maria came waddling into my room, shifting her vast bulk from one rickety leg to another, and announced, 'Signorina, I have worked in this house forty-eight years. Boys have come, and boys have gone, but there's only been one Beppe. *Keep him.*'

And so, at the end of the month, his wages were raised and, to Beppe's obvious delight and pride, he was taken on permanently.

The increase in his self-confidence made itself felt immediately. No longer would he spend his evenings with the scratchy pen. He went out for strolls down the main street in search of adventure. He soon found it. I began to wonder what were my moral responsibilities for this 'orphan' of twenty-four, who had come, on my account, from the small village to the sophisticated tourist centre. No longer was the table cleared in silence at night. Instead, in his strangely Arabic voice, he kept up a stream of songs, both ancient and modern, about *amore, amanti* and *bionde*. His work finished, we would hear the songs slowly receding down the garden path and, hours later, we would be awoken by their return, faintly at first in the distance, then slowly growing louder as he climbed the garden terraces. Night after night, it was the same; but his work never suffered. I summoned my counsellor, Maria. She shared my anxiety in a place where all the good girls were locked up after dark while their fathers, husbands and brothers went off to enjoy themselves with the foreigners. Yes, he *was* engaged. Yes, Maria thought the *Padrona* should speak to him.

Beppe, summoned in his turn, grinned and admitted that he had a girl in the north. He meant to marry her — she was a good girl, who worked hard and didn't gossip — but before tying himself in matrimony, he wished to have five years of liberty. He showed me a photo of his *fidanzata* which he carried on him, but his stand was firm. The girl would have to wait. The singing went on . . .

At Christmas I gave him three well-earned days of rest. It was not until later that I learned that he used these to *fare la fuga* — to elope. That is, he had taken his *fidanzata*, in the tiny village where he was born, from her parents' house to his own, and from that moment she was a marked woman. Unless he married her in the not so distant future, the girl was ruined. No man, whatever her charms, or, more important still, her dowry, would look at her. And this is in a country where there was then no other career for a woman than marriage.

After a day or so of sobriety and early nights, the singing began once more. Down at nine o'clock, back at midnight. Letters and cards began pouring in from the north:

'Next time you show your face in this place, you'll be married at once!'

'We have all the licences ready.'

'The wine is ordered — and the meat.'

'The priest is waiting.'

Maria and I agreed that it was time for another interview.

Beppe was adamant: 'Rather than be married, I prefer never to go there again. I would rather lose my land, my linen and my bicycle — yes, even my *bicycle* — than show my face there again . . .' I felt more than a little sympathy, which I managed to hide.

Some friends, beset by the everlasting servant difficulty in England, asked whether I would be willing to solve the problem in an altruistic way by letting them take Beppe home with them. The chance was one I felt I could not reject without a word to him, so I asked him if he had a friend who would like to go.

He jumped at the suggestion. '*I'll* go!'

I warned him that it wouldn't solve his difficulties: 'Remember you'll have to return in a year.'

'I'll marry the girl first, and then I'll find a way of staying for ever.'

'How?'

'I'll marry an English wife there, and then I can stay.' His intentions were apparently 'trigamous', I thought, as I remembered the girl — if indeed it was only one — in town. On my advice the friends withdrew their offer, and matters went on as before.

One week, however, his morale cracked. A dental abscess was the cause. Each day the pain increased, as did his resolution not to go near a local dentist. He went on working, sadly and slowly, without sleeping, without eating, and all the time the swelling grew. He was obstinate and deaf to all our prayers and warnings, until at last, after four days and nights, the pain broke his resistance, and off he went to the clinic.

He must have been in the dentist's chair when the postman brought another card from the north. Maria and I looked at one another: 'Better let him have a little sleep

115

before we let him see it,' we agreed, and we hid it for a day.

We never knew what was on the card, but the effect on him was galvanising: 'I must go home at once. There is nothing else I can do.' I gave him two days off.

He returned, true to his word, at midnight on the second day, a sad, crestfallen figure, his face still sore and swollen. He went silently to bed. The next day Maria told me that it had been both his twenty-fifth birthday and his wedding day. With what enthusiasm I could muster, I offered my congratulations, and invited his wife to come, as my guest, for a fortnight's honeymoon. With great dignity, he announced: 'That is very good of you, Signorina, but I must decline. While I am here in this town, I wish to pass myself off as a bachelor of nineteen.'

A week passed in work and silence. On Sunday, his day off, he appeared with an enormous English Grammar.

'But Beppe, aren't you going out?'

'No, Signorina, I'm never going out again.'

'But why? How? What do you mean? *Never* again?'

'Never, as long as I'm in your service, *never* shall I go out again.'

Instead he was going to master the English language.

The valiant attempt to keep his marriage vows lasted little more than a week. Then the singing began again. I watched, helpless. Maria agreed that there was nothing we could do. But my sympathy began to shift towards the neglected wife.

Two months passed. Beppe remained the perfect servant, but our anxiety grew until one day Maria burst in: 'Signorina,' she cried, 'you must *do* something — he is now scenting his eyebrows and his moustache!' I agreed, but *what?* (If only he had not been such a perfect servant in this all too imperfect world . . .)

Mercifully the problem was solved for me by the culprit himself who, somehow brought to his senses, erupted shortly afterwards into my room, and without any ceremony burst out: 'Signorina, I *must* have my wife here or I shall go mad.'

I replied with the greatest calm, 'You know I have invited her. Go and fetch her, and she can stay here for a fortnight.'

'I must have her always.'

'I don't know her yet. She must come on trial, as you did, and then we can all decide together.'

'I must have her here for ever or I shall

117

leave your service!'

'Perhaps — we shall see.'

Disgruntled, he departed, and the next day I found myself wondering how I was to welcome Franca, a poor little, unwanted bride of eighteen, who had never been in a train before, who had never gone out alone, who had never seen a house like this or spoken anything but her local dialect.

I received the couple at the top of the steps, and presented her with as bridal a bouquet as possible. She was yellow with anxiety and fear, but managed a wan smile.

'Isn't she pretty, Beppe?' A lie, but a necessary one.

'Not so very,' came the disgruntled answer from a husband tired after dealing with the inevitable travel sickness.

Franca was, as he had said, a good girl who didn't gossip. As she recovered her balance she began helping Maria, and was generally pleasant and useful. At the end of the fortnight, it was tacitly agreed that she should stay. Months passed, and during all that time the bride never left the house. On Beppe's days off she was left behind with old Maria and her nephew of eight, while her husband disported himself (respectably?) according to Maria, with his friends on the Corso, or in the newly opened cinema. In vain I tried to tell myself that I needn't feel too much pity: women of her class had been accustomed for centuries to watch their men go out and enjoy themselves, alone or in entirely male company. But my feelings about women's rights were strong. I *had* to interfere. After much patient persuasion, Beppe at last took his wife out to one of the many religious processions in the town. He even gave her a new dress. We watched them from a distance, and on their return many compliments were paid to Franca: 'Beppe, your wife was the prettiest girl in all the *festa*.' Our efforts were received in ungracious silence. Only much later did I have a further chance: 'Beppe, you two were the comeliest couple in all the crowd.' This time the compliment was greeted with beaming smiles on both their faces, and the joint dates gradually became more frequent.

That summer, while I was away from the island, I had a letter from Beppe:

Dearest Signorina,
I have to inform you that my wife this morning brought to the light of day a beautiful little man. All goes very well

with me. He is to be called Vitus. Your unforgettable slave,

Beppe.

Deeply buried in the past were his extra-matrimonial adventures. Beppe became a most devoted father and husband — in that order. Once, even, when it was suggested that he might, exceptionally, work on a Sunday afternoon, he drew himself up to his full four feet eleven inches and said with great solemnity, '*That* is the time that a man has a duty to take his wife down the Corso. It would not be right to neglect it.' The suggestion was dropped.

And now, amazed and fascinated, I was to watch the gradual transformation of Franca from a modest, hero-worshipping wife into that terrifying thing — a nagging Sicilian matriarch.

Beppe, from the moment her pregnancy was recognised, became very solicitous. He offered her his arm on every occasion: 'She mustn't fall, my son is in there,' he would say, pointing to her swelling figure. Franca was, after all, the channel through which he was going to reproduce his wonderful self. Sicilian women in those days were quite used to this attitude. To produce a son was the main aim of their existence, and men tended to take all the credit . . . Franca basked in the unaccustomed sun of his attentions, and when she produced the son and heir she was even more coddled and spoiled — after all, she was the dairy at which the wonder was fed and she had an abundance of milk. She was avaricious and she knew that it was a saleable commodity. So, after a few months, she took a foster child whose mother had lost her milk. The fee for a wet nurse was settled by long-established custom: a certain sum in lire and a large beefsteak a day. But Franca lost more than she earned and the real cost was great. Her own baby never fed from her again. When put to the breast he yelled and screamed, and nothing would induce him to suck. Beppe then took over with a bottle while Franca continued to earn her beefsteak. It was the beginning of lasting trouble between mother and son, and probably led to Franca's growing antagonism towards me.

One night Beppe called me urgently. His precious baby was ill, he couldn't get his breath. It was 11.30 p.m. Even if I went down to the village — in those days we had no telephone — would I be able to persuade a doctor to come out at that hour? Very unlikely. If it was really a matter of life and death, then I would be prepared to make a scene, threaten a scandal and insist on his coming, but if it was just a question of the fears of over-anxious parents, I had to keep my big guns for a real crisis.

I had a guest at the time whom we had dubbed 'The National Monument', by reason of her narrowly patriotic British views and her likeness to William Nicholson's portrait of the ageing Queen Victoria. She had been that symbol of rectitude and dignity, a London Hospital sister, and late in life she had married a rich patient, recently widowed. She was not accustomed to go abroad alone and I had been asked to take especial care of her. She had previously only left the British Isles in the care of her protective husband and was apt to be tiresomely lachrymose. I felt that an appeal to her professional past might serve to distract her from her present distress. She might also spare me a fruitless night journey to get the doctor.

Already she was in bed and very flustered by my request: 'I know nothing about children — haven't seen one for years . . . But if you really think . . .'

I assured her that her opinion would mean everything to us: whether I must go for the doctor at once, or whether we could safely wait until the morning. With her long, white plait of hair trailing over the collar of her pale blue, quilted dressing gown, she nobly came out — duty called — to their small cottage in the grounds. Franca was lying in the huge bed with her baby, Vito, in her arms, and to me he looked ill and very pathetic with his pallor and his breathlessness. The National Monument became once more the professional. She took his pulse and temperature and asked a few questions, with me as interpreter, and then, to my immense relief, pronounced her firm opinion that the child had some bronchitis; nothing dangerous, he should be kept warm. The doctor's visit could safely be postponed until the morning. Most Sicilian children suffer from bronchitis. In this mild climate they are dressed as for the North Pole. Head — above all, the head — feet, everything, is swathed in the heaviest of wool. At that time even the prams were fitted with plastic windows, which just allowed enough air to reach the well-covered child so that it wouldn't be suffocated. Not a breath of fresh air was knowingly allowed to enter a house at night, and the poor little over-clad things readily sweated and fell ill. They developed little resistance to disease.

Vito survived and grew into a charming, intelligent and sensitive child. Once I was very ill with undulant fever caught from the bite of a tick. It seemed to me that there were two Sicilians who knew how to behave in a sickroom — Vito and my dog Mischineddu. They came and sat, until turned out, one on each side of my bed, silent, sad, motionless, for hours on end — in striking contrast to their elders, who were capable of making an uproar out of nothing, shouting their heads off, in my room, over the small question of what I should have to eat that day, if anything. The calm devotion of child and dog meant much to me and helped my convalescence.

Vito made rapid progress at school. After one term he came to my room, early one morning, with the result of the American presidential election. In carefully formed, capital letters he had written GION CHENEDI. He had heard it on his radio and knew I would be interested. Italian spelling is strictly phonetic and Vito hadn't hesitated. He was clearly very bright. Poor Franca: when she should have been at school the war was on and she was illiterate. She resented his attachment to me.

'*Lo ho due muglieri* — I have two

women,' he would say, *'Mamma e la Signorina.'*

Franca found this hard to take, but she had violently, if unwittingly, disrupted the physical link between them, and she had neither the imagination nor the patience to forge a different one. A hard and deprived childhood had left her no time for play. Her family was large, and money short. When tiny, she used to tell me, she would be sent out before dawn to pick baskets full of white, scented jasmine flowers which she had then to thread on to the withered heads of 'umbrella plants'. These would be sold for weddings and other celebrations. She remembered the damp cold of the early mornings when her fingers froze. Her family needed the money she earned. She could baby-talk with her son, but she could not tell him stories or invent games, so Vito came to me. He loved my stories, games and songs. I tried in vain to draw Franca into our play, but no, she could not. Also she was once again pregnant, and self-absorbed.

She began to bully Beppe, telling him he was a fool to be so good to me: 'You must insist that she should pay you more — she must give you longer holidays — you're a fool to work overtime for her.' And so on.

Her gossiping with the neighbours, with its hostility to me, increased and was disturbing, and she was furious when, once, they were on holiday he got up at 2.30 at night, a week before they were due to return, in order to catch a train to come and see if I was all right and managing without him. It involved a long walk to the station and he missed the train, poor man. Her derision for this act of stupid devotion to duty was hurled at him for months afterwards.

One day, after he had been with me for several years, Beppe announced joyfully that his sister, who had emigrated to the north of Italy to a town in the foothills of the Alps sixteen years before, was coming, with her unknown husband, for a holiday in Sicily.

'Beppe, this is wonderful. You must be there to welcome her as soon as she sets foot on Sicilian soil. Take the day off. Go to Messina and meet them off the ferry.'

He was thrilled. The great day came and, to my surprise, there was Beppe, still working.

'But I thought you were going to Messina?'

'No. Franca didn't want it.'

How long had she been able to command, I wondered?

The sister came. She was an unappetizing piece: bewhiskered, be-trousered, chain-smoking. Those were the days when no Sicilian woman wore trousers. Women from the north who *did* might find that old women would come up to them and take a piece of the trouser material between thumb and finger, scowling severely, as they asked, 'Are you a man or a woman?' (Ten years later all the girls were in jeans.) Beppe's sister was short and thickset like him and was not really made for trousers. But she had come to show the benighted southerners, known by northerners as *terroni,* or people of the earth, how a sophisticated woman from the north was free to do as she pleased and was quite liberated from the old, narrow ideas of the south. Where she now lived, life was wonderful. Women could work and earn so much more than down here. They could put their children into nursery schools while they did so. They had a bathroom in their flat, and a television set. She didn't notice that Beppe and Franca had all these advantages except the factories — a television set was already on order. Or, if she did notice, she decided to smash her brother's contentment. This was only too easy if she worked through Franca. The latter was deeply impressed by all the boasting and posturising and was unable to see, as I did, that her guest had lost all the natural grace and dignity that is the hallmark of the Sicilian countrywoman.

Beppe came to me one day and asked if Franca could have a week off to go with 'her sister', taking the, by now two, children to the village where they had been born.

'But Beppe it is *you* who should have time off, it is *your* sister who is here.'

'No, Signorina. Theirs is such a great and wonderful friendship that I would not stand in the way of their being together. Franca loves her; she was timid at first, but now it is so different . . .'

Was he glad to get rid of the two of them, I wondered? So Beppe stayed behind and the three — the sister's husband was invited as well — and the two children went off.

When the week was over the sister and her husband left. Franca was red-eyed with weeping. She went on for hours and hours.

'Beppe, why is she crying so?'

'Signorina, you must know that she has lost a great and wonderful new sister. She was at first afraid of her, but gradually they grew to like each other and now it is terrible that they have to be separated.'

The crying went on throughout the day. The next morning, Beppe, white-faced and exhausted, reported that she had allowed him no sleep, she had sobbed throughout the night. It continued all the next day, varying between groans, soft whining and heartbroken sobs. A veritable marathon of a weep . . .

I made an attempt to dam the tears. 'But what are you crying for?' I asked.

Between increasing sobs, she blurted out, 'I have lost my best friend.'

'But she's *not* lost, she'll come back. She can write.' Then, desperately, trying to see whether severity would help, I said firmly, 'Stop it at once!'

The answer was increased tears pouring down her cheeks . . .

The next morning a weary, but smiling, Beppe announced: 'It is over. She has stopped.'

High time too.

The mystery of the weeping was cleared up just a month later. It had been the only weapon for the determined Franca to wear him down and to make him accept her plan. They must leave the backward south, and go to the splendid north of her fired imagination. She must be near her dearest friend. They would be rich, richer than they could ever be if they stayed stuck here. On the day after Christmas, which had been marred by an ill-tempered, pouting Franca refusing to take part in any of the festivities, Beppe came into my room: 'Signorina, I have sad news for you. We are leaving at the end of March. All of us.'

'Why?'

'Because she wants to go and get rich with my sister.'

'But Beppe, you have been to work in the north and you didn't like it and you came back.'

'Signorina, if it was my choice I wouldn't go. If it wasn't for the children, I would stay with you and let her go alone.'

'No, Beppe, you married Franca, not me. You must either control her or follow her.' I hesitated, to let this sink in, then: 'Why don't you control her?'

'Because, Signorina, I am frightened of what I might do. You have never seen me in a temper.'

I had, and had found it truly terrifying. One day he had come rushing down the stairs, white hot with rage: 'When you have a moment I wish to speak with you.'

'As you see,' I had hastily answered, concentrating on my writing, 'I am very busy now. When I have a moment we will talk.'

To my relief he had blustered out of the room. I ran round to that wise old body: 'Maria, what have I done to make Beppe so furious?'

'It isn't you he's so raging against, Signorina, it's Catena.'

Immensely relieved that it was the gardener Buneri's daughter-in-law, I told Maria that she could now send Beppe in to me. With me in the lordly bishop's throne I left him standing: 'And what is all this about?'

He shouted, 'She insulted me!'

'But how?'

'She shook, not once, but twice, a blanket out of the window just as I was passing underneath . . . *Twice!*'

'But was it really so terrible?'

'It was an intended insult.'

'But was it really necessary to put yourself a *second* time under the window, when she was shaking blankets?'

He relaxed and we both smiled. His loss of control had been brief but while I thought I had caused it, I had been really frightened by his rage.

And now the Franca problem: 'I am frightened of my rages: twice I have nearly killed her. Once I took a knife. I could have cut her throat, but something saved me. I turned it on myself. Look, I still have the scars on my wrist. That brought me to my senses. Another time, so angry was I, I nearly got my hands around her neck. Instead I seized two tea towels and twisted them until I tore them in two. I am terrified of my temper and of my strength. I can't control Franca without losing it. I gave way after two nights without sleep because of her terrible nagging and weeping, and I promised that we would go.'

'But *you* know what it's like up there and she doesn't. She has no idea what frost and cold in the north can be. She doesn't know what it's like to be a southerner speaking a dialect not understood — and despised. Or to be one of the few to be unable to read or write. She has never seen a factory or shared a flat or kitchen with another family. She can have no idea what it's like, and all is made worse during the long winter. She can hardly imagine it!'

'I've said all this to her, but she won't listen. She says that if I won't agree she'll start weeping again. And, Signorina, I can't face that.'

'But why March?' It was obvious, but I asked.

'Because she thinks it'll be warm up there by then. But *I* know that there could still be snow. It can go on and on . . .'

Hoping to make him assert himself against her ignorance, I tried to shake him: 'You won't leave in March, but just as soon as my lawyer tells me how much notice you must give. I expect it's a month. That means you'll have the worst of the winter there. Of course I can't wait until the spring to find someone to take your place, I must find someone now while there are people looking for work. Think it over very carefully in the next day or so, and then let me know what you decide.'

Franca used her power and was adamant.

Poor little man; they left in January. It was coldish even here, and we never have frost. The two children, by now six and four, were gay and smiling. They had been filled with stories of what the new life was going to be — trains, mountains, snow, cousins, games, truffles (costing more than diamonds as they do?) and other lovely things to eat . . . I suggested that perhaps it

133

would be wiser if they left some of their bigger furniture in Sicily, in case they didn't like life up there and wanted to come back. But Franca insisted that everything must go. All she left were three bottles of rancid olives, which she had failed to preserve, and with which she deliberately blocked what is politely known as the 'Vater' so that I had to have the plumber take the floor up, and a huge nail which, witchlike, she hammered into my favourite tangerine tree. She knew, as I did not, that were it not discovered in time, it would have led to the tree's slow but certain death. Citrus trees cannot stand nails.

Not long after, my neighbours received a letter: 'All is wonderful — far better than there.' He was earning twice as much, their relatives were kind and affectionate, Franca would soon get work, the children were happy in a nursery school and so on and so on. Far too good to be true, I thought. Then a year's silence. Gradually the news of the real situation filtered through. Things were not so blooming. A few months later another sister was sent to feel out the position here. Could they come back? Alas, I had no longer any need of them, having found an ideal couple who were to stay with me for over thirty years.

And so, poor Beppe had to return to the remote mountain village where he had been born and to what casual outdoor work he could find. He had kept a small, dilapidated house there and he settled into it once more with Franca and their two children — another was on the way. All Franca's dreams of wealth and success had evaporated.

Once, he had to come to our town to collect birth certificates and other official documents. He told our neighbour that he wouldn't be seeing me, he felt too ashamed. But the neighbour insisted that he must. He had to pursue me to a restaurant where I was lunching with an old friend who knew his story. We gave him a warm welcome, but he was ill at ease in his best suit which was mainly worn at funerals, and was embarrassed with us. He was thinner and looked much older.

'Signorina, life is not easy; we all make mistakes and we have to pay for them.' He deserved a better fate.

About twenty busy years went by during which I often thought with affection of the little man, and wondered what had happened to him. No one here had seen him or had any news, so I decided to try to find out. With a friend who had known him, and who had also returned after a long interval, we drove to the northern coast of the island and then up a narrow, winding, mountain path. When near the village, which must once have been attractive but had suffered much from war, poverty and unemployment, I asked an old woman, dressed entirely in black, if she knew Beppe. She answered in pure Sicilian that he was dead. I was shaken, but then I remembered that, as most firstborn sons in these villages are called after their paternal grandfathers, duplicate names are common. She still insisted that he was dead, so I asked for his sisters, who were twins. This made her think again. I described the family, citing Christian names of his wife and children, and slowly the old woman became more helpful. Was he the one who had gone away and come back? Had he lost his wife and married again? *That* Beppe lived on the Piazza — she didn't know the number, but it was near the shop, everyone knew *him*.

Much relieved, I walked up to the Piazza and hesitated a moment while deciding whom I should ask for help. Suddenly I found myself being hugged and kissed by a very excited little woman: 'Signorina, Signorina, it really *is* you . . . I knew that you would come here one day. I can hardly believe that at last it has happened! It is a dream come true! The Madonna must have led you here!' It was one of his twin sisters, now fifty years old or more. 'My brother will be so excited, so very, very happy. He always speaks of you. He always hoped . . .'

'But where is he?'

'He's working but he'll be here in a few minutes. He's on a building site. It's heavy work and he's not so young, but they all want him and he's never without work. But it's hard.'

She led us into the diminutive old house. The tiny entrance, which evidently served as a sitting room, was almost entirely filled by a vast modern sofa and a matching armchair, also huge. She made us sit down while she remained, beaming, in front of us. She would not sit with us but stayed standing. By this time a crowd had collected outside, determined to miss none of the drama.

I asked, 'And Franca?'

'She died; her heart was bad.'

It brought to mind a peasant who had once told me, as if complaining of having been done down, that his newly married daughter-in-law had died of heart trouble:

'She wasn't marriageable goods,' he said. But Franca had lasted longer.

'And Vito?'

'He's married. Soon I shall be a great-aunt. He's an accountant, with a good job in the city. He's done really well.'

Good news. A steady, pensionable, white-collar post remains a universal and, for most, an unobtainable dream.

'Maria will soon be coming in. She works in a factory and lives with us.' It costs a lot to marry a daughter, as maintaining dignity over it all is essential and debts can pile up. 'And I've got another niece — she's working too.'

At that moment Beppe came rushing in. The crowd had already told him the good news. I found myself being hugged again and again, but then he drew back: 'I'm in my work clothes, I forgot . . .'

I cut him short, my delight at finding him again so obvious that he saw that I didn't mind. He said that he must go and clean up.

Soon, a changed and polished Beppe returned bearing a tray with a plate of the special Sicilian almond cakes and a bottle of Scotch, a drink seldom downed in that village I would think, but he had remembered my weakness for both and had rushed out to buy them. We drank to all our healths, to our everlasting friendship, to England, to Sicily, and to the future grandchild; there were tears in Beppe's eyes and almost in mine. Meanwhile we had been joined, very timidly, by the new wife — but she was not so new now. She was dressed entirely in black with a black kerchief on her head; a typical, hard-working Sicilian peasant. She spoke no Italian, only Sicilian, which I can understand if it is not too different from the dialect of my province and is not gabbled too fast. But I was not tested, she was far too shy. I tried to put her at her ease but she remained standing, as if almost stunned by this apparition from her husband's remote past. All the women stood and only Beppe drank with us.

'Signorina, now we have met again, we must keep in touch. I have no telephone, but give me your number and I will phone.'

'And you must come back as my guest, with the Signora, and with Maria, who is so proud to have been born in Taormina.'

But he has never come. He phones at Christmas and Easter, but he has never come back. Perhaps he cannot face a return, or to see his successors happily in the house that he could have had, and working in the job that he could have had, if only he had not let Franca become the matriarch.

Another four years, another visit . . . The house is much larger than we thought. This time Beppe with tremendous pride showed us how it stretched behind the entrance where we had sat, and had a back door on another road. He had restored and painted it all since he had retired on a good pension. He cultivates his land, which lies outside the village, selling or freezing what the family doesn't eat. Two enormous freezers are in his new kitchen and they are full. He is a proud house-holder, a proud grandfather and, it seems, a contented husband. This wife certainly looks up to him and he is clearly the master.

Concetta

Old Maria had valiantly managed to cook for much larger numbers than she had been used to in Don Roberto's days, but the poor old thing was failing. One Christmas Day, she indulged herself a little and broke her diet. On Boxing Day, I heard loud shouting coming from the direction of the kitchen; I called down to them to be quiet and let people go on sleeping, but the sounds increased, so I went to investigate. Then, for the first time, I heard the bloodcurdling sound of the Sicilo-Arab lament for the dead: Beppe and Buneri were mourning Maria, who had seized up and suddenly collapsed. She had always hoped to die in harness in the beloved house and happily her wish had been fulfilled. I could not mourn: despite the shock, I could only feel glad for her.

After the death of Maria and the defection of Beppe, the only help I could get was a few hours from a very pregnant daily. Somehow I managed to give two meals a day to a full house, with some help from guests. I had also the duties of a *locandiera* to cope with: taxes, insurance, notification of guests to the police, shopping and also attendance at the many funerals of my uncle's devoted friends. My absence would have caused offence. After six months of this I was whacked and I decided that there wasn't much future in it.

One day Peppino, the gardener who now worked two days a week, asked me whether I would like his wife to work for me. I would have had her for her smile alone: it had shed happiness on our children's Christmas parties.

'When can she come — at once?'

'No, not until her grandfather dies.'

With solemn face and voice I asked how old he was.

'Eighty-seven.'

'Is he happy?'

'No, he drinks too much and he wants to go.'

At intervals I asked after the grandfather. As I was to learn, most people looked after by Concetta get better. However, one day Peppino abruptly asked if the whole family could move into the little house in the garden *at once*.

'And the grandfather? Has he died?'

'No, but the family is accusing us of

keeping him to get hold of his pension. It isn't true, Signorina.' And I knew it wasn't.

They moved in, four of them, a boy of eight and a girl of four. For the first time I saw the extent of the disaster of three years before when their house, in the hills behind Taormina, had been struck by lightning and they had lost everything except their lives and their night-clothes. At that time I had been balancing on a financial razor's edge and when I heard that the village was helping I thought that let me out. I am ashamed to this day, but their dignity and pride had deceived me. They had held their heads high and never begged. It didn't take long to arrange their pitifully few possessions, and the next morning Concetta was ready for work.

'I'm afraid I don't know how to cook,' she said.

How odd, I thought; she had a family to feed and she was intelligent. To myself I said, as so often, *Pazienza, pazienza.* To her, 'Then I will teach you, as I did Beppe.'

I went into the kitchen the next day for the first lesson to find her making a birthday cake for Peppino far beyond my powers.

'But I thought you didn't know how to cook?'

'Oh, I know how to cook for us, but not for you.'

'But I love Sicilian food.'

I was reminded of Maria. The first time I had asked her to boil me an egg, she said: 'But I don't know how.'

'You must have done them for Don Roberto?'

'Oh yes, I know how to do them for *him* but not for you.'

Concetta is with me still. She is a superb cook willing to try — and succeed at — all the many local and foreign recipes I give her. She collects herbs in the countryside and makes delicious dishes with them. She is an expert gardener with 'green thumbs', as they say. She deals with babies, children — even problem ones — with sure, intuitive handling. She knows all about the wild birds and flowers. She was a wonderful nurse when I acquired three fractures of my ankle, tactful, efficient, cheerful and with the necessary sense of humour. Hers was the safest arm when I was relearning how to walk. In addition, as a huntress of hornets she is unique, unlike the pest control officer who considered even a wasps' nest too dangerous to tackle.

After more than thirty years I am still amazed at her reasoning powers, her innate taste, her wisdom and her strength, both physical and moral.

She has had a hard life: first with the Fascists when, instead of studying in her little mountain school, they spent time doing the *Passo Romano* while the boys shouldered their tiny rifles. During the war they were refugees in mountain caves, and she and her cow — she tended it although she was only ten — helped to avoid starvation.

In those prolific days, strangely, she was an only child. She and her mother, saving to build a better house after the war, did a milk round before school. One day her mother, astride a donkey, measuring out the milk, was thrown on to her head when the donkey reared, frightened by a dog. She was brought home dead. Before the year was out Concetta had a stepmother.

She eloped with Peppino, a school companion, when she was nineteen. He has been a very good husband and they have worked together and overcome the disaster of the loss of their house.

I like to think that the happiest years of her life have been spent in Casa Cuseni. She has taken advantage of everything we had to offer and made friends among my guests. Once, as she looked at the many gifts she received from them, she said, 'I have never left the province of Messina, yet I feel I have been all over the world — at least, my photo has.' Her real beauty has grown with the years and she is very photogenic.

And now the son, Nino, is the champion chef of Taormina, with a magnificent gold medal on a chain hanging from his shoulders, and the daughter, Mimma, is a specialised teacher married to a surgeon. The five in the family (for years she and Peppino 'adopted' his nephew, a problem child, as she was the only person who could handle him) have four cars between them — five if you count the doctor's.

Before the latter's arrival in the family there was a crisis when Nino, aged fourteen, put his right hand in a moving ice-cream machine when he went to work in a bar during the school holidays. The employer's wife had the presence of mind to switch off the current while her husband ran out to insure him. He was taken at once to the local hospital. I was in England at the time, receiving letters on the lines of: 'I hope this finds you as it leaves us — we are all very well.' I was therefore shocked to find, on my return, Nino with his arm in a sling and three fingers paralysed. The treatment was massage each day. For a wild moment I thought of flying him back to England, but I told myself he was Sicilian, and must make use of Sicilian services or they would never improve.

Everyone who could have helped seemed to be on holiday and there was no doctor or friend whose aid I could enlist. I waited in great anxiety until a leading Swedish plastic surgeon returned to his winter home and told me that one of his best students, who had worked with him in Stockholm for four years and had married a Swedish theatre sister, now working with him, was Professor of Neurosurgery in Catania. We got the boy to him at once as a private patient and he diagnosed a smashed tendon and a severed nerve. We wanted him to operate but, under the health service scheme which was all that we could afford, Nino had to go to the Ospedale Traumatologico in Palermo, the site for which had been donated by an Englishwoman, Delia Whitaker.

A pathetic couple set out: the father anxious about a long journey to an unknown town; the boy in a huge sling, with an unusable hand and frightened of what might be done to him. All I could do to help was to phone the Anglican padre — I was not a member of his congregation but he was a kind man — and ask him if his manservant could find Peppino a cheap room where he could stay. The padre said at once, 'Don Peppino will be my guest.' A great relief to all of us.

Father and son took with them a huge, brightly coloured cockerel, a magnificent bird.

'Why ever, Peppino?'

'It's a present for the surgeon.'

Its feet were tied, but at least it was upright in a basket and not upside down.

'Couldn't you wring its neck before the journey, the poor thing?'

'No, the doctor must see that it is fresh.' And off the three set. (An American friend who had married a fascinating, handsome, young Sicilian intern in New York without ever having been to Sicily was later to tell me that she had been appalled when, on their first Christmas in Palermo, the balcony of their flat was crowded with live kids, lambs, hens and turkeys that had to be rapidly dispatched, or fed and watered, until they could steadily eat their way through them. Freezers were rare in those days!)

Peppino is known to the hospital staff in Taormina as one who had some training as a nurse when he did his military service, and he is given visiting and other privileges. But in Palermo no one knew him. He felt totally lost. He was told in the ward that he must leave the boy, who of course had never been separated from his family, and could only visit in three days' time. Protests were useless until another patient walked up, put his arm around the disconsolate father and whispered, 'Give the nurse 1,000 lire and when you reach the gate porter the same, and you'll see.' He did, and was allowed to visit daily. Feeling much better he walked down the steps and immediately ran into the very new Mayor of Castelmola, his birthplace. I suspect that the Mayor, on his first visit to the Sicilian capital, was feeling as lost as Peppino and was pleased to see someone with whom he had been at elementary school. They walked along arm in arm and soon the Mayor saw an *onorevole*, a Christian Democrat deputy, whom he knew. So all three walked along together, and a far happier Peppino arrived to a warm welcome from the *Riverendo* who allowed him a free phone call each night to the anxious Concetta on the other side of the island.

The operation was beautifully done and the end result very good indeed.

'Don Peppino is a perfect gentleman: he left a bottle of gin when they went home, and I wasn't there to say goodbye,' said the *Riverendo*. It was a graceful touch from someone who had never drunk any spirits himself. He must have been horrified at the price, but only the best could be offered.

Their great event of each autumn is the *vendemmia*, when Peppino and Concetta are the proudest and happiest of hosts up in their mountain property at Lupinaria, the land of the lupins. In the loveliest, unspoiled countryside they have their old, stone house near a spring. Available water is the most important factor in Sicily. We all go up early to pick the grapes, cutting them off the vines and piling them high into baskets and tubs which used to be carried up to the stamping ground on a donkey, but are now taken up the steep incline on the backs of strong, young men friends of Nino's. They tip them on to the *palmento* where three or four stout bodies trample them down, fruit, skins and all, hour after hour. Once barefoot, they now wear Wellington boots. The purple juice pours through a hole into a strainer basket below and, through it, to a lower stone floor from which it is scooped up in a *quartara*, a four-litre metal measure. The next day skins and pips are crushed once more, by a great rock suspended from a centuries-old beam. The only time, years ago, when I helped in the first crushing, I looked around for somewhere to wash my feet — to the huge amusement of all. You wash your feet after, not before!

Meanwhile, Nino, his chef friends and our hostess are preparing a tremendous meal with gallons of wine. Course after course is served at a sit-down banquet in the upstairs room next to the bread oven, which Concetta has persuaded them to build for her so that she can bake bread as her grandmother did. Up to thirty-five people can be fed till none of us can eat or drink more. Their table rivals mine in overcoming all differences of language, class, age and sex, as we drink to our beaming hosts in the powerful wine of last year. Miraculously, all cars arrive back safely: the wine is not only strong it is *sincero*, that is, pure grape with no chemicals added. It causes no hangover, unlike its opposite, *vino sofisticato*. And the strong, black coffee which ends the meal doubtless helps to clear the drivers' heads.

In Sicily, when the law required those without a surname to choose one, a nickname often became the family name. Thus Quattr'occhio could have been the first man to wear glasses. Could Bev'acqua (drink water) have been an alcoholic? Or was he just mean? Is it significant that Concetta's maiden name was Genio? (genius)

Her arrival was the best stroke of luck that could have befallen me or Casa Cuseni.

Mrs Dylan Thomas

I think it must have been in the early 1950s when, just as I was leaving London to return to Casa Cuseni, a psychiatrist with whom I had previously worked suddenly warned me: 'Wyn Henderson and Caitlin Thomas are in Italy and will probably land on you in Taormina.' Alarmed, I said: 'Hadn't I better refuse, saying that the house is full to overflowing? I don't think I could cope with Caitlin in my museum of a house.'

'You will if you're wise,' she answered.

Some weeks later, I got a letter from Wyn, an old and penniless friend who was supporting herself by being watchdog to the now rich Mrs Thomas — *Under Milk Wood* was paying huge royalties. Caitlin, Wyn wrote, was hoping to write a book. It was to be called *Left-over Life to Kill*. It would be a brilliant success, Wyn was sure; all she needed was a peaceful place in which to write it. Meanwhile, all three of Dylan's children were travelling with them and they would like to come to me.

It was easy to answer firmly that I would not be able to put them all up. But Wyn persisted: she had told Caitlin that I would be the perfect person to provide her with inspiration; they had sent the children to school in England and now could I put up two of them?

Again, I answered I was full. I knew Caitlin was drinking heavily, Sicilian wine was everywhere available and very strong. I couldn't picture myself as a patient, long-suffering hostess for perhaps months. The third letter I didn't answer.

One glorious night when there was a full moon and Etna was deeply covered in snow and bewitchingly beautiful, I saw two figures coming up the terraces of the garden. I just had time to see that one, an assisted blonde, her hair dazzling in the moonlight, had a large wicker basket out of which was sticking a large, half-empty bottle of wine.

'Daphne, you never answer letters. So here we are.'

'What a libel!' I exclaimed.

I kissed Wyn and said: 'I'm sorry, but I'm afraid you're out of luck. My house is being spring-cleaned and painted, and I'm leaving tomorrow for an archaeological dig on the other side of the island.'

They were crestfallen. I had to settle them somewhere, but didn't care to send them to a hotel when I had no idea how badly Caitlin might behave. Almost next door was the family *pensione* of simple Sicilian neighbours who would probably be only too anxious for some clients, as times were still bad for tourism. I went over to ask them and they were delighted. I left early next morning.

After ten days I was back, to find a desperate letter from Wyn. She had looked after Caitlin first in Ischia and then here. In Ischia Caitlin had acquired a lover; he was a tough Sicilian type and he beat her. Wyn had decided she *must* separate them, and this was why she had come to Taormina. Caitlin had seemed willing as she didn't enjoy being beaten. But she now regretted his absence and had written to Gio, who had turned up here and they had disappeared together. (Caitlin had meanwhile told Wyn that I was everything she had fought against all her life!)

Wyn on her own was very welcome. She was an entertaining companion when not deeply distressed about Caitlin's fate. She had been threatening a libel suit against Peggy Guggenheim who, in her autobiography, had written about 'Wyn Henderson of the hundred lovers'. After a week, I found myself saying 'Ninety-five, ninety-six, ninety-seven. Well, I don't think you have much to complain of!' Her intimate friendships had, it seemed, been mainly with the authors of books on my library shelves.

Months later, the erring couple turned up again, but didn't ask to stay with me. Caitlin had quickly made friends with the red-headed Irish doctor in the top flat. They enjoyed teasing each other with insults. One evening he invited her out to dinner warning her: 'Don't bring your brats — I won't have them.' Of course, she brought Colm and Aeron. I saved the situation by saying they could come to me. (Caitlin had by now taken her fifteen-year-old daughter Aeron away from Dartington School in England and placed her in a Catania convent boarding school, poor girl. Catania had turned out to be Gio's birthplace, just fifty kilometres away from Taormina — too near.)

I cooked the children a meal and meanwhile suggested that they should go to the library where they might find an interesting book. As I went to call them I heard Aeron reading, with the lovely Welsh lilt that was Dylan's, the Opies' nursery rhymes she had found on my shelves.

We had a pleasant meal, ending with fruit salad.

'I'm afraid there's no maraschino,' I apologised.

'Thank goodness,' Aeron exclaimed. 'We *always* have maraschino!'

In due course Caitlin packed the children off to school somewhere and settled down with Gio, who once, making a heavy ham of a fist, declared: 'I govern with this!' The last time I saw Caitlin she was walking on teetering high heels down my steep garden path, dressed in a tight-fitting coat and skirt, without a blouse. 'Gio doesn't like them.' Out of the side of her mouth she pushed the angry words: 'This little-woman business isn't going to last much longer.'

But it did. I believe she and Gio were together in Calabria until she died years later. No one was more surprised than I when I received a message that Caitlin sent me her love and admiration. Her memory had clearly betrayed her.

Can I have dreamed it, or did it really happen that when in drink she once cartwheeled down the Corso?

The Godfather

In general people know two things about
Sicily — both of them alarming: Etna and
the Mafia. Curiosity about the latter is great
and never satisfied. In my early days it was
seldom mentioned by the locals. Occa-
sionally someone, when asked directly
about it, would immediately deny its existence. If I mentioned this to other Sicilians
they would look wise and say: 'One who
says that is certainly One of Them.' And
that was about as far as I dared enquire.

One day my friend Franco, a law student, told me an astonishing story. In his
small town, up a valley in the foothills of
Etna, they celebrated *Carnevale* with the
greatest excitement. There would be
dancing and festivities for twenty-eight
nights before the arrival of Lent. The men
of the place were jealous of the honour of
their wives and daughters, which was
closely linked with their own. This meant
that no respectable woman would be
allowed to go out to dance with the men;
they would be shut in their houses while

the men enjoyed themselves. The lack of dancing partners was met partly by boys dressed as girls (Franco told me that one night he had gone as a Spanish *belle* with painted eyes and lips, and dangling ear-rings, while the next he became a man again and went as Hercules in his mother's hearthrug). But the main source of part-ners was women hired from Catania at a price. The bargain was made in advance by the men of the town. I wondered whether it was only for dancing that the Catanesi were paid? Improbably perhaps, I am inclined to think so; jealousy in Sicily being what it is, the husbands from Catania probably kept a strict eye on proceedings. They can hardly all have been pimps?

This year, Franco told me, the men from Catania regretted their bargain and claimed more. This was refused. So they created 'rough house' every night, breaking up the party and threatening to wreck the hall. In vain the priest tried to pacify them; the police seemed helpless they were so outnumbered.

Someone suddenly said, 'Why not call Don Ciccio [pronounced Chicho]?'

He was evidently a superman. He came down from his mountain and had only to walk, arms folded, eyes flashing, with no sound coming from him other than his footsteps, and all the trouble-rousers vanished and the dancing went on.

Fascinated, I asked who this was with so much power.

'The head of the Mafia in these parts.'

Of course I wanted to know more. Franco seemed willing to oblige, unlike others. In those days I had a naive view of the 'Honoured Society'. I pictured it, like Robin Hood, taking from the rich to give to the poor, and generally protecting the weak at the same time as they enriched themselves. This was well before it developed into an international, ruthless organisation of drug-pushing millionaires.

Pleased by the interest he had aroused, Franco said suddenly, 'Would you like to meet him?'

'Indeed I should; but how could I?'

'I'll bring him to call on you.'

I was sure he was boasting. How could a young law student bring such a man to visit me?

Some weeks later, after dark, there was a knock at the french window of the study. I opened it. Franco was there.

'Are you alone?'

'No.'

'How many?'

'Why do you ask?'

'Because I've brought Don Ciccio with me and he's a bit shy — he hasn't shaved today.'

As most Sicilian men hadn't, it didn't seem a likely cause of his shyness. I had only a couple of friends with me: the husband was the Colonel in charge of education in the British Army of Occupation in Austria and his wife was a Cambridge don and a successful novelist.

Reassured, Don Ciccio entered, blinking at the light. He was a wiry little man, quick-moving, sunburnt, almost shabbily dressed; a scar over one eyebrow and dropped eyelid made him hold his head back and up, thus adding to the general impression of ferocious arrogance. He wore the simple working dress of any peasant, but we sensed his power at once. Later the Colonel was heard to say that he had never met anyone so conscious of his own superiority in whatsoever company he might find himself.

Don Ciccio sat on a sofa beside the fire into which, now and again, he would spit with well-directed force. Gingerly I took my place next to him and asked what he would like to drink, painfully aware of the limitations of my tiny cellar of very ordinary wines. (We were still living on the minute post-war tourist allowance.) Franco had told me that my guest produced his own wine which he sold to fortify inferior brands for export. Without enthusiasm he accepted a glass. Franco, to my surprise, had told me that I could ask him anything I liked. Boldly, I asked him how he had joined the Mafia.

Ignoring the question, pontifically he started to answer, *'La nostra Italia* — I don't know whether any of you has ever seen her on the *carta geografica?'* (Except for him we were all of us university graduates.)

At this Franco began translating in excruciating French.

Don Ciccio furiously slapped him down, shrieking, 'You shut up. You know nothing about it, *shut up!'*

'Scusi, scusi, I only meant to help,' almost whispered Franco.

'I will speak and when I reach a suitable place I will stop and the Signorina will translate. You shut up!'

Bravely Franco came back, 'You will have to speak Italian' (meaning not Sicilian). *'Parlo tecnicamente Italiano.'* But it was clear that he was much happier in his usual form of speech, the very different dialect into which he kept slipping.

He started again, '*La nostra Italia* is shaped like a leg.'

And he seized the nearest to him — which was mine. I don't think he was aware that I was on the end of it. Holding it firmly with one hand, with the other he illustrated his points.

'Here off the toe are we Sicilians; *on* the toe is Reggio; then Naples; then Rome; then Florence.'

At each town he gripped the leg in a vice of steel. I wondered what would happen when he reached Genoa . . . But thankfully he stopped at Florence and replaced the object. My mounting anxiety prevented me from grasping his next gambit. But when he stopped I asked him how he had proved his superiority to all other men — a question he took at face value.

'Simple,' he said. 'When I was a young man, if there was a fight to be fought I won it. If there was a mountain to be climbed I got there first; a river to be swum and so on. If, Signorina, you would like a display of my prowess, all you have to do is to lie flat on the floor and make yourself stiff like a corpse, and a corpse is a very heavy thing, and I will put a sash around your waist and — with my teeth — I will lift you to the height of my shoulder!'

His teeth were shining and numerous; they seemed to be more than those of a normal man, as the Colonel remarked later. Half of me was tempted to do it, the other half knew that I was heavier than I look and it would be a bad beginning to our friendship if he could only lift me an inch or two off the floor. (Later, when supping with me in a bistro, he was to seize a heavy chair with his teeth and swing it up until the legs hit the ceiling causing the plaster to fall. Interestingly, the owner did not protest.)

I changed the subject: had he known my uncle, Signor Kitson? I had by now learned to pronounce it in various ways before it was recognised. None of them struck a chord.

I tried again: 'He was called *L'Egregio* — the egregious one.'

'No.'

'Or Don Roberto?'

'Ah, Roberti; he was a great friend of mine. He was under my protection: an individual was giving him trouble. All Roberti had to do was to walk arm in arm down the Corso with me and that fixed that! There was no more trouble. Because he was under my protection he could drive all over Sicily night or day in his open car and no brigand could have laid a finger on him.'

I only wish that my mother, his sister, could have known. She would have been spared much worry about his travelling in an open car all over the island which was known to be full of brigands only too eager to waylay a rich foreigner. Her fears and protests had been ignored and no reason given. Perhaps it was not very respectable to be under Mafia protection even in those far-off days?

I asked about Don Ciccio's family. When he was eighteen months old his mother had gone to the US, and not returned, leaving him behind with his grandmother who had brought him up. He now lived with his 'aunt' (like so many priests, I reflected).

'My mother was a very beautiful woman — blonde. I have never seen her since she left me,' he sighed. 'Although all the women I want are at my disposal, I haven't married because I want her to choose me a wife. One day I shall go to *Newi Yorki* and see her again. She has had many children. One of them is champion boxer of the Marines. Signorina, you must come to my house and tell me what it is that they have sent me. It's a *macchina elettrica* but you plug it in and nothing happens.'

'What's it look like?'

'It has a face like a clock and a magic eye, but you plug it in and nothing happens.'

I suggested that it might be a television. Perhaps New York didn't know that television had not as yet reached Sicily.

'No!' he rapped out.

'A radio?'

'No' again.

'Have you asked an electrician?'

'He knows nothing about it.'

'Then why do you think that *I* should be able to tell?'

'Because there are words written in English and you could read them.'

I promised that one day I would call on him.

He then got up to go, bowed low, kissed my hand and said with dignified emphasis, 'Signorina, I place myself entirely at your disposal. If there is any individual that is displeasing to you, you have but to let me know and . . .' He made a great sweeping gesture of his arm accompanied by a contemptuous snort.

'*Any* individual? A foreigner? An American?'

One was being particularly tiresome at

the time and it would have been nice if he could have been made to leave Taormina. My imagination raced; would he protect my house against burglars? Could he get me precedence in buying a new car when the war damages came through? Settle the boundary disputes that lawyers had tried to but failed? I thought it best to return to the unwanted American.

'Yes, we have excellent communications with *Newi Yorki.*'

'Don Ciccio, you are most kind, but how do I call you if I need you?'

'Simple. You ring the central line to my village, and I will come at once.'

There was no other line or any private telephone to that remote medieval mountain village.

With an imperious wave of farewell to my guests, he backed out of the french window, followed by Franco.

That night I lay awake thinking about the possibilities. Would he be able to stop the ceaseless pestering of tiresome young men, or *pappagalli,* who so infested our walks in the town? He probably would — but how? I could picture knives being brought out and me hanging on to one arm trying to pull him back, and him shaking me off: 'You leave this to me. This isn't woman's work.' And the throats would be cut. Sadly I decided that I could not risk calling him.

A few days later Franco appeared again in a state of some excitement: 'Please, you must call Don Ciccio.'

'But I don't need to; why should I?'

'Because I want to know why he has been summoned urgently by the Principessa Campobello di Fichera to deal with something very important. He wouldn't tell me, but I'm sure he would tell you.'

'Why in the world?'

'Because, when we left you the other night, I asked him what he thought of the Signorina and he answered, "Didn't you hear what I said to her? I don't place myself at the disposal of *any* woman".'

Flattered, and though full of curiosity at Don Ciccio's strange link with the aristocracy, I firmly refused to call the central line — to Franco's disgust. So we never knew what problem faced the Principessa.

Some time later, Don Ciccio paid me another visit. It was early morning and he found me in the garden. Without delay he explained that he had had to come to Taormina to pay his taxes (this aspect of him as a law-abiding citizen with such mundane duties was surprising). He said that he was 10,000 lire short and asked me to lend him the missing sum — of course he would repay it in the near future. In my reduced circumstances I hesitated: either this would be a wise investment which would ensure his immediate help should I ever need it, or it would seriously increase my ever-present money worries. I went up to the house pondering the problem, with him by my side. Both house and garden are of a size and beauty that lead people, especially Sicilians, to regard me as a very rich woman (which in effect I am — in capital terms), but such a house eats money and I have always had to be very wary about people who try to borrow. Ten thousand lire was then a substantial part of my income. Lending it was a hard decision. It could have been curiosity as to the fate of the lire and a wish to test Don Ciccio's honourable intentions, or perhaps a fear of refusing him, that led me to give him the money. I made it clear that it was a big sum to me and that I would only lend it to a special friend.

He took it with warm thanks and then, raising his voice and speaking with great emphasis, he launched into a stream of advice: 'Signorina, I know this world. You must trust *no one*, neither your brother, nor your sister, nor your father, nor your aunt. Only your mother can you trust — she is of the same flesh. You must stay on the horse till the end of the journey with the knife in your hand.'

Odd when his mother had been his first betrayer?

I let several weeks go by before deciding to visit Don Ciccio in his mountain hide-out. I telephoned Franco and asked him to arrange for me and two friends — Jocelyn Brooke, the poet and novelist, and a Swedish guest — to see Don Ciccio at home so that we could pronounce on the *macchina elettrica!* Would he please act as guide and chaperon? Franco was delighted — he liked being seen with foreigners, who in those days were not numerous. He insisted that we should first have lunch with him and his mother in the small town which had so vigorously celebrated *Carnevale*.

We arrived at a large, gloomy, mid-nineteenth-century *palazzo* in the main street, with ugly furniture and thick curtains over the windows which added to the gloom. Sicilians at that time entertained rarely in their homes, and we considered it an honour to be invited. As always they wanted to save face before strangers and a great deal of trouble had been taken by Franco's rather shy mother, who was a widow. We started with very sweet vermouth accompanied by sweet biscuits. It was shortly after noon. Then we sat down round a huge oak table and dish after dish was served by a far from elegant — and probably grossly underpaid and overworked — servant. Franco apologised for her: this, he said, was only his country house and we must excuse any shortcomings. (I very much doubt whether he had any other.) The shortcomings were certainly not in the matter of food or drink. Course followed course. Despite our protests, our plates were piled high time after time and, as soon as we emptied them, wine glasses were refilled almost without our noticing. Sicilians like their food to be appreciated, and they find it difficult to believe that a firm 'No thank you' to a second or third helping means just that. In my time I have eaten heroic meals in the cause of fraternisation. My companions were not so practised. Our hostess spoke no English and two of her guests had only a few words of Italian, so eating and drinking tended to take the place of conversation. We made our way through great heaps of pasta, then fish, meat, vegetables and cheese followed by cream cakes and fruit. It was all delicious. Next, very sweet Marsala. Mercifully there were tiny cups of espresso coffee when at last we came to the end.

By then we had been steadily eating and drinking for three hours. Franco announced that Don Ciccio would be waiting for us and we must go. The coffee had made me just capable of driving my new and rather small car about ten kilometres to the village of Motta. We snaked up the winding, narrow road, with one hairpin bend after another, through the glorious hilly country. High above us we could see the medieval village perched on a huge, precipitous rock. Franco told me to stop. He stood up in the car, put his hands to his mouth and let out a long and piercing whistle. Immediately there was an answering call from behind the rock above us and Don Ciccio appeared, silhouetted against the sky. He waved to us and then with an agility that would have done credit to a mountain goat and was amazing in a man of his age — he must have been around fifty — he ran, hopped and skipped down the almost sheer hill face.

'Signorina, welcome,' as he kissed my hand and shook those of my friends.

It was a very different Don Ciccio from that of his first visit to me. Today he was meticulously shaved, he wore a smart dark suit more suited to the city than the country and under it he had an exquisite shirt of pure white silk, obviously custom made.

'You must come and see my land first and then my house.'

I began locking up rugs and coats in the boot of my car.

'There is no need,' he said curtly.

In those days of austerity after the war new clothes and rugs were all but unobtainable.

Daringly I demurred: 'But Don Ciccio, people don't know that we are your guests; people are poor and these would be such a temptation.'

Without another word he took off his cap and laid it upside down on the bonnet and then said, 'Follow me.'

Surreptitiously I stole a look at the cap. It was a very ordinary affair with apparently no name or distinguishing mark on it. But our belongings remained there for the best part of three hours on the road only half a kilometre from the poverty-stricken village and no one laid a finger on them or the car.

We were still sluggish after our gargantuan meal, and greatly relieved when he led us up the high rock where we had first seen him by an easier, kinder path than the one he had run down. Standing at the very top, outlined again against the sky and very much monarch of all he surveyed, he proudly pointed out his large property far down in the valley below. It was green and beautifully cared for with olive and almond trees, vines, artichokes and beans.

Then he pointed out other properties: 'That one there, he's good, we don't have to use much persuasion, he gives to the poor.' (The Robin Hood side of him — but persuasion?) 'That one' — pointing in another direction — 'he's tough and we have to insist a bit.'

We walked on to the village. Unexpectedly and so quietly that only I could hear, he said, 'On this spot a man was murdered.' (By him? Who knows?)

We reached the medieval village clinging to the steep escarpment of Ice Age rocks: the church in the middle with long-ago builders' signs carved boldly on its walls; the streets barely wide enough for one car to pass; and the smaller pathways with steps cut into the rock. Except at the height of summer, the sun could barely reach most of the houses. In one of the narrowest, Don Ciccio stopped, pulled out a large key and bade us welcome to his home where he said he lived with his aunt. She was not there to receive us.

The house could not have been more simple. The stone walls were bare with no plaster; the stairs were of rough wood with no covering; the ground floor had one room used for storage; the ceiling was low, adequate for Sicilians, but taller northerners had to stoop. Apart from one tap in a corner there was no sign of any plumbing. The room on to which the stairs opened had a stove and gas cylinder. It was a strange background for our so elegantly dressed host. We followed him into the other small room where the only furniture was a narrow truckle bed occupying the whole length of one wall, a small round table with some plates and glasses on it, and five very ordinary wooden chairs with string seats.

The only object to distinguish it from the humblest peasant's house was the *macchina elettrica* on a shelf on the wall. This was taken down — almost with contempt. He plugged it in and nothing happened. We all agreed that it was a very old and quite useless crystal set. I broke this gently to Don Ciccio. *Newi Yorki* had

clearly disposed of this old set to the sup-
posedly dumb, remote Sicilian half-
brother.

He accepted our verdict dubiously and
with ill grace and then he turned to the
very ancient, framed photograph of his
mother and aunt. Neither of them was
good-looking to my way of thinking, but:
'As you see,' he said, 'my mother is a very
beautiful blonde.'

She was neither beautiful nor blonde,
but I admired her with enthusiasm, which
pleased him.

'One day I shall go to *Newi Yorki* and
meet her and she shall choose me a wife.'

It seemed to me that it would be a cruel
meeting with, in all probability, a stout and
blowzy Brooklyn housewife. How much
happier for him if he could preserve his
fantasy. My opinion fortunately was not
pressed; food was more important at that
moment.

Our host first drew out from under the
bed a bottle of red wine that he had made
from his own grapes. He pulled the cork
and exclaimed with pleasure at the curious,
mouldy-looking substance revealed: it
looked rather like a fat white grub curled
around the rim to seal it properly. He
removed it with his fingers before he filled

our glasses. Despite our reluctance to consume any more wine, we knew we had to accept. He then knelt down again and pulled from under the bed a huge loaf of the heaviest home-baked bread; next came a barrel of olives swimming in oil of the strongest flavour; then came a huge slab of pecorino cheese — far from my favourite; last, a hunk of the fattest smoked bacon I had ever seen. We were all too aware of our already overtaxed stomachs as we watched the preparations with alarm. Once again our plates were piled high. Don Ciccio cut the bread against his chest with a sharp knife; then a thick slice of bacon was placed on each piece. Desperately we begged for mercy, explaining that we had eaten too much and too recently. Don Ciccio's eyes flashed; Sicilian hospitality was at stake. He was used to being obeyed. He wouldn't take a refusal. I had experienced rather similar situations before, and I have mercifully a strong digestion, but my poor friends had not. They were only just learning that one could not insult Sicilian hospitality, however outrageous.

Out of the side of my mouth I hissed, 'Eat, *eat* for the honour of England.'

And we did, under the fierce eye of our host; only a piece or two disappeared into bag or pocket. The strong wine helped to wash it all down. Our host beamed as he achieved our submission.

At last we were allowed to go: we staggered down the stairs and steps and reeled along the narrow streets, grateful for the fresh air and the few hundred yards to walk to the car. Don Ciccio picked up his cap from the bonnet, put it on his head, shook hands with the men, kissed my hand and that of my Swedish woman friend. Sated as she was with fatty food, she still found this 'superman' fascinating, unaware that he had whispered to me, 'She is beautiful, but too old!' She wasn't old, but her hair was an exquisite white — which any Sicilian woman would mistakenly have dyed — and it framed eyes of dazzling blue.

Don Ciccio, who was not a driver, told me how and where to turn the car around. By this time I was obeying every command with no opinion of my own and only too anxious to get us all safely home.

The next day, and the next, both my companions spent in bed nursing their livers and taking only sips of water. I, with more practice, survived — but only just . . .

Our next meeting was by pure chance

months later, perhaps more than a year. The famous botanist Collingwood Ingram arrived with an introduction to me. He had been assured — by whom, I wondered — that in Sicily I would be able to show him places where there were unusual wild flowers. He was accompanied by his wife, a silent, long-suffering woman, and they came in a very old Austin saloon car. It was still difficult, if not impossible, to buy new cars and this one had been to many distant countries and looked as if it had tackled many rocky, ill-made roads.

Collingwood Ingram was a bit of a dictator, used to getting his own way. He insisted that I should spend a day with him. I suggested going up the Alcantara valley and warned him that it was pretty wild and, as there would be no café or restaurant, we should take a picnic. No, he didn't want to; nor would he start early so as to get back in time for a late lunch.

We set off, but it was some time before he found something that really excited him. Then: 'We *must* go on. Surely there must be *somewhere* we could eat?'

His wife had been sitting at the back steadily knitting, in silence, as she had doubtless done during tours of China,

Afghanistan and South America in search of flowers.

'I *told* you that there was nowhere. We must go back or stay hungry.'

Suddenly I saw Don Ciccio in the middle of a tough-looking group of men. 'Would you be prepared to eat with the head of the Mafia?' I asked. 'He's over there. If any man can arrange to feed us, he can.'

Collingwood Ingram was intrigued and nodded. I went up to the group. Don Ciccio kissed my hand and welcomed me warmly. His companions melted away.

'Of course I can get food — over there in that house.'

We left the car and were taken into a simple peasant home where Don Ciccio was clearly a welcome guest. The housewife, undaunted by the unexpected presence of three unknown foreigners, began preparing a delicious meal of bread, pasta, eggs and tomatoes.

We sat ourselves down on hard chairs in the bare room. Collingwood Ingram was fascinated. The knitting continued.

'He's wonderful. Would he let me draw him, or would he be offended?'

'I think he'd be both flattered and delighted.'

Don Ciccio agreed and at once adopted

an arrogant pose, leaning his head back with one arm hooked behind his chair back. Collingwood Ingram sketched quickly and Don Ciccio demanded to see it.

'Not up to much — very poor,' he asserted.

Cowardly, I modified my translation.

The food fortunately arrived at this moment. Everything was spotless and tasty. We all ate heartily and drank strong Sicilian wine. At the end of the meal I tried tactfully to pay. Don Ciccio firmly refused with a wave of his hand. I didn't see *him* offer any money but our hostess was beaming. Perhaps it was an honour to entertain friends of Don Ciccio? But she didn't look as if she could afford to.

We went back to the car, and then to my amazement Don Ciccio said he was coming with us. He sat himself in the back of the car beside the knitter.

'On!' he shouted, waving his arms towards the driver.

Collingwood Ingram, as surprised as I was, obeyed silently.

A few kilometres on, in the great valley at the foot of Etna which towered above us, I suggested that we should stop and look for flowers. Somehow — I didn't see how — Don Ciccio possessed himself of the botanist's knife. At first Collingwood Ingram didn't notice; his attention was on a certain plant. What colour were the flowers? I had never seen them in bloom, so I asked Don Ciccio if he knew.

With no hesitation: 'Blue!' he pronounced.

'Are you sure?' I asked, anxious that the National Museum should not be given false botanical information.

He almost spat out the words, 'What does it matter? This is child's play.'

Collingwood Ingram looked at the plant carefully again, and said that he'd like to take one with the root. He then discovered that he hadn't got his knife. Don Ciccio pulled it out and in a flash he had plunged it into the soil and brought up a mutilated root.

By this time the botanist was dancing up and down in a rage. 'Daphne,' he yelled. 'Get that knife away from that lunatic!'

Somehow I managed it and Collingwood Ingram went down on his knees and got up a specimen, this time whole. We went back to the car where the knitting needles were still clicking away.

'On!' again shouted Don Ciccio; and again Collingwood Ingram obeyed.

Another five kilometres on: 'Stop!' came firmly from the back seat, and again the order was obeyed — it seemed to have become a reflex. A splendid-looking peasant woman with flashing dark eyes put her head through the window lowered by Don Ciccio. A long conversation in pure Sicilian followed. I could see Collingwood Ingram getting impatient, but he said nothing.

At last Don Ciccio wound up the window. And 'On!' came the cry from the back.

'A beautiful woman — at my disposal night and day.'

Anxiously, in view of the knitter, I translated. It was received in silence.

By this time Collingwood Ingram was getting anxious about the time. He didn't like driving in the dark, and Taormina was about thirty kilometres away. 'Stop!' came once more from the back and we stopped. Don Ciccio got out and advanced on a splendid painted cart by the side of the road. No owner was visible. Don Ciccio took the whip and cracked it three times. At once a man appeared from behind a hedge. The two men embraced and started a long conversation, again in Sicilian. It seemed the business was important. Minutes went by; there was no sign that the discussion was approaching an end. I felt I *had* to intervene to prevent outright insults or even fisticuffs between the botanist and the *mafioso*. Timidly I advanced on the two and said that the Signor Dottore was not very young and must get back. Don Ciccio graciously told us to proceed.

'But how will *you* return?'

'I have other means.'

Only the cart seemed visible on the vast plain. It didn't look as if it would get him back to his mountain home. But he waved us on and stayed. It had not been a very successful day botanically, but at least Collingwood Ingram had got a splendid photo of a magnificent piece of topiary. Two cypress trees growing side by side had been cut into the likeness of our British Queen Mary: bust, toque and all. She had once passed that way when staying with the Duca di Bronte, the then Duke's uncle. 'Now there's a *real* Queen for you,' Turiddu had once said, and many Sicilians felt the same. The day was not wholly lost. The photo was enlarged and filled a whole page of the *Illustrated London News*. Collingwood Ingram was the brother of the editor.

On his short visits to see me, Don Ciccio

had often said that he wanted me to come with him on a *schittichiata.*[*] (pronounced skitikiáta) in the spring. He would take me to meet *brava gente*. It sounded intriguing but possibly alarming. He assured me that they were special people and I pictured myself and my friends, whom I had hastily suggested should accompany me, being welcomed into the very bosom of the Mafia. To my relief Franco was to come with us. Surprisingly Don Ciccio didn't appear to mind being driven by a woman. We drove up and up, along a winding and ravishingly beautiful road with the Sicilian spring at its best. We reached one of the highest villages in Sicily where the snow had melted only that morning. Instead of the toughs I had expected we were welcomed by his uncle and aunt, an old couple, he with one arm (the other had been lost in the First World War), his wife respectable and motherly. Great were the embracings. She had obviously done much to help the poor *bastardo* long ago abandoned by her sister. They were proud of his worldly success — but how much did they really know? We watched,

[*] Sicilian dialect. The word means a festive picnic in the country among friends.

fascinated, as we saw Don Ciccio assume the role of attentive son. Only a scar over his eye suggested the violence of his life.

We spent a long, boring and hungry morning with their granddaughter and her fiancé, a prissy young man who was an elementary school master heavily aware of his importance in this remote and backward village. We examined and admired her trousseau; we expressed amazement at the beauty of the matrimonial bedspread painted with putti floating on pale blue clouds; we admired the hand-embroidered sheets that she had been collecting since childhood. Our foreign presence attracted a small crowd of villagers outside the house. Few foreigners had ever been in the village except during the war and they had certainly never seen a woman driving a car.

At long last, at about three o'clock, we sat down to a great *spaghettone,* a dish of utterly delicious spaghetti ruinous to our figures. We were hungry. To my surprise it was the head of the Mafia who humbly waited on everyone and was the last to sit down and eat. Conversation once more was strained, with my friends confined to smiles and gestures.

After the meal the room was cleared for music and dancing to an old gramophone. Don Ciccio continued to surprise me. He was the first Sicilian I had met who couldn't dance; he had no rhythm and had little control over his feet, which trod heavily on mine. Most Sicilians seem to be born dancing, but not he who was so nimble on mountains. He even expressed regret but, ever resourceful, he disappeared to return a few minutes later saying, *'Adesso che mi sono profumato i capelli, puo' darsi che andrà meglio!'* (Now that I have scented my hair perhaps it will go better.) But it didn't.

While he was trying with Ingeborg, with no more success, I chatted with the aunt and learned that the conspicuous scar over his right eye was due to his falling downstairs when he was two. It certainly added colour to his Mafia side. Did the old people know of his other life? I wondered yet again.

It was an astonishing yet tame *schittichiata*, but surprise was still in store. In the car on the way back he reverted to his arrogant, commanding self, insisting that we should guess who was the greatest hero of all time.

We started with an Italian: *'Giulio Cesare?'*

'No!'

'Napoleone?'

'No!'

'Winstoni Churchilli?'

'No!'

We avoided Mussolini, knowing that our host had been in a Fascist gaol. We tried no Pope, as he was believed to be anti-clerical. Roger of Sicily? No, again. Who else could we suggest? We knew his knowledge of history was scanty.

He broke our silence with a contemptuous, *'Martino Lutero,* of course!'

'But why?' I exclaimed. Luther was about the last name I would have dreamed of offering.

'Don't you remember, Signorina, how in the year 154– (I forget which but I am sure he was right) when he arrived in Rome, he knelt down and said *"O Roma città perduta"?'*

This agreement with Don Ciccio's own view of the accursed city, the capital of the hated *continente* as the Sicilians call it, sufficed to place his hero on such a pinnacle — and perhaps his antagonism to the Catholic Church came into it? It was a surprising end to a surprising day. Don Ciccio was no longer the modest, considerate nephew. He was once again the leader of men with no doubt of his superiority to all of us.

I think that two or three years went by before I had a 'safe' reason for summoning my protector. By this time he was no longer calling me 'Signorina' but 'Mr Dafferty', partly, I supposed to show that our friendship had progressed and partly to show that he was a man of the world, familiar with the English language. That winter the four highest villages in Sicily were completely cut off by snow. The houses there were not built for this; the people's only form of heating was provided by small charcoal-burning *scaldini* which warmed little but their feet; their clothes were inadequate and they had limited stocks of food. Their suffering must have been intense. The government arranged for some supplies to be dropped by helicopter; the church appealed for funds, but money (even if the food and clothes it could have bought would have helped) was useless, all roads being impassable. I thought immediately of Don Ciccio: one of the villages was where we had had the *schittichiata*. I began collecting essentials.

I was walking down the Corso when my friend Madame Rosa called to me: 'Signorina Daphne, that English friend of yours, the one you told about my collecting that money after the floods in England, has sent me 5,000 lire — all that was left, he said, of his tourist allowance. He said he was ashamed that it was so little but he wanted to show that an Englishman did not forget.' (If anything was left of the small sum then allowed us, it was certainly illicit. He had not stayed in a modest hotel.) 'He wants me to get it to those poor people up there. How can I? I don't know anyone there and no one can get through. Could you do anything?'

'I think that perhaps I might. Give me the money. I will buy things and put them with what I already have.'

The Anglican Church never understood why I did not contribute to their fund. I got my help there several weeks before they managed it. That evening I rang the central line in Motta, and at eight o'clock next morning Don Ciccio was on my terrace. I was busy with something I couldn't leave, and called down to him from the balcony that I would come down as soon as possible.

I asked an English friend, a grandmother, 'Mary, please can you go down at once and entertain Don Ciccio until I can come?'

With great presence of mind, before breakfast on a Monday morning, she seized a brandy bottle and there she was when I arrived, swilling brandy with the head of the Mafia. As they had no words in common apart from *Buon' giorno,* drinking once more had to take the place of talking. Don Ciccio had poured the stuff straight down his throat. (It is a trick that takes long practice, as I discovered when I tried.)

I had filled two large holdalls and quickly explained that I knew that — if any man could — he would get these to Santa Domenica to his aunt.

He bridled at once: 'My aunt has no need of charity!'

'Your aunt,' I hastily interrupted, 'is an honest, God-fearing woman who will divide these things amongst the poorest, those who are most in need.'

'Take your pen and write, Mr Dafferty.' And he pompously dictated a letter explaining the situation. He ended with an emphasised 'N.B. — you know what that means, Mr Dafferty?'

I nodded.

'*Nota bene:* This help is to go to the poorest!'

He refused more drink, to my relief, and then swung the two huge bundles on to his shoulders and back and started down the garden path. I accompanied him to the gate.

There he stopped, placed the holdalls on the wall and said, 'But Mr Dafferty it is for *you* that I would wish to do something.'

'That's very kind of you, but you see I have no need. What would you suggest?'

'I will give you an example; I will tell you the story of the little Baronessina. She was very young, she was very beautiful and very rich. An elderly *avvocato* wished to marry her and asked her parents for her hand. But he didn't please them.' (The Baronessina evidently wasn't consulted.) 'So they said no. So he kidnapped the Baronessina. You realise of course, Mr Dafferty, that had there been any publicity, had the police or the press known, she would have been unmarriageable. So they summoned me and within twenty-four hours she was back at home *perfetta* and *completa*.' (The kidnapper was clearly a slow starter.) 'Of course Mr Dafferty I hope that never . . . But if . . .'

He bowed, took up the huge bundles

and departed. A lesser man would have been ashamed of being seen as a beast of burden. I never needed to call him again.

Next time I saw him, I was driving across the island to the north coast with my gardener, Peppino. We were going to buy young orange trees. Suddenly I spotted Don Ciccio in a group of men. He had already seen me and would have been grossly offended had I not stopped. Feeling embarrassed in front of Peppino about my strange friend, I went towards the group. Don Ciccio was delighted to see me and we chatted for a few minutes. Rather sheepish, I got back into the car.

Peppino to my surprise said, 'I know that type of man.'

'You do? How?'

'You remember I told you about the patient in the hospital, who was kind to me when I was feeling lost in Palermo and Nino's hand was so bad? The one who told me to tip the nurse and then the porter, and how after that I could visit daily? Well he was one of them!'

Once again the Robin Hood aspect.

Several years passed without my seeing or hearing of Don Ciccio. I didn't know whether he was dead or alive. Then in 1989 Jonathan Hunt, the biographer of

Jocelyn Brooke, whose description of Taormina and my house I quoted earlier, came to stay. He was hoping to learn something about the two winters that Jocelyn had spent at Casa Cuseni. When I suggested it he jumped at the chance of seeing where Don Ciccio had given us the gargantuan meal, also described in *The Dog at Clambercrown*. We drove up the corkscrew road to the mountain village.

Little had altered. The same group of old men were playing cards in the bar where not a woman was to be seen; *they* were either hidden in the houses or carrying huge loads of firewood, or food for animals, or their families, on their heads. There were a few cars parked dangerously in the far too narrow, curving streets. I had entirely forgotten which was Don Ciccio's house among the buildings in the medieval heart of the old Motta. We had to ask many times — and yet I was certain everyone knew of him. The inhabitants stared at us with ill-concealed curiosity, but for some reason they didn't want to tell. At last a man in a shop pointed it out. We scrambled off the main street down steep steps to a narrow path, wide enough only for pedestrians. We recognised it because there was a large mourning notice for the death of his aunt. The house was even smaller than I had remembered it. I knocked loudly and a fine-looking, dignified, middle-aged peasant woman, with a brightly coloured kerchief on her head, opened the door a crack. She looked surprised, but yes, Don Ciccio was in.

'Will you please tell him that Mr Dafferty Kitsone is here and hopes to see him?'

As soon as he heard my voice, he called down the stairs, 'Come up, come up!'

His welcome was spontaneous and warm. He was in the small bedroom where we had eaten. It seemed that nothing was changed except for one addition. The same single truckle bed was against the wall still bare of plaster; the food was still stored beneath it. There were three simple kitchen chairs, and a table on the middle of which, among the plates, glasses and medicines, was a bright scarlet telephone of the most modern design. It was a shrunken, grey-faced Don Ciccio. He was not well; he was 'coughing out his lungs from too much smoking'. But his eyes still flashed as he reproved me for not having warned him of my visit.

'I would have liked to have given you a meal — now I can only ask you to favour me with this.' He pointed to his simple dish of beans and pasta.

A meal was just what we were determined to avoid. I explained that I had to get back for urgent business at home. He looked as if he would have liked to command us to eat, but he was too weak to go on insisting.

'In any case how could I have let you know?'

He pointed with pride to the one and only luxury object in the room: 'You could have rung.'

'Yes, but I didn't know you had such a wonderful thing,' I congratulated him, continuing: 'Don Ciccio, not long ago I had a burglary: my beautiful ear-rings, a ring and a little marble statue were taken. If I had rung you would you have been able to get them back?'

'Of course, but only if I had known at once. It is too late now.'

So he still had his contacts . . . With whom? I shall never know. But I do at times wonder what a son of his is up to in London. Hardly Robin Hood activities?

One day I shall go back to Motta. But I don't think I shall find Don Ciccio. He still owes me the 10,000 lire . . .

Don Roberto

Vincenzino

Beppe

Daphne and Don Ciccio

Daphne in 1948

Daphne with duck. *Photograph taken by Henry Faulkner and posed by him!*

Inauguration of Macrì's theatre

Marketing in Giarre

Henry Faulkner at the Taormina Carnevale

Bertrand Russell at Casa Cuseni in 1949

Roald Dahl   Tennessee Williams

Caitlin Thomas

The terrace

Daphne with Concetta and Snoopy

The *salotto* at Casa Cuseni

Daphne in the garden
at Casa Cuseni

The Brangwyn dining room
at Casa Cuseni

The *salone* at Casa Cuseni

Daphne

Concetta with her granddaughter,
Daphne

Social Work in Sicily

Our straitened circumstances meant that, during my first visit, Eve and I had to be meanly economical. This was not so difficult after years of war and austerity. Britain was still in the grip of the latter; luxuries of any kind were scarce. Sicilian food was a delicious change with its tasty bread, garlic, fresh sardines, olive oil and all the citrus fruit at its best. It had been sadly lacking at home. Yet we should not have enjoyed it if we had had more money to spend; it would have separated us from the great majority of the Sicilian people, who had suffered much more severely than we had. Often, after hours of queuing for their meagre rations, they would find that supplies had run out and had to leave empty-handed. As so often happens in so much of this unfair world, the rich and privileged could afford to eat in expensive restaurants and keep the produce from their estates. On the few occasions we were invited out, we gazed in amazement at the great hams, huge cheeses, kilo slabs of butter, none of which we had seen for years.

Outside, in all probability, would be thin, ailing children pressing their hungry faces against the glass doors to be hastily shooed away with the starving dogs and cats. It was not an experience we enjoyed or wished to repeat.

As soon as we felt a bit settled in and could undertake problems outside Casa Cuseni, the social worker in me had begun to function and I asked about the Hostel for the Aged Poor. This refuge, mentioned earlier, had been founded by a Dutchman, Grandmont. After his death my uncle had been its President for twenty-five years, during which time every lira had had to be raised, there being no government provision. Notices would be posted in hotels asking people not to give to beggars — they often managed to collect more in a day than honest, hard workers — but to help the hostel. Being English, Robert could guarantee that the money would be honestly spent. He had also been persuaded to organise fund-raising events, and when he sold a picture he would exclaim, I am told, 'Today my poor will eat well!'

From my earliest years I had heard about the hostel, with the dozen or so old people and the devoted nuns who looked after them. I was horrified to learn that now they were near starvation. The nuns were no longer in charge. Instead, a blind man and his fierce wife were wardens and they were said to be stealing what little food there was. In fact it looked as if twelve old people would be thrown out on to the street all because one Englishman had died. Most people seemed to think that the football team was of greater importance. Something *had* to be done. In despair I turned to Turiddu, still with us in those days.

'Simple!' he declared in his melodramatic way. 'It is the tradition of the house to organise a lottery when the hostel is in need.'

'Of what?'

'Always a lamb — and two of your uncle's paintings. The tickets must be cheap; Don Roberto insisted on that, as everyone had to be able to buy one — never more than fifteen lire.'

'But how do we get a lamb?'

'Simple: we go down to the monthly market on the beach and bring a little one up here. He will grow fat on the grass above, and be a great prize for anyone.' Turiddu rejoiced in being in charge and arranging matters — as long as I produced the cash.

One beautiful morning we started down the rocky path to the beach where a fair was held each month. We soon overtook an old couple leading a sheep and two lambs. In pure Sicilian, which I couldn't follow, and with a great deal of shouting and waving of hands and arms, a bargain price was fixed. I suggested therefore that there was no need to take the poor animal all the way to the beach when he would have to be dragged up the hill again. The old man thought it was a good idea, but his wife, evidently the manager, was against, so we all continued down.

While we looked around at the crowded and gay scene with peasants, horses, pigs, sheep and, alas, songbirds in cages, Turiddu kept an eye on his lamb. Soon we saw him advance angrily on the old woman. She was sitting bolt upright on the sand with her legs stretched out in front of her, a kerchief on her head to keep off the hot spring sunshine, munching away on a piece of bread and pretending to be not in the least interested in Turiddu. Obviously she had insisted on the whole troupe coming down because she had hoped to find a more generous purchaser. She continued munching steadily, feigning deafness as his voice rose higher and his gestures became fiercer. But suddenly she gave up and took the notes he was waving, with ever-increasing fury, in front of her nose. 'Martino' was ours at the price first fixed.

He was a splendid animal and surprisingly clean; he had clearly been laundered before his sale.

'Turiddu, why Martino?'

He looked at me pityingly for my ignorance: '*All* lambs are called Martino.'

The acquisition of Martino proved to be only the first hurdle. Turiddu told me that the draw for the lottery always took place on the day of a main religious *festa*. It would have to be, for us, either on Easter Sunday or later on Corpus Domini when the town would be crowded with the faithful coming from surrounding villages to join in the procession. I would have to go and ask the Archpriest to 'give' me one of those days, so I went to the *Arcipretura* and was graciously told that Corpus Domini would be ours. Only a few days later I discovered that he had given the same day to some university students so that they could stage their rag. This was serious. Turiddu looked upset. On that day, he said, they would go wild. Few respectable women would venture out and all the shops would barricade their windows. They might easily kidnap poor Martino and would certainly insult the four attractive girls who had promised that they would accompany him, hoping to sell last-minute tickets. What were we to do? He told me that I must go and beard the chief student (he was later to become a corrupt mayor) and implore his help. Generously he agreed that we could have the first part of the ceremony and be left in peace; they would perform later on.

Meanwhile another difficulty cropped up. We had noticed that next door, on a flat roof, a middle-aged man would often wander up and down gazing longingly at us in the garden below. Turiddu said he was a lawyer, but *pazzo* — mad. He was offering to buy a whole book of tickets in return for an introduction to the Signorina.

'Of course we must accept.'

Turiddu, very firmly: 'It would not be suitable.'

'Why ever not?'

'Last time he got an introduction he pestered her for months.'

'The tickets aren't selling too well, the offer's rather good.'

Very firmly indeed: 'It would not be suitable.'

I yielded.

The day arrived. Martino, by now fat and strong, was encased in resplendent harness of red and yellow braid, the colours of Sicily. We were all dressed in our best clothes, though the Sicilian girls were much smarter than us, rationed as we still were in England. We started down the Corso. Almost immediately the students' rag overtook us. Dressed as Red Indians they careered about on small motorbikes firing off popguns and crackers. Martino bolted into the nearest shop, dragging his signorina with him and creating havoc inside, but the shopkeeper was kind: this was a work of charity, and he liked the signorinas. After this unpromising start the students mercifully kept their word and disappeared — possibly they had forgotten they had ever given it?

At last we reached a piazza in front of a small church, just after the religious procession had arrived. The *pazzo avvocato* rushed up and bought a single ticket asking for change from fifty lire. He had introduced himself and now considered he knew us. He was not to give us anything like so much trouble as the younger *pappagalli*.

The piazza was a dazzling sight, with brightly coloured bedspreads hanging from the surrounding balconies and the roads and alleys covered in many-coloured flowers. (How many, I wondered, had been stolen from my garden?) There was the Archpriest in magnificent vestments, bearing the Blessed Sacrament in a gold and jewelled casket, flanked on either side by minor clerics also in splendid robes. We placed ourselves on a small platform at the edge of the piazza, up a flight of steps which afforded some protection against the excited, pushing crowd of the faithful.

I exclaimed, 'This is like being on the balcony of Buckingham Palace!'

'Only the Royal Family doesn't have to work so hard for its footing,' said Eve.

The Archpriest uttered a short prayer and then raised the Host. People fell to their knees, crossing themselves, and then, totally unexpected by us, ear-splitting fireworks, rockets and, it seemed, bombs were let off. It was a most infernal row and we, who not so long before had been bombed in all seriousness, did not enjoy it any more than poor Martino. We managed to control him and prepared for the draw.

The procession moved on, but people stayed behind to watch us. I had been told by the irreverent that generally the Arch-priest did the draw and that he would hide the winning ticket in the folds of the ample sleeves of his cassock — doubtless a libel as he would, of course, still be processing. To show that our lottery was above board, I picked a small girl, rolled up her sleeves and told her to show her naked arms to the crowd. She took a ticket out of the glass bowl which had been well stirred round by us. The number was 563. Turiddu yelled it out and right down at the edge of the crowd a man came waving his ticket. He managed to reach us on the steps, not an easy task, but his triumph was short. He had 566. No one else came forward nor, distressingly, did they for the next two numbers for the much-desired pictures. We were becoming embarrassed, but there were by now two more prizes: someone had given a rabbit, sadly still alive, and a friend had offered to sketch a portrait of the fifth winner. Mercifully the numbers for both of these came up, but the rabbit was not there to be given away in the sight of all. We had decided that we could not expose *two* frightened animals to the racket, or control them, and that it would have to be fetched by the winner the next day. Our lottery was beginning to look like a total fraud.

Just as we were wondering what we were

going to do with poor Martino, as the crowd and noise had died away, two women came up the steps: 'I knew this morning that I was going to win this lottery,' the elder one said, and she didn't seem at all taken aback that she now had charge of this large animal. She had a garden and would put him in that. Thankfully we handed him over. This was the beginning of a long and faithful friendship with Madame Rosa, the most affectionate and admiring friend of the British. I never knew what Martino's fate was. I expected he must have ended at the butcher's like all his kind. But anyway he served a good purpose; there was some money for the aged and at least their need had been generally advertised. Perhaps some people might even have felt moved to help. Today, years later, the hostel still survives and is in the hands, once more, of the devoted white nuns.

Once a social worker, always a social worker. In England, with Dr Friedlander's Child Guidance team, I had been closely concerned with conditions in institutions for children without families, which in those days — and possibly now — left much to be desired. The plight of the

Taormina orphans was tragic. Over fifty of them were living in a convent run by the 'black nuns', so-called to distinguish them from the 'white nuns' who were considered to be of higher social status. The convent was in a corner of the town, between the prison and the slaughterhouse. The youngest child was three and the oldest eighteen. The only time they emerged to the outside world was at funerals when they followed the coffin, dressed in gloomy black, mouthing prayers for which the nuns were paid per yard according to the distance covered by the procession. Rumour had it that when the girls reached the age of seventeen they were asked, would they become nuns or tarts? It was not phrased so vulgarly, but that was what it amounted to since their only experience of the outside world was at funerals. Few had any hope of support from relations or hope of earning, except in domestic work in which no girl would long remain a virgin or consequently have any hope of finding a husband. In fact, theirs was no choice at all.

What could be done? The first step was to have an introduction to the Reverend Mother. My uncle's dear doctor, much beloved in the village, agreed to take us to the convent. A gloomy building in which hours of prayer were observed daily with dull, monotonous intoning. The Reverend Mother received us graciously with abominably made tea and delicious cakes. She was a bulky Sicilian woman with kindly eyes, in contrast to the repressive atmosphere around us. The doctor explained that we wanted to help in her splendid work with the poor girls and that I should like to invite them to a *piccola festa* at my house. To our surprise the Reverend Mother accepted at once and thanked us for our goodness. We agreed that, as fifty-two was too many, there should be three *festas* on different days. Two nuns would of course have to come with them each time. I nodded, relieved that there were not to be more.

As we took our leave with bows and handshakes, she said to the doctor, 'They are Catholics, of course?'

'No, but they are Christians.'

To her credit she did not withdraw her consent. It was in the days before the Archbishop of Canterbury had called on the Pope and when many Sicilians, hearing the word *Protestante,* would hastily cross themselves.

A week later we received seventeen girls

and their two chaperons. They were stiff and joyless and all in dark uniforms, except for the youngest (aged three) who had only just been taken in. She had not yet been measured and was still in normal clothes. She clung to an older girl and was most of the time on the verge of tears. It was in the days before the welfare state, with its grants, and many probably had a heartbroken mother or father, recently widowed, whose only solution was to put their child in an orphanage.

My guests seemed incapable of spontaneous action. When invited to sit or eat, they listlessly obeyed. In an attempt to breach the deadly uniformity, we had prepared small buttonholes of mixed flowers, each one different, and we persuaded the girls to choose. With encouragement they slowly thawed as we pinned them on to their tunics. Food is good for warming things up and we led them to the tea — or rather soft drinks — table. Once we got them seated and grace said by the nuns, they had to be told: 'Take a bun . . . begin to eat', etc. As soon as possible we left them to the warm, Sicilian care of Maria and her helpers, with their reassuring dialect, while we invited the nuns to have some cocoa and buns in the next room. To my surprise, abandoning their charges, they came.

Then one, looking half curious and half frightened, pointed to the large fireplace and asked, 'What do you do in there?' She wouldn't say what she thought we did. I explained that we lit log fires to keep us warm in the winter. She still looked unconvinced and fearful. Could she possibly have thought that it was an altar for black mass? Every so often they would cross themselves and refer to our religion 'of no value' and call upon the Madonna to help us. All we could do was to smile in a friendly way — fortunately our elementary Italian prevented further religious discussion.

'Tea' over, I persuaded the eldest orphan to come with me to see the geography of the house, in case of urgent need on the part of the little ones.

Screwing up her courage, she suddenly said, 'Signorina, I shall pray for you every night of my life.'

'Thank you very much.'

Emboldened, she continued, 'It must be terrible to have a *falsa religione!*'

I smiled, hoping to convey that it didn't worry me unduly . . .

We collected on the large terrace, with

its amazing background of snow-covered Etna, and began to teach them Hunt the Slipper, Grandmother's Footsteps and Musical Chairs. It was hard work, but gradually they thawed and in the end were giggling and more nearly normal. Even the nuns joined in and were enjoying themselves so much they stayed and stayed until the sun went down and it was chilly. Still they didn't leave. Poor things: as ex-orphans themselves possibly they too had never played?

Ice had been broken and this continued with the other parties. These became annual events. A year or so later, we had nuns playing Blind Man's Buff and even jumping on to the low walls to escape the groping hands of my gardener, Buneri. Later, all of them wanted to be invited and we ended with many more chaperons than two.

My suspicions about the nuns' fears of a black mass were confirmed when we were invited to a 'theatrical entertainment' for the Reverend Mother's name day. The devil, disguised as a wicked woman of the world dressed in silks and pearls but exposing nothing more than her face for decency's sake, was seen tempting poor, innocent girls with promises of wealth and happiness. They yielded and went from bad to worse until the devil, triumphant, went too far and led them to a black mass. At that moment they all made the sign of the cross and, with a hideous shriek, the devil pulled off her finery down to decent underclothes and dived under the black curtain. Slowly the tempted climbed back to grace. So I had been wrong about their never having any relaxation in the convent!

Later, on various occasions, I was to do my poor best to get round the unpardonable delays in paying pensions to the aged whose right to have them had been officially recognised. Often months, or even years, would elapse before anything was paid. So that my visit should produce an unusual effect and not be forgotten, when I went to the Messina office for social insurance I took with me three most attractive, young foreign girls. Miss Phelps, followed by them, caused a sensation as they passed through the outer offices to the head. Without them I should have been palmed off with a minor official. Alas, the ploy was of little avail; the pensioner died in extreme poverty before the money arrived and neglectful, uncaring relations pocketed the arrears.

One day I phoned the local post office to ask whether the pension of my septuagenarian old friend — whose brain was to say the least of it woolly — had arrived. It would have been so much simpler if she had agreed to sign a paper appointing a delegate to collect her two pensions, one in respect of the death of her father in an air raid in Rome over forty years before, and the other her own. But she clung passionately to her right to be given the money personally. As she was incapable of walking the whole distance, I would drive her to the nearest parking point, which was seldom very near. The old Signorina wanted the post office man himself to pay each 10,000 lire note into her hand. The first time we went I had checked that the authorisation to pay had arrived, but I hadn't thought of asking whether there was money to pay it. There wasn't!

The pensioners were waiting in a cold hall where there were few seats. Mostly the attitude was *'Pazienza, pazienza'*. But an old dame who had walked slowly from one end of the town to the other, followed by all five of her cats, was not patient. While I demanded to see the manager, she shrieked her imprecations at all the authorities, responsible or not. The manager was said to be out collecting money from a bank halfway down the Corso. Probably he was having an espresso on the way back. What need for hurry?

Meanwhile the cat owner was yelling her head off: 'It must be that old cuckold of the Monsignore who has gone off with it, curse him! Or the Mayor? He knows that I voted for his enemy. When I had to go into hospital with my legs, *he* saw that the doctor cut the nerve so that I should never be able to walk properly again, curse him!' People tried to calm her or at least make her moderate her shrieks.

From the hidden office emerged the sub-manager. 'Out with those cats!' he shouted.

'What,' she shrieked back, 'my *bambini?* They follow me everywhere. *They* know I need the money for their fish. They have the right to be here while we wait for that imbecile of a manager. I don't budge till I have it.'

At last the manager, unlike us refreshed and rested, turned up to find the angry crowd thirsting for his blood. The money was paid out and receipts signed, with mostly illegible scrawls, and the journeys home could begin. I invited the cat owner to come to my car: 'To save your poor legs.'

'And my *bambini?*'

'You can bring them too; there is room for you all in the back.'

They were sleek, clean and well fed on, I suspect, better food than the Signora allowed herself. She hesitated and then, grudgingly, accepted. I offered an arm to each old woman and slowly the three of us, followed by the five, made our way to the car. To my alarm I saw that one tyre was completely flat and the car unmovable. Confirmed in her distrust of all wheeled vehicles, the Signora wouldn't wait. I calmed my Signorina and placed her in the front seat while the wheel was changed. Three-quarters of an hour later we passed the Signora and her followers. With her 'nerveless' legs she had managed half her monthly journey back. But, like the Signorina, she would continue to collect the money herself. Was it that, for both of them, it signified the little bit of power they had left, as did their insistence on hanging on to their bunches of old, and now useless, keys?

Later on, I again made an indirect effort to engage in social work. In the distant north-west of Sicily, the very heart of the Mafia area, Danilo Dolci, the so-called

'Gandhi of Sicily', who was an architect, poet, social reformer and a courageous fighter against injustice, had begun his work. As he said, he had 'only hunger with which to fight hunger', and he started fasts, to the death if necessary. He also organised 'upside-down strikes', telling unemployed men that they might as well do some useful work as rot in idleness. With them, be began to build a much-needed road. To avoid the possibility of violence, he persuaded them to leave at home the knives with which they cut their bread. When the police ordered them to stop, he made them all lie down in the road and offer no other resistance. Danilo, a heavy man, was the last to give in and was arrested. He was charged with trespass and went to gaol for several weeks. In court he was able to denounce many of the injustices in this desperately poor area. He also gained further attention through his remarkable books; he was opening windows from Sicily outwards, and inwards from abroad. In several countries committees were set up to raise money and to encourage volunteer workers. Unfortunately, the latter were not always well chosen or trained for this difficult and pioneering work in such a backward area, and some of them were overworked and had serious breakdowns.

Too far away to take an active part myself, and also too busy, I tried to persuade Danilo to use Casa Cuseni as a place where people could rest *before* and not after a breakdown. He came to see me and the house, but he never realised what it could have meant to his well-meaning and overworked helpers. However, many of them, as well as the victims of an earthquake in the same district, did gain from peaceful stays in Casa Cuseni that helped them return to their stressful lives.

Archaeology

Until about my sixth year in Sicily my interest in archaeology had been indirect. It came from my link with Arthur Evans of Knossos, who was a Phelps cousin and had been brought up when his mother died shortly after his birth by my great-aunt Frances Phelps, his stepmother. For twenty-five years he had devoted his skills and private fortune to the excavation of Knossos in Crete. I only met him once when he was over ninety and blind. I was a child, but the memory of the old man is still vivid.

In 1953 I had an introduction to a Romanian archaeologist who had recently arrived in Gela on the south-west coast of Sicily, which had been founded by Greeks from Rhodes and Crete in the seventh century BC. A friend staying with me insisted that we drive across the island and find out what was happening in Gela. Unfortunately she was a bad asthmatic, and in a bar in the magnificent golden baroque town of Noto she suddenly threw the worst attack I had ever seen. Unable to speak, she signed to me that I must at once give her an injection. There, on steps high above and in front of what seemed the whole male population of Noto — there wasn't a woman in sight — I had to jab an unsterilised needle into her thigh. The effect was magical. She recovered long before I did.

We drove to Gela where we were surprised to find in this poverty-stricken town a modern hotel owned and run by Scandinavians. Before bed I suggested, partly to calm my still shaken nerves, a walk along the pier. Two foreign women arriving in a car with no man to drive was a sensation in this remote town. A woman came up to us, stared and then asked excitedly in pure Sicilian: '*E quanno comm . . . ?*' When were we to begin? Her dialect was more than I could cope with and the conversation ended.

A little later a policeman came up. Again the stare, then: '*E quando iniziano?*'

'Begin what?'

'The circus!'

Our appearance was so strange to local eyes that we could only belong to the expected band of performers.

During the night a great wind came up driving billowing masses of sand against the windows of our room and causing a further asthma attack, but this time Joan was able to cope herself. This was the sand that had come, centuries ago, even faster than the attacking Carthaginians, deeply burying the Geloan walls. It was these that two keen and active archaeologists, one Piero Orlandini from Parma in north Italy and the other Dinu Adamestianu, a Romanian refugee from Communism, had begun excavating, moving rapidly and boldly with a bulldozer thousand of tons of sand on to the sea side. Speed was essential in obtaining results if further grants were to come from the ministry in Rome. Next morning we met the two archaeologists. I was delighted to be told that Arthur Evans had come here with his father-in-law (Professor Freeman whose four-volume history of Sicily had ended in 267 BC!) and without the help of aerial photography had, from ground level, made a plan tracing where he thought the walls, several kilometres long, must lie under the sand. He had guessed right.

The first time Don Bastianu, as the workmen called him, came to Casa Cuseni he identified four artefacts in the garden as fourth century BC and Greek. My uncle had evidently discovered them when the foundations of the house were being dug, had admired them and, without being able to recognise them for what they were, had rescued them, placing a lion's head above the pool at the entrance to the garden with a stream of water coming through its mouth; he built a funny little face ('made to amuse a child', said Don Bastianu) into a wall; the broken pedestal of an 'arula' or small family altar, which to Don Bastianu's horror, old Buneri, the gardener, had turned upside down and filled with earth in which he had planted geraniums. The fourth was a complete amphora now safely placed in the house. Dinu excitedly exclaimed, 'Of course the Greeks would have had a villa here, they wouldn't have missed this view. This site and that of the Greek theatre are the best in Taormina.' There are three Greek wells in the garden providing essential water. We still use them for irrigation.

The two archaeologists had created a remarkable team of workmen in Gela from unpromising material in this town of despairing poverty. Not long before our arrival the men had been embittered, unemployed, illiterate Communists to a man. Now there wasn't a Communist among them. The *Dottori* had hand-picked the most likely in the trial run and offered them permanent jobs on one condition: that they learned to read and write.

'*Impossibile!* How can we?'

'There's an evening class to teach you.'

'It's run by a signorina of twenty. How can we, married men of thirty, sit at *her* feet?'

'We've spoken to the Signorina and she's willing to have you.'

'But we *can't*. The classes are held during the *passeggiata* when we go up and down the Corso to meet our friends. It's impossible!'

'Well, it's your choice.'

Within six months all of them had learned to read and write enough to keep records on the dig; shortly after, they became experts at identifying shards as Greek, Roman or from Turkey and could even guess what century they dated from. Both *Dottori* told me they had never had such intelligent, willing workers ready to put up with real hardship on remote mountain digs, when they even slept in open Greek tombs. The *passeggiata* was forgotten, as were the highly prized *festas* in Gela. After long days of hard, hot work they would sit in the dark listening, thrilled, to the history of their distant ancestors. They were proud of their achievements and devoted to the *Dottori* who had made them possible and transformed their frustrated lives. I was reminded of the gratitude of the ordinary people of Taormina to my uncle for having respected them. Seldom did people higher up in the social scale do so — except at time of elections . . .

My time to be respected came when Piero and Dinu asked me to translate their *Guida di Gela*. 'It will mean little cash but much honour,' said Piero. It was not an easy task, as I had learned Italian technical terms and was ignorant of the English, but I was given time and in due course the translation appeared. I was the guest of Gela when the splendid new museum was inaugurated and blessed by a cardinal.

In the museum among the hundreds of superbly arranged exhibits one had the place of honour: a magnificent, life-sized horse's head in terracotta. It had been found in a well which is now incorporated into the museum. My contemplation of it stirred a vague memory: 'They found a horse's head in my uncle's time in *our* well at Casa Cuseni,' I suddenly remembered.

Immediately Dinu was alert with interest: 'Who? What? Where?' When I had only just arrived and was sunk in a myriad of problems, and understood Italian with difficulty, one of the staff had mentioned it. I tried to get him — or her, I can't remember who it was — to describe it. 'It was *antico*.' 'How big?' 'About this . . .' And they demonstrated a size slightly smaller than an average horse. I had wondered whether it had been sculpted or whether it was the skull of a famous military horse, or a winner of races, which I vaguely believed used to be honoured and preserved. The informant's Italian was mixed with Sicilian and being both weary and busy, I had given up and forgotten all about it.

Immediately I returned from Gela I questioned Maria, who was still alive at the time. She knew nothing. 'Then it must have been Buneri or Turiddu.' But both swore that they had never known anything about it or mentioned it to me.

Once more I had to give up, to Dinu's immense disappointment, but even he, on his next visit when he tried to extract information, drew a blank although he was fluent in Sicilian and of course experienced in cross-questioning the local people about finds they might have made. He was convinced I must have dreamed it, but I *knew* I was not mistaken. I hadn't even known then that people fleeing from conquering enemies would throw treasures they couldn't take with them into wells, hoping one day to return and retrieve them. They seldom did, and archaeologists always searched wells carefully.

Years later I was sitting beside the Thames picnicking and reminiscing with Eve, when she suddenly asked, 'What happened to the Greek horse's head?'

Much surprised, I said, 'How do you know anything about it?'

She replied, 'I was shown it in a shop in the Corso.'

I pressed her for every detail she could remember about it; the size seemed right and this was of course the only description I had extracted years before. It *must* have come from our well. And so I realised that when we had congratulated ourselves on still being possessed of all that we had found in the sealed house, we were badly mistaken. I only hope it ended in some museum and not in private hands to be gloated over. Certainly the antique dealer had been handsomely enriched at our expense.

The protection of archaeological finds,

especially in Sicily, is almost as important as their discovery and preservation. Mafia bosses were well aware of their value. They would spy upon the *Dottori* from afar with field-glasses and note where they appeared to have found promising sites. The Gela area was huge; not only was there the city, but several hilltops, spread in a fan shape behind, were fortified to afford further protection against enemies attacking from the sea. After exploratory digs to confirm first impressions, it was not often possible to safeguard discoveries throughout winter, and bad weather and the *tombaroli,* or grave-robbers, would move in for the pillaging. Often they would bore holes large enough to pass a small boy through to the tomb and he would hand up to them treasures buried with the dead. Not only did they steal but they caused sad damage to the tombs themselves.

Once I was lunching with Piero in the hotel at Gela when a waiter told me there was a man wanting to speak to me. He was not asking for me by name. This seemed odd. Did he not know me? After lunch he came forward carrying a parcel wrapped in newspaper. He said it was a Greek vase. Would I like to buy it? Piero was just behind me so, although full of curiosity, I virtuously said no. Piero, who had the right to confiscate immediately any contraband, stepped forward saying *he* was interested. Strangely the man didn't know who he was; it seemed odd that he had not taken the trouble to learn the identity of the only two men with the right to confiscate. Encouraged, the would-be seller opened the parcel. He wanted 12,000 lire for what looked to my unskilled eyes to be a black, two-handled crater in perfect condition. Piero carefully examined it, turning it over and over, then finally said he wasn't interested. Disappointed, the man wrapped it up and went off.

'Whatever was all that in aid of? What is it?'

'A black crater.'

'Genuine?'

'Yes.'

'Then why didn't you confiscate it?'

'We already have three others like it. If we confiscated everything we are shown, we should have no friends among the peasants. We want them to bring us their finds instead of going straight to the Mafia.'

It seemed reasonable, but I would have liked to buy that vase.

The loyalty of the workmen to the *Dottorti*, now known in dialect as *I Picciotti*, was severely tested, but it held. They knew that the finds belonged to the State and they fully realised that their scientific importance meant that they must not be spirited away.

Alas, Gela is now one of the most violent and murderous towns in Sicily owing to the desperate battles between rival Mafia gangs fighting to gain control of the drug traffic and the oil that has been found in the neighbourhood. Both *Dottori* have long since retired, but the splendid museum and walls remain.

Puppets' Godmother

As children in England, we had all been excited by my uncle's many, brightly coloured
paintings of the Sicilian puppets theatre,
with its crowded audiences of men, old and
young — there never seemed to be any
women. In my early years at Casa Cuseni,
as soon as I had coped with some of the
major problems and had a little free time, I
decided to find out where we could see a
performance. 'Impossible in Taormina. Why
do you want to see them? We have the
cinema. Only the lower people enjoy them.'
I persevered, and at last an antique dealer
told me he thought they could be seen in
Catania. He didn't know exactly where, but
it would be in a rough quarter and unless
we were under the protection of Guglielmino, a *carrozza* (driver), whom we could
probably find near the fish market, we
would almost certainly have everything
stolen, even the wheels off the car. We set
off to find Guglielmino. He gave us a great
welcome and took us to his house, which
was meagrely furnished, the only impressive

piece being a huge radiogram upon which, when he had covered it with a cloth, his wife served us bread, wine and cheese. He then took us to the theatre in another shabby back street of the city.

The theatre was not large and was absolutely packed with excited, noisy, small boys who were kept from rushing on to the stage and slipping under the curtain by a fierce-looking man with a heavy stick, which every now and then he brought down with a great 'wham' on the wooden stage front. The boys hastily retreated. The only women in the audience were my two friends and myself, while behind the scenes the only one was the *puparo*'s wife who spoke the women's voices. This was a special children's performance. When I asked a small boy why there weren't any girls he looked at me, with all his male superiority, and asked witheringly, 'What would they understand of the story?' He did not agree with me that perhaps they could be given a chance . . .

The tradition of the Sicilian puppets is a long one with its roots in the epics of Ariosto and Tasso. Before the coming of cinemas and television, most villages would have a small theatre, which would be crowded nightly by peasants and fishermen. Like Elizabethan groundlings, they would boo and cheer and take an active part in the eternal battle between the *Cristiani* and the *Pagani*. The former were knights, coming from all over Europe to fight under the leadership of Charlemagne against the peril from the East. Intriguingly they included Astolfo, 'the Englishman, the boldest, the most resolute and the first to fall at Roncesvalles'. Could he have been a Norman? There were the Frenchmen Orlando and Oliviero (Roland and Oliver), and heroes from Denmark, Spain, Germany and other countries. The serialised plays, with nightly performances, could take anything up to thirteen months to complete. The various stories are typical Sicilian mixtures of honour and treachery, cruelty and mercy, valour and cowardice, with pagans converted at the point of the sword. Christians appear, on the whole, to be more bloodthirsty than their enemies as the pile of pagan dead should always be higher than that of the *Cristiani* until the last great tragedy of Roncesvalles and the death of Orlando.

We so enjoyed the whole performance that we were determined to discover a theatre nearer Taormina and were delighted when, one day, in a little back street in Giardini, only four kilometres away, we saw boldly painted posters announcing the imminent arrival of Emilio Sollima's puppets from Giarre. In a private house, rented for the occasion, hens were being driven out of the living room as the owner erected a small stage and simple wooden benches. We asked if we could attend. Sollima was flattered that foreigners were interested, and even more welcoming when he heard who my uncle was — 'that great patron of art'. I told him that we should bring a famous philosopher with us: 'Then we must build him a throne.' I discouraged this; he was a modest man and would prefer to sit with the rest of the audience.

Once again we found ourselves yelling for the *Cristiani* and booing the *Pagani* and the wicked traitors, with their hideous faces, who betrayed Orlando and his warriors to the enemy.

After this my fame as a patroness of the art spread, which was embarrassing in view of my impecunious state. One morning early, an alarming-looking character, with a bandanna on his head and dangling gold ear-rings in his ears, turned up on my terrace begging for my support for yet another group. To my surprise, he accepted my regrets and left without a scene. Then a more soberly dressed man from Acireale, a good forty kilometres away, was sure I would help *him*. Of course I could help no one with cash and I could certainly not take a second group under my impoverished wing.

A year or so later, I received a sad letter from Sollima saying that he had no choice — he had to live and support his wife and son — he had sold all his puppets, scenery and posters to an antique dealer. 'An artist's life,' he wrote, 'is rich only in adversities, with no satisfactions.' He would work in a factory distilling alcohol, and Augusto, his nine-year-old son, was determined to study and become a mechanic. In those years he was only one of the *pupari* whose hearts were broken by the loss of their beloved knights and pagans which, over the years, had become as precious as their own family and almost as alive. Whenever I see puppets hanging in a shop I know that behind them there is a broken-hearted artist and his family, mourning the puppets as they struggle to accept a life shorn of romance, in a humdrum job far removed from a theatre.

The silver lining to Sollima's failure was that I was now able to give some help to the Acireale theatre, which was more securely based as the town council had made a small grant, realising the potential for attracting tourists. I went to see Emanuele Macrì there. He gave me a great welcome and with pride showed me his theatre in a shabby back street in this beautiful baroque town: 'Signorina, in order to be a puppeteer you have to be a poet, a sculptor, a painter *and* a blacksmith.' He could have added, 'And an actor.'

Backstage was hanging motionless, like dead men, a magnificent array of paladins, Muslims, court ladies, giants, dragons, griffins, magicians and guardian angels, some of which, he told me, weighed up to forty kilos.

'Would you like me to make them come alive?' And in a trice knights and infidels clashed and clanged against each other; heads were cut off, bodies were slashed in two — vertically and horizontally. The pile of dead grew, all to the rhythmic beating of his and his son's feet on the floor of the bridge from which they worked the heavy figures.

The theatre he had kept just as it was in his adoptive father's day. I was surprised to hear of an adoption and asked him how he had escaped the fate of most lone children, put in an orphanage run first by nuns and then by priests. His saviour had been Mariano Pennisi, a *puparo* famous all over Sicily who had somehow found time to become a champion cyclist. In those days cycling was the most passionately followed sport in all Italy. In the early years of the century he would ride all round the island and, when stopping in Messina, he had made friends with the Macrì family. In 1906, just before the birth of Emanuele, he had become their *compare*, or honorary member of the family, by consenting to be the baby's godfather. In December 1908 Messina was devastated by one of the most disastrous earthquakes ever to hit Europe. Eighty thousand were killed. Mariano at once got on his bike and somehow reached his friends' house to find it totally destroyed. With his bare hands he pulled out the bodies of the parents and the two older children but, amazingly, found the baby Emanuele still alive. Somehow he got him back to Acireale. (I like to imagine that my uncle may have helped them as he spent hours at rescue work in the Taormina station, where trainloads were arriving of those dead, dying, wounded and being born.)

The *puparo* adopted the baby as his son, bringing him up among the puppets. From childhood he learned to work and love them, and got to know all the legends by heart. When, he said, the old man was on his deathbed he constantly bemoaned the fact that there could be no worthy successor — no one had the same skills. One night he secretly dragged himself out of bed and to the theatre to watch Emanuele. With immense pride Emanuele told me that the old man returned to his bed murmuring, 'I have a worthy successor.' A day or so later he died.

At my next visit Macrì asked me if I would honour his puppets by becoming their godmother. Thinking of what would be one of my main duties, I said nervously, 'You know I'm not a *rich* woman?'

'Signorina, I'm not thinking of *money*,' he said reproachfully, as if it were the most filthy and unnecessary thing in the world. 'All I ask is your interest.'

Much moved, I promised him he should have it to the best of my ability, thus becoming almost certainly the only person in the world with thirty or so Christian godchildren and as many pagan ones. I was then solemnly introduced to them one by one.

Shortly afterwards, the post brought me a small visiting card with 'Emanuele Macrì *Artista del Folklore Siciliano*' on it, beside a sketch of a furiously fighting *paladino*. On the back was a typewritten message:

Dear Miss Phelps,

I beg you to accept a few pictures of the Theatre with my grateful compliments, also a specimen of Acireale sweets.

The theatre is now waiting for its inauguration which you have graciously accepted to perform. A Friday at your election will be the favourable date for me and my puppets. Will you please let me know when you have decided to inaugurate the theatre and also kindly advise the number of friends you will bring with you.

Your most obedient servant,
Emanuele Macrì

This was the first I had heard of the proposal!

I put notices in all the hotels and managed to collect two busloads of tourists of several nationalities. Expecting a simple ceremony, I was mildly alarmed to find the Mayor and the whole town council present with local photographers who never left me alone throughout the afternoon. I had prepared a short speech with tributes to Macrì and Pennisi (I had been asked always to refer to him as *Illustrissimo*) and then another one, in English, saying something of the tragic history of Emanuele and sketching the history and plot of the scene we were about to see. The stage curtain was down and across it were tied scarlet and yellow ribbons, the colours of Sicily. Macrì bowed low and handed me a silver salver with a pair of scissors on it. I cut the ribbon and the curtain went up on a crowded stage, with the splendidly crowned figure of *Carlo-magno* (or Charlemagne) addressing the dazzling array of his paladins resplendent in their gold, silver and black armour. In the background lurked a most villainous, leering traitor. As usual the audience was enchanted with the performance and Macrì's impassioned acting as, from the wings, he declaimed the voices of each character with all the fervour of his Sicilian heart. I was given a large bouquet and a little marionette Orlando by Macrì's beautiful daughter and, presumably having seen that I had played my part well, the Mayor hastily sent out for a huge box of the famous Acireale almond cakes. I think he was pleased — and probably surprised, as he had not seen puppets since he was a small boy — at the prospect of tourist money being attracted to the needy town.

On my next visit I asked Macrì where I could buy a copy of the book from which he worked. He took me to a bookshop and tried to get me to buy Ariosto and Tasso. I refused this and asked again for *his* book, from which he worked. Sadly he shook his head: 'Impossible, it is out of print and I only have two.' I was with a friend and money was still so short that I was unable to invite him to lunch, but only to coffee afterwards. He arrived at the bar with a parcel which he handed to me. It was what I had asked for. Of course I said that I couldn't accept such a sacrifice, it was essential for the theatre. He opened it. Already he had inscribed it: '*Alla Signorina, Questo mio libro pregiato perchè mi è sempre custode gelosa*' (To the Signorina, this my precious book, because she will always be a jealous custodian). He then asked me to spell out my name. All he knew was that it wasn't Kitsoni! I spelled it out for him letter by letter D-A-P-H-N-E P-H-E-L-P-S and he painstakingly filled in the blank. Begged to accept, I agreed to take it, thinking that if there were only two copies it would be as well if they were not in the same place in case of fire or other disaster, and I assured him that I was only the custodian and would return it if ever he needed it. The text was in Italian, the date was 1890, but the many woodcuts were clearly much older, and fascinating in their naive vigour. Inside the book there was a photo of himself depicted as the scholar he liked, with some justification, to consider himself, studying a large tome. On the back he had inscribed in Italian: 'To the most impassioned foreigner [presumably me] who through the Bard of the Age of Chivalry [presumably him] transports on iridescent wings of fantasy and human poetry . . .' It ended with a great, flamboyant signature. It was difficult to see who had transported whom, he had so lost himself in his flowery vocabulary. More simply, he once exclaimed: 'I think I'm the happiest man in all the world. I have my puppets around me, I have their godmother with me and I have my wife and family.' Then, guiltily, 'My wife and family come first of course.' But I fear they didn't . . .

As befitted one living in the world of chivalry, he was a passionate royalist.

Whenever we met he would raise a glass: 'To the most beautiful queen in the world, Elizabetta.' I solemnly joined in. He planned to make a puppet each for the young Prince Charles and Princess Anne, but as business picked up he never had time.

Macri's lifestyle created problems for his family, particularly his attractive twenty-year-old daughter. Three times she became engaged. Once I found her sighing over the portrait of a dashing young man in naval uniform; she had a large pearl on her ring finger and a full bottom drawer. Later I received a photo of her clutching the hand of a different hero in uniform, but both engagements were broken off by her father: the men 'had not the necessary chivalrous behaviour'. The third fiancé was also in uniform, he was a policeman, but alas he too failed to meet parental expectations. I hope the poor girl was eventually allowed to marry.

Salvatore, the son, took matters into his own hands, following an attractive American girl, whose father had a museum of puppets from all over the world. He imported a group of Sicilian puppets and built a special theatre for them and Salvatore in New England.

Macrì's own fortune changed when the Italian ambassador to Belgium, a native of Catania, had the imagination to arrange a visit to Brussels for my godchildren. I was invited to accompany them, but made excuses. I might have found chivalrous living for a week too intense.

I received an excited postcard: *'Grande trionfo dei nostri pupi.'* After that Macrì, who before had never left Sicily, was invited to north Italy, to Prague, Paris, Helsinki and once more to Brussels. Each time it was a *grande trionfo,* and I was quite sure that this was the truth. But his great ambition was to go to London. I did my best, but there was the problem of finding a suitable theatre, the main difficulty being the space needed for the manipulation of the long iron rods.

After this, honours came pouring in: he was given the title of *Cavaliere del Lavoro* in Rome; famous writers such as Quasimodo, the Sicilian poet and Nobel prize winner, came to see him play; Peter Ustinov made a film with him and his puppets; Giorgio di Chirico was enchanted by the 'cocktail of colour'. In Macrì's visitors' book were names from all over the world, including China, Japan, Russia and the Americas. When he could by now have had a princess, a duchess, an ambassadress for his godmother he remained faithful to me, an impoverished Englishwoman without a title. How typically Sicilian was such loyalty.

Sadly, Macrì never did get to London. He died suddenly in his late sixties after a particularly fierce evening of ferocious battles. In a hot sweat he walked home; there was an icy wind sweeping down from the snows on Etna. Pneumonia carried him off in a few days. But his puppets survived. The town council had by now realised the importance of the money they brought, and began to support the theatre.

Policemen

In a small town like this there are five different kinds of policemen, all with various functions. First, the Carabinieri, famous for their magnificent ceremonial red and blue uniforms. They are paramilitary and theirs are the lives most at risk as they deal with terrorists, *mafiosi* and the toughest criminals. Second comes the Commissariato di Pubblica Sicurezza, with whom all foreigners have to be registered, and they are responsible for the safety of the many prominent visitors, both Italian and foreign, who come to the town. During the Cold War they used to consider themselves the main defence against Communist infiltrators. Their duties often overlap with those of the Carabinieri, either of whom could deal with emergency calls and theft. They are said to be jealous rivals. Then there are the Finanzieri, or Financial Police who deal with tax offences of every kind, and with customs. Fourth come the Vigili Urbani who are local men dealing with the regulation of shops, markets, parking, etc. They are the ones who used to be given mountains of gifts on 6 January, the Feast of the Epiphany, mostly from motorists and shopkeepers anxious to have a blind eye turned to offences. Their pickings could be considerable. Lastly, the Polizia Stradale, or Road Police, who are active mostly outside the town on motorways and other main roads.

The Captain of the Carabinieri

The Captain of the Carabinieri was a handsome man and fully aware of it. He expressed to Don Carlo, who was only too anxious to please him, that he would like to be invited to meet the Signorina. I decided that tea might be a suitable time and enquired whether he had a wife. He had. So I painstakingly wrote a letter to invite them both. They duly arrived, he in what looked like a brand new uniform with a sword which he detached and handed to a minion to hold. The Signora was delighted and delightful. I guessed that it was the first time she had been invited to accompany her husband. First Ladies were then unknown in Sicily. He, on the other hand, seemed a bit disgruntled, but on the whole I thought it had been a success and we should be able to expect his help if needed in the future.

A few days later Don Carlo came up with another message: now might he be invited *without* his wife? This was a tough one. We did not want to be obliged to rebuff him. If offended, he could make my life impossible. I slept on it. The very next day a vision appeared on the Corso; all male eyes were on a beautiful girl with golden skin and long blonde hair. Dressed in the latest fashion of brief white shorts and shirt, she had a golden spaniel on a studded leash: the niece of the American Ambassador in Rome. The Captain took one look and forgot all about the English Signorina in her drab, post-war wear.

The Sanitary Policeman

Attached to the Vigili Urbani is the sanitary policeman. He too is a local man and deals with public health matters in housing, hotels, shops and markets. He is also supposed to deal with pests such as rats, hornets and wasps.

As I held a licence letting me have paying guests, I soon had a visit from him. At once he told me that he had been a great friend of my uncle, who had promised him 'two big pictures'. I received this news coldly and changed the subject; so many people said they had been promised so many things, one even claiming that the house was to be his . . . The policeman became less smiling and began looking for trouble. Beds were stripped to see if they were clean; my compost heaps were insanitary (they weren't); fly screens were to be installed everywhere, obstructing the Etna view and so on. I was sure that more trouble threatened for the future and I began to check up on him. Had he really known my uncle well? All agreed that he had. Was it likely that promises had been made? Again, probably, they had. At his next visit I asked how and when he had first got to know Don Roberto.

'I shall never forget it. I was eight, my father had remarried and our new mother hated us children. Your uncle found me crying by the road and he stopped and tried to cheer me up, inviting me to his garden. He chatted and joked with me and said I could come back when I felt like it. On the next visit he offered to teach me to paint, so I saw a lot of him. He saved me and I shall never forget. I still paint.'

Of course he got the two big pictures. They were a grand investment: because of our consequent friendship I could have had my house fly-blown and rat-ridden, my drains could have been inefficient and my compost heaps allowed as long as they could not be seen from the road. Fortunately, I respect hygiene and was never a public health risk . . . I fed the friendship by giving him stamps from all over the world. 'Who in Taormina has stamps like these?' he boasted, as I handed him yet another valuable batch from the Museum of Modern Art in New York whose creator, Alfred Barr, was a keen supporter of Casa Cuseni and was much amused at so innocent a form of bribery.

The Financial Policeman

We had had a jovial Christmas and I was still in bed on Boxing Day when, at 9 a.m., I was told that tax officers had arrived and demanded to see the *locandiera*'s accounts. I had been warned by a Sicilian friend either not to keep any, or else to keep two versions — one for me and one for the police. I had followed the first advice. Quickly I dressed and went down to the library. There were two of them, in uniform, with revolvers at their hips. They looked fierce and determined. I felt the need to soften them up and smilingly offered coffee, vermouth, tea — what would they like? The younger one, a brigadiere in spectacles, was stern and refused my offers, while the older one, of lower rank, looked as if he'd like to accept. My next tactic was to say that my papers were upstairs, and one by one I produced some receipted bills. I took my time going up and down.

On my fifth descent the Brigadiere said severely, 'Signorina, you are wasting time.'

'I'm very sorry, Brigadiere, but you see I am a foreigner and all this is so new to me I get confused. I am trying to learn.' And I offered a timid smile.

It had a softening effect and the Brigadiere, looking round him, said, 'You have many books. Are there any Italian ones?'

I nodded.

Eagerly, he asked, 'Would you lend me some?'

'Of course, I'd be delighted. Are you a great reader?'

'Indeed I am. You see I'm the only unmarried one in the barracks, so I am left on night duty a great deal and I read and read. I've finished my books.'

And so our friendship started.

He soon learned that the Signorina had many guests including several young girls, one of whom exclaimed joyously: 'He dances divinely!' I felt that they were probably safer in a brigadiere's arms than they would have been with less disciplined partners. He would often drop in of an evening without his uniform. He said he had recognised that I was *'una persona seria'* and that he could trust me. Gradually I learned his story. He came from a devout, Catholic family near Naples. Owing to the war, his father had lost all his money, property and health and it had become essential for the sons to seek steady, pensioned employment. What could be better than the Finanzieri? 'We hate it, but I can arrange myself and fit in; but my brother is a poet and for him it is hell.'

One evening when he dropped in there were no pretty girls but instead a distinguished Fellow of All Souls, Denis Mack Smith, who was writing a history of Sicily, and Mr Mitchell, an old American lawyer who had been head of the legal department of Procter and Gamble — and he knew a trick or two. The ardent Catholic was dazzled as the old lawyer told of his visit to Rome and his private interview with the Pope. Then, casually, he let fall that he had also had half an hour with the Minister of Finance. Antonio, as he now was, was deeply impressed; not only was he given a medallion of the beloved Pope John, but he was meeting someone obviously on good terms with the ultimate financial boss.

'Do you think that he could get me transferred to nearer my family?' he whispered to me as he left.

I promised to ask. The lawyer went up to bed. The historian stood with his back to the fire warming his behind, which we call 'cock-sparrowing' in our family. 'Isn't it amazing how these old Republicans get around? *Anyone* can have an interview with the Pope — it's not difficult — but *half an hour* with the Minister — that really is something!'

Next morning a contrite Mr Mitchell came down: 'Daphne, dear girl, I have a confession to make. I realised that that young man could play a very important part in your life so I spun a tale. I never saw the Finance Minister!' He was ready to lie, despite his stern Episcopalian faith, to help me and Casa Cuseni. Also, he was grateful because we had nursed him through a nasty illness and had even produced a Swedish doctor to look after him.

Fortunately we never had to confess to Antonio. A few days later he was borrowed by the Road Police to help check dangerous driving. Seeing a monstrous instance of overtaking on a blind corner he had stopped the driver, fined him on the spot and was beginning to write out a receipt, when up came his Colonel: 'He's a friend of mine, you can't fine him.' Bravely Antonio stood his ground, mainly, I guess, because the receipt — with a copy — was all but complete and could not be cancelled. The Colonel shouted, 'You'll pay for this!'

Sure enough Antonio was sent to a punishment station on Lipari. In summer it would have been tolerable, but in winter with hotels and restaurants shut, and no foreign women around? I felt it was a good excuse to go and see that amazing, pumice stone island again. My surprising companion was Jo, Viscountess Forteviot, the widow of a Scottish whisky millionaire. On the journey I discovered that she had previously always gone abroad in their private plane, with his valet and her lady's maid. Actually, she enjoyed roughing it with me. Her Ladyship was much impressed when we were met at the quay by a handsome, uniformed policeman who rushed us round the island in an official jeep, and then took us to lunch in the best restaurant in town. (I never saw anyone pay.) Once again the young man was impressed when I said that Jo was Macmillan's cousin and that the Prime Minister, whose name was then probably the only British one known to the Italian public, had spent his holiday with her in Perthshire.

Again Antonio got me on my own: 'Signorina, do you think your friend would ask Macmillan to help me to get out of here?'

'I don't know . . . I can ask.'

Jo took the request in her stride: 'Oh yes, I think so — a word to the Ambassador would help. I'll ask him.'

Antonio was still more impressed with the *locandiera*'s friends, but I think he did his full time on the island.

Something like forty years later when he has been pensioned for a long time, he lives happily near Naples and is a married man with a family; he still comes to visit me on his holiday.

The Road Policeman

In due course I was able to buy a very necessary car. As I was a foreign resident, the British government gave me privileges over taxes and waiting lists. I bought an

Austin A40 sports car. She was a bit of a tank, but she needed to be if she was going to tackle the third- and fourth-grade roads I was hoping to explore in remote Sicily.

I had not foreseen how conspicuous I would be in my car that people said was 'blond, like you'. I was then the only woman driver apart from the occasional tourist. *'Una* femina *che guida!'* people would shout as I passed. They didn't believe a woman *could* drive and they would follow me into a shop to see where the man was hidden who would surely take the wheel. When I stopped for petrol, crowds would gather as grandparents, uncles, aunts and cousins would be summoned to see the phenomenon.

One cold, wet, windy day a tiny, elderly figure appeared at Casa Cuseni with an introduction from an Oxford professor. She was Miss Carlyle and I had been one of the last students to be coached by her father who, in his turn, had been the last ever college fellow to lose his job when he married. She was writing a book on the resurgence of southern Italy and was armed with introductions from the then Christian Democrat Prime Minister, Segni. They had provided her with two nuns, disguised as social workers, to act as guides and interpreters. She was convinced that wool had been pulled over her eyes and she had not been given the truth. Searching questions had been evaded. She wondered whether I would be prepared to go round the island with her on a second tour. I abandoned house to the staff and we set off.

My companion was a Scot and determined. She wrote endless notes; she interviewed all kinds of people. We stayed in modest hotels in out-of-the-way places where two women in a car — open, at that — were a sensation. Once we were turned out of a *locanda* and referred to the red light alternative; an inn careful of its reputation couldn't put up such creatures without a man — they were certainly up to no good. My companion laughed: 'Well we're used to scandals in my family — my father lost his job because he got married! But it's the first time *I've* been suspected of immorality!'

We pushed on through villages which had only seen foreigners during the war. One morning we were driving along an unasphalted, pockmarked road through wild, uninhabited country, raising clouds of dust in front and behind us. We were about ten kilometres south of Piani dei

Greci, a settlement founded to the south of Palermo by Albanian refugees in the fifteenth century. On Mussolini's first visit to Sicily, the Palermo police had everything taped for the great man's visit: anyone suspected of anti-Facist feelings was arrested, walls were lowered so that no sniper could hide behind them and so on. After three days of triumph Mussolini suddenly, and unexpectedly, said he wanted to go to Piani dei Greci. The only way the police could protect him was by placing him in the large car of the Mayor — who was also head of the Mafia. It is believed that he tapped his guest on the knee and boasted: 'While you are my guest you needn't be afraid. No man would dare to harm you.' Mussolini never forgave the insult and from then he determined to put the Mafia down. He never succeeded.

The sun was too pleasant to be shut out by raising the hood, so we pulled on headscarves and put on dark glasses, tolerating the gritty dust. Suddenly two road policemen on powerful motorbikes appeared in front of us adding to the swirling clouds of dust. Zoom, zoom, they overtook us in the opposite direction. In the grey gloom of dust we were stopped. I wound down the window and began pulling out my documents. The one on my side was not interested in them He leaned over the door, a large wedding ring on his finger, and excitedly enquired, 'Are you from *Birminghammy* University?'

We looked at each other in utter disbelief.

He repeated anxiously: *'Birminghammy?'*

We hadn't misheard. Recovering, we said we were both from a university near there but not, we were afraid, from Birmingham.

He looked bitterly disappointed.

'But why do you ask?'

'Because there was a signorina from Birminghammy. She came to Sicily for her holiday. We met. It was a *fulmine* — a thunderbolt! We danced together for four days and four nights. Then she left me. She gave me no address, but four times a year she sends me a postcard. I cannot answer.' He sighed deeply. 'I *did* so hope that you were from that university.' Then, as he straightened, no longer leaning on my car, he changed to official abruptness: 'Show me your documents. Two women have no business to be here alone on a road like this. They're wicked people around here.'

'But surely it's safe in broad daylight?'

'Yes, perhaps,' he grudgingly admitted.

'But don't drive around here at night.'

'I wouldn't dream of it. I'd be far too frightened.'

'We have a saying: "If you see a Greek and a wolf, kill the Greek and leave the wolf." They're bad people round here.'

At that he saluted. I bowed in reply. They returned to their motorbikes and once more disappeared into the dust.

Bertrand Russell

One of my first thoughts on finding myself in occupation, if not possession, of a house — and such a house — was that I could try to repay the generous hospitality that I had received from the Bertrand Russells when I was stranded in the United States, unable to return to England because of the war.

I had met them in 1940, when Bertie had already been in the US for a few years. He had taught first at Chicago University and then at the University of California in Los Angeles. I had only myself to support, but he had a wife and three children under eighteen. It was therefore a serious matter for him when, through the machinations of the Episcopalian Bishop Manning of New York, he was declared a corrupter of youth and unfit to teach logic to the young of New York City College because of what the Bishop called his immoral, salacious views.

One day while we were in Berkeley, David, a British Commonwealth fellow who had known Bertie and his wife 'Peter' in Oxford and Chicago, saw in the paper that Lord Russell was on holiday in the High Sierras at Lake Tahoe. Also I had discovered that I had met Peter at Oxford when she was at the beginning of her relationship with Russell. He was then sixty-one and she twenty-three. I clearly remember Peter, at the time unknown to me, unexpectedly sitting down one day beside me in the common room and pouring out her feelings about the affair. I sat silently listening to the stream of emotions. She was tall, slender, with gorgeous Venetian auburn hair and she had been one of the first women to be an '*Isis* Idol'. Up till then they had generally been handsome young men with political ambitions, leading athletes or distinguished actors in OUDS, the university dramatic society. She enjoyed startling people with her wit, her provocative views and her pipe smoking — it was a very little pipe and the same colour as her beautiful hair. I knew nothing about their surprising marriage — his third — and I think I must have been abroad when it happened. I had been puzzled when Americans, hearing I was at Oxford in the early thirties — women students were not many at this time — would say: 'Then you must have known Lady

Russell?' I had denied it. It was when David said the same that I realised that my strange acquaintance of one morning seven years before was now Countess Russell. When David suggested that we should drive over to Lake Tahoe I was full of curiosity and delighted by the idea.

We had thought that we might have a picnic with them and then explore the beautiful lake on our own. However, we met with an enthusiastic welcome. They insisted that we should stay with them and we did, for several days. At that time they were justifiably embittered about Americans and their treatment of Bertie. Although many liberals had spoken up in his defence, he had not been allowed to appear in court himself to state his point of view, as the case was not against him personally but against the College. As a result, they were feeling homesick as well as saddened by the desperate situation in Britain, after Hitler's conquest of Europe. They were delighted to have English guests, especially David — an old friend who could discuss philosophy and semantics. They were also amused by the stories of my hand-to-mouth existence working as a char etc., while I waited for a boat to take me home. I was very careful not to get involved in abstract discussions with Bertie! But fortunately, as well as charring, I had dined with a judge of the Supreme Court, slept in Katharine Hepburn's vast four-poster bed and tea-d with Mrs Henry Wallace when she was the Vice-President's wife. My penniless adventures in the US were very different from theirs.

By this time Bertie was free from financial anxieties as he had achieved a new post: teaching philosophy at the Barnes Foundation in Pennsylvania. We thought, therefore, we could accept their pressing invitation to stay with them. I discovered that at Cambridge, fifty years before, he had proposed my young mother for membership of the Fabians. He was also pleased to know that I was a cousin of 'the enchanting Jane Harrison of Cambridge'. At their insistence we stayed for an exciting week and in my impecunious state it was a godsend. When we left, they insisted that we *must* stay with them in Pennsylvania. As yet they had no address, but, they assured us, the Barnes Foundation would be able to find them in Merion.

Barnes, a pharmacist, had made a fortune with his creation of Argyrol, a throat medicine, and had invested most of the proceeds in art. His collection consisted mainly of French Impressionists which he had bought before Impressionism was in demand — but there were also El Grecos, Goyas, Picassos and so on. He had built a gallery at Merion and hung his pictures in unorthodox ways, putting, for instance, a glowing young Renoir blonde next to a gaunt El Greco saint. At first he had admitted all and sundry, but one day he found visitors laughing and jeering at the more startling Picassos. In a furious rage he had shut the galleries, declaring that his treasures were not to be insulted by ignorant nit-wits. In future only those who had taken his special course in art appreciation would be allowed in. His paranoia made him stick to his resolution that no one, but *no one*, should see his pictures without having first taken his course. I believe that even distinguished experts who had crossed the States and the Atlantic were refused access. (Barnes was later killed in a road accident when he insisted on what was not his right of way.) Bertie was to be paid a most generous salary, for two or three hours a week lecturing on philosophy as a background to the course.

Mercifully David was unfit for military service owing to some careless surgery in California, and as women were still not allowed to cross the Atlantic, I felt no guilt on staying in the US.

Many months later we arrived at the main Philadelphia station, having driven from San Francisco in a car lent to me by friends. I was to stay with the elderly, distant relation with whom I had left a suitcase 'for six weeks' while I seized my 'only chance' to see the Pacific. That had been October 1939. We were now in April '41.

David tried to phone the Foundation. Impossible: there was no entry in the directory. Enquiries answered that no one was to be given any information. He drew a complete blank. I was sure my 'aunt' would know and I phoned her.

She laughed and said, 'You'd better bring the young man here. You certainly won't find out anything tonight. We'll sort things out in the morning.'

I was anxious to collect the suitcase that I had left so many months ago, before recent earth-shattering events. I had turned down her offer of a home for the duration: the ease and comfort would have suffocated me when friends and family were facing danger and hardships.

In the morning I was taken off to a swell luncheon in the company of some wildly rich women. We had dropped David off at

Merion, wishing him good luck, but my aunt was dubious about the prospects of his success in tracing Bertie. As usual in such company I had to listen to outrageously anti-Roosevelt sentiments and to views about — and apologies for — the way 'the devil in the White House' had treated my King and Queen when they had visited in early 1939. I had tried to assure them that their Majesties would have been delighted at their reception and would not have been 'insulted' when offered hot dogs at a picnic at Hyde Park, Roosevelt's country place; in fact they would have been delighted to be given typical American food. This, however, was received with snorts of indignation from the ladies — clearly *they* had never tasted anything so vulgar!

I then tried to change the subject and said how grateful we were for lend-lease under which Britain had acquired essential merchant ships. (I, with a very common American surname, had been signing every petition I could come across, urging its passage through a largely isolationist Congress.) But I was told that 'poor England' should have no faith in the man whatsoever: 'Why, if he meant business he would have put down the unions.'

Severely shaken, I murmured, 'We are *fighting* Fascism, you know.'

There was a horrified silence which my aunt broke, saying, 'We are having the most extraordinary time trying to find Lord Russell. We can't even get in touch with the Barnes Foundation where we know he's teaching. Daphne's friend is invited to stay with the Russells, but we just can't find them.'

Whereat one of the guests said, 'He's the tenant in my house at Malvern.' And she gave me the telephone number.

Meanwhile David, having discovered the Barnes Museum and enquired for Lord Russell, had met with suspicious hostility. When he had persisted, a tough Irish policeman had threatened to manhandle him. All he had been able to achieve had been a conversation with a taxi driver who said he knew Bertrand Russell by sight — was he an old gentleman with a shock of white hair who rode a bicycle? We knew that Bertie after completing, in nine years, his great book *Principia Mathematica*, had gone for a ride on a bicycle and during it had decided that he no longer loved Alice, his first wife. He had come back and straightforwardly told her so. This was why Peter always discouraged bicycle riding! It did not seem likely that the old gentleman was Bertie.

David transferred to Little Datchet Farm, Malvern and I followed him a few days later. We stayed in the Russell household for about three months, still waiting for the chance to sail. It was an almost unique experience shared, I think, only by the nursery governesses of Bertie's children. By then Conrad, aged three, was the only one at home.

Bertie was working on his future bestseller *A History of Western Philosophy*. He would disappear for most of the day, just emerging for meals. In the evenings, while David and Peter washed up at one sink, Bertie and I would be at the other. As always, he couldn't keep his hands off any woman, but I was firm; he did not attract me physically, but the scintillating wit which flowed over the sink each night was riveting; his stories of Gladstone, Aristotle, Mirabeau, Galileo and so on were as vivid as if he had met them that morning and chatted over the garden wall. They enchanted me.

Conrad adored his father and Peter was a devoted, spoiling and admiring mother.

As far as possible we made ourselves useful. I remember driving Bertie to meet

Einstein; like any chauffeur I stayed out-side, of course. I helped in the garden and with shopping, and on the free days of Geneva, the black cook, and her husband Charles, I helped in the kitchen. It was a godsend to two English waiting to get pas-sage home. We just hoped we weren't taking advantage of their hospitality.

One day Bertie emerged from his study in the midmorning and suddenly an-nounced that he had been doing accounts and had found that they simply must get rid of Charles and Geneva. He couldn't afford to keep them on. He was abrupt and definite. Peter looked appalled, but waited to make her protest until the evening. It was the kind of dramatic, hysterical scene that was to confront Bertie more often in the future. She appeared, rather reminis-cent of Lady Macbeth, in her long white nightdress with heirloom Russell lace spread over her outstretched arms, her eyes half open.

Her voice, at first quiet, steadily rose to hysteria: 'Bertie you make me your slave. I have to do everything for you — you sacri-fice me rather than this stuff. You don't want to sell it; it is easier to make me slave even more than I do.' And she wandered round the room shrieking her accusations.

Bertie, not always a very sensitive husband, took Peter's arm and gently steered her to bed. In the morning there was no more talk of sacking Charles and Geneva and they stayed on long after David and I had left.

Later, the inevitable quarrel with the paranoid Barnes was to erupt and Bertie was dismissed. It was brought about, I believe, by Peter's insistence on knitting for 'Bundles for Britain' throughout Bertie's lectures. When Barnes had remonstrated with her she had angrily asserted that the lectures were elementary, real kid's stuff, surely she could continue knitting for this wartime cause? Barnes insisted they had to go and later Bertie sued him for breach of contract and won his case for compensation.

While we were at Malvern we heard almost the first encouraging war news: the sinking of the *Bismarck*. And I was sitting beside Bertie when the amazing news of Hitler's attack on Russia came through. We began to hope.

Despite the world situation, we managed to have three happy, peaceful months in that really beautiful countryside with two generous and kind hosts who wrote warmly that they missed us when we left and inviting us to come back if we couldn't get passages. But at last we sailed for Britain in August 1941. Men had to go in one convoy and women in another. The passage took twenty-two stressful days.

Two years later, Peter and Conrad arrived during a lull in the bombing and came to stay in my London flat. I remember his half-brother John, later the fourth Earl Russell, turning cartwheels on my bomb-site garden in the uniform of a naval AB to amuse Conrad, then about five. There seemed to be real affection between the three. Bertie followed in a still later convoy, and they rented a flat in Marylebone. Their hospitality continued and was particularly convivial as Harrods had just delivered, unordered, a crate of twelve bottles of the best whisky apologising to 'Your Lordship' for being unable to send more. Whisky was then almost unobtainable. They had fortunately mixed him up with his dead brother, the previous earl. It was very generous of them to share it with us and we revelled in it.

By the spring of 1949 the allowance of £35 a year was conceded for foreign travel although, in general, strict austerity was still the rule. In 1950, now living in my uncle's beautiful, if a bit war-battered, house I was able to invite the three Russells to stay. Peter refused, saying that she was so ill she couldn't possibly inflict herself on anyone — she'd be a *complete* wet blanket — but Bertie would be going with Conrad to Aix-en-Provence where he was to receive an honorary degree and they would come on to Taormina. I was ambivalent about the situation: on the one hand Peter's presence would be a protection against Bertie's philandering, on the other she would have been criticising him in her now continually attacking way. On the whole, I was glad that she had cried off.

This was in the early days when Julian Trevelyan and Mary Fedden, who were then deciding to get married, were among my guests. Julian and I went off to Catania airport in his old four-seater to meet, as we thought, Bertie and Conrad. Instead, the first person to descend from the plane was an exquisitely dressed Peter with a dark brown ostrich feather in her hat, very high heels and an elegant, long, rolled umbrella. I was taken aback; it was difficult to be welcoming. I should have to turn one of my other guests out to a nearby *pensione* and in order to arrange this I must occupy one of the seats in Julian's car. I hoped that

Peter, the unexpected one and much younger than her husband, would volunteer to go by bus, possibly with Conrad. But no. Bertie, in his late-seventies, faced the sixty-five uncomfortable kilometres.

By this time I was not sure what terms they were on, but I had no choice: they had to share a room. Bertie was delightful; charming and undemanding. He was a devoted father and he adored Conrad; it was the old man who accompanied the eleven-year-old to the beach 800 feet below when Conrad wanted to see the lava rocks and pumice stone or collect shells, and he was endlessly patient with the demanding child. But Peter was not happy. Jealous of Bertie's popularity with the other guests, she sulked. She was full of aches and pains and instead of being, as in the past, the centre of attraction with her beauty, her daring conversation and her pipe smoking, she was unhappy and isolated. The situation did not please her.

I guessed that in their room the little man was being henpecked; and he surely was. I asked him if he'd like a separate room.

'It would be an unmitigated relief,' he said in his precise, emphatic voice. 'She declaims and I am the public meeting!'

So I moved to a camp-bed and he had a peaceful room to himself.

Some days later a Sicilian friend invited me, Bertie, and some others of the party to a moonlight picnic and fishing expedition. Serious fishermen would never go out at full moon, but the sheer beauty of the shadowed cliffs and black rocks when the moon was bright and the sea alight with its beams, was breathtaking. What did it matter if we failed to harpoon sardines, drawn to their fate by powerful lights as we gazed through glass-bottomed buckets? Rocco, the fisherman who owned buckets, lights and boat, had known that the haul would be nil and had brought a splendid large fish which he grilled on a wood fire.

Sicilians, oddly, are abstemious and often they amuse themselves with practical jokes against the physically much larger northerners who are unaccustomed to the strong Sicilian wine. Disastrously, and purposefully, Rocco mixed the wines. Except for Mary, who knew she had to drive back up the hair-raising mountain road, we all indulged and were soon astonished at our scintillating wit.

Bertie sat on a black lava rock, his shock of white hair glistening in the moonlight, and was, of course, the wittiest of the lot.

Until then he had been 'Bertie' only to Julian and me, and Lord Russell to the rest, but now he became 'Bertie' to everyone. We ate and drank happily until midnight, but when we got up to leave we found our legs were distinctly uncertain, although our heads still seemed brilliant. 'This is most disgraceful. I was a tee-totaller until I was forty — my wife was a temperance reformer. I'm as drunk as a lord — but it doesn't matter because I *am* a lord!' was Bertie's comment.

More used to the wine, I was able to offer him a steadying arm and we slowly climbed up the road where Mary was waiting with the car. She drove beautifully. I helped Bertie up the many terraces of my garden, telling myself that everyone would be in bed and thinking how fortunate it was that Bertie had a room of his own where he could sleep it off with no one being any the wiser.

I was wrong. Lights in hall and stairs were lit. The door was flung open and there was Peter, furiously pale in scarlet dressing gown. As Bertie and I stood blinking in the sudden light I had time to notice that it clashed with her hair before she screamed: 'Daphne, how *dare* you go out without Conrad? You know how he adores fishing.' (I didn't.) 'The poor child. Daphne, you ought to be ashamed of yourself!'

Bertie slowly took out his ever-comforting pipe, lit it, escaped to the lavatory and locked himself in. Almost at once another blinking couple turned up: Mary supporting Julian, who was tall and double-jointed. He had cheerfully drunk the treacherous wine.

'Julian!' yelled Peter. 'It's a man's job to put my drunken, senile husband to bed!' And with that she rushed upstairs and slammed her door.

I was worried about Bertie who, I thought, needed protection. *I* could hardly give it as we were both in the dock, so I asked a motherly friend, who had not been at the picnic, and so had not aroused Peter's anger, to go and see that he got to bed unbullied.

I fell asleep at once on my camp-bed and awoke late next morning, deeply embarrassed. Peter, I felt, had behaved abominably. How could I appear as a gracious hostess when I felt insulted and furious? My problem was solved for me by a call from the terrace below: 'Signorina, Signorina.' I looked out and there was a taxi driver come, he said, to fetch the Signora who was flying to England today. And there was Peter dressed once more in her beautiful town clothes, rolled umbrella, feather and all. That was the last I saw of her.

For the next few days Bertie was bruised and quiet. He begged us to be patient with the insistent Conrad who was chanting, in his high-pitched voice, 'Wine bibbers, wine bibbers!' to the lot of us. The child, said Bertie, was deeply disturbed by his mother's departure. Doubtless it was so, but he seemed more concerned with his collection of lava and the prospect of the eclipse which would be seen clearly from Sicily in a few days' time. Abusive telegrams succeeded one another and Conrad would open and read them. Finally, ignoring Bertie's request for lenience, I rounded on the brat: 'Conrad, as long as your father is in my house, telegrams addressed to Russell are only to be opened by him. Understand?' It had little effect.

Bertie, the adoring father, had once told me that all the sufferings of his second and third marriages had been worthwhile because of the intense joy brought by the children. Now he said, 'A boy will of course side with his mother — and she will tell him what a villainous man I am. He will believe her.' Conrad did.

After 1952, and his fourth marriage, I only saw Bertie twice. I was seldom in England, he was in Wales, and I knew that he had no further need of my support and sympathy. But I will always remember him during the time between these marriages when I was 'holding his hand': on one memorable occasion he rang me, inviting me to dine with him. He would be catching a very early train from Wales and would go at once to a meeting, to discuss with other sages from various countries the possibility of writing a history of the world which could be accepted by all as a 'true' version. It seemed a daunting task! He would come to the flat just off Eaton Square where I was staying, around six o'clock.

He arrived on foot and after drinks we walked, arm in arm, nearly a mile to the restaurant where we ate a not very exciting meal at the still-controlled price of five shillings. The waitress recognised him and was thrilled. At that time he was very much in the public eye.

'I am quite relieved,' he said, 'that you are here to chaperon me!'

We then walked back to my flat where he made a last, light-hearted, attempt on my virtue. I did not find it difficult to refuse him . . . He put it down to my inhibitions, which made me laugh. He settled down to interest me with a fascinating account of all his loves and marriages, his wit sparkling throughout.

At about midnight I said, 'Bertie, I've got urgent matters to cope with tomorrow. I don't know about you, but I need sleep!'

He insisted that I should go part of the way to his hotel with him — as far as Hyde Park Corner. Among the stories he told on the way was one of Churchill's reluctance to accept that dangerous animals and snakes at the zoo must be put down for fear of their being liberated in a blitz. Imitating perfectly the famous manner, he said that Churchill, having sadly given his consent, was heard murmuring to himself: 'Seems a pity, bombs a-falling, lions a-roaring, fires a-raging — seems a pity.'

'Bertie, I *must* go home.'

'I can't let you go alone, it wouldn't be right.' And he turned around once more and back we went.

This time I insisted that he return alone. The whole day was an amazing achievement for a man of his age — eighty, I think. He had shown no sign of weariness, but was his usual scintillating self the whole of the evening.

The last time I saw him was when I went to Penrhyndeudraeth with Kathleen Nott, the poet, philosopher, novelist and wit. I did not then sympathise with his extreme views on disarmament, whilst enormously admiring his outstandingly courageous struggle. That he, at eighty-nine, preferred to go to gaol (to the great embarrassment of the government), and had actually sat up all night on a pavement to fight for other people's future, was to me a sign of greatness. But I hadn't the courage to argue with him — my lack of logic would have been mercilessly pounced upon!

His many letters to me are brief, affectionate and mostly concerned with practical plans for meeting. They are unimportant except to me.

Siciliana

A Generous Heart

She was about fifty when I first met her: her slender figure, her fiery temperament, her flashing eyes, between exquisite antique earrings dangling below her dark curls, showed how devastatingly attractive she must have been when young. She had married early and one year later had left her lawyer husband taking with her their only child, a girl. For the next forty-eight years — there being no divorce in those days — she lived in devoted sin with Carlo.

Carlo felt, with some reason, that one of his duties was to try to rein in Madame Rosa's extravagant generosity towards those in trouble and less well off than herself. Benevolence towards the needy was fairly rare in Sicily. All social work was in the hands of the Church; the public was asked to contribute to the nuns' charitable work and their help would probably only be given if the recipient was sure to vote Christian Democrat. In general the public, rich and poor, would feel their duty done if they dropped small coins into the hands of beggars. But Madame Rosa would do more — much, much more — providing medicines, foods and even mattresses and beds for the sick and needy. One day I asked her why she was so different from the others.

'Signorina, I have known suffering and unhappiness and I *must* help when I see it. I was in the Messina earthquake when I was eight years old; I was buried for hours and hours and when they pulled me out, kind people sent me to the north to be looked after. Records were not kept because of the confusion and chaos and I was lost to my family for eight whole years. My people couldn't trace me. People had meant to be kind and help, and perhaps saved my life, but by the time I was able to return to Sicily there were only two old aunts left. They were wonderfully good to me, but they weren't my parents. That was how I learned what suffering is and now when I see it I *have* to do something.'

She did so much that Carlo and her daughter had to hide money in case she gave it all away . . .

At a time when Britain's post-war popularity was steadily declining, since we had no money to spend, and our critics were numerous and destructive, Madame Rosa continually sang our praises. Years before, an Englishwoman had given her an embroidery shop. It was one of the first in the tourist town and she made it pay. She never forgot the debt to England. As our empire slowly melted away, the pound steadily fell and English visitors grew scarcer and poorer, she blew our trumpet for us: we were the best, the kindest, the most honest and the most faithful friends. Proudly she would show her book with the names of 'My Boys', the soldiers of the Eighth Army who had arrived in Sicily in 1943, many of them after years of sand and blood in the African desert. Immediately they appeared she had gone to the military authorities to get permission to open a 'tea room' and here she had welcomed officers and tommies alike. The 'home from home' meant much to them as did the warmth of her welcome and their comments in her book showed it. Many of them over the years came back to visit 'Mamma'. (She also made much-needed cash with her teas.)

Several years later, in 1953, she thought that Britain again had need of her, and off she went to the police to get permission to collect for the victims of the floods in East Anglia. This achieved, she stood for hours outside her shop saying, her hand outstretched to all and sundry: 'Come, give, give for the English, they did so much for us, they are kind and good and now they have need.' And people gave: Americans, Germans, Italians and others. This little Sicilian with the large heart collected the impressive sum of 300,000 lire, mostly in 100 and 50 lire pieces — about the equivalent of £700 at the time.

Later, typically impulsive, she suddenly realised that the Dutch also had suffered in the same high tides and storms: 'They too were good, they too have need', and she gave half of what she had collected for the British to the Dutch. It never entered her head that the poor of Sicily had much greater need than either, and less — far, far less — help from the state.

A year or so later, Queen Juliana of the Netherlands came to stay in a modest but comfortable hotel in the town — the very hotel which I had run in the absence of its Dutch owners and where I had faced the problem of the Baronessa and the rats. She was at a low ebb in her fortunes: a 'witch' had failed to cure her daughter's blindness and her husband was in England with his mistress. Her small escort was a few helmeted bodyguards on motorbikes, and two or three ladies-in-waiting, friends from her university days. Her hostess told her of Rosa's gift and the Queen, followed at a distance by her bodyguard, went to call on her in her tiny shop.

An excited 'Mamma' stopped me the next day as I passed by: 'The Queen was *wonderful* — just like you or me. She sat there in that very chair where you so often sit, and talked and talked. She stayed on and on and I gave her tea. Then when she got up to go, she seemed such a poor, lonely woman that I put my arms round her and kissed her on both cheeks!' Then, realising that this was *lèse-majesté:* 'The Queen kissed me first of course.' I was not convinced . . .

Soon the press and radio were buzzing round the shop. Madame Rosa was handed a microphone. She had never handled one before but, never hesitating, she gave the Queen a great build-up: her humanity, her dignity, her simplicity, even her wit. I hope the Queen heard it. She had had a poor press as she had complained about the endless photographers stalking her with tele-photo lenses whenever she left the hotel to go walking, swimming or shopping. She was far from photogenic, but her face would light up when she smiled — as she seldom did then. Madame Rosa had even made her laugh.

Next year the Queen returned in the royal yacht. Followed by Bernhard, her husband, and three princesses, she went to call on Rosa and thanked her again.

It was a long time before I managed to tell the British Ambassador of Rosa's devotion to us, and he too, nobly, went and had tea with her, so at last she was suitably thanked by official Britain.

Madame Rosa had a second, very different, ambassadorial encounter. In the darkest days of the Cold War, when the Pope threatened to excommunicate anyone who voted Communist, the Russian Ambassador in Rome came to stay at the San Domenico, the one luxury-class hotel in the town. Led in by his wife, who wanted one of Rosa's exquisite hand-embroidered blouses, he arrived, grim and unsmiling, in her shop. His lady tried on several and decided on an expensive white silk blouse, but it needed some alteration. Rosa could get it done in a day, she assured them, and she took up her scissors to cut it on her client. But first she wanted a deposit. The Ambassador refused. Rosa insisted. He still refused: 'Don't you know who I am?' His wife smiled and signed to Rosa to begin. Courageously, doggedly, she refused again. Finally it was the Ambassador who was made to yield and the deposit was paid. She was the one person to defeat the surly bear. She won his respect and he even smiled as they came to collect the blouse. People said it was the only time.

One fine day Madame Rosa learned that she was at last a widow. She didn't want the trouble of getting married, but by now her daughter had married one of the leading lawyers of the town, and she insisted that her mother should make an honest man of Carlo. So to our amazement a small bowl arrived with *confetti* in it, or sugared almonds, which brides and grooms always give to their friends. With it was a card with their two names and the date of their wedding.

'I didn't want to do it,' she says now, 'and I've been regretting it ever since!'

The English Way

Even in youth Donna Anna can never have been a beauty. In old age her body was like an ill-shaped pear, her face re-sembled a shrivelled brown berry with a few long and stained teeth, but her eyes were shining black and little escaped them. For many years she had been the bringer-in and layer-out of human beings. She had had no training in these complicated jobs, but she 'adapted herself' as she needed the money, and fortunately births and deaths were numerous in the little town. In addi-tion, tonsils and adenoids were taken out (by a qualified surgeon) on her kitchen table and a rent was paid for the service. Long ago her husband, after the birth of their only child — mercifully a boy, as a girl would have required a dowry to buy herself a husband — had left for the US and after one or two letters she had never heard from him since. That was thirty long years ago. The son had grown up just in time for the Second World War and he had been taken prisoner in Albania and ended up in a German camp where he was held for several years. He returned, but he married almost at once, and once more Donna Anna had to fend for herself. The important news of his safety and of the marriage was sent post haste to the Bronx, but it, like all the rest of the news from Sicily, was met by stony silence. The father, it seemed, had severed all ties with his past this side of the Atlantic. All the same, the neglected ones went on hoping.

One evening in June the son came rushing up to my terrace: 'Signorina, Signorina, my son has come out — you must come and see him.'

'When?'

'Now, at once.'

'But how old is he?'

'Ten minutes. Come quickly.'

'But your wife must be tired — shall I come tomorrow?'

'No, you must see him at once — he's wonderful.'

I promised to come as soon as I had finished my supper. I lingered over it hoping to give the by no means robust mother a slight breathing space. I asked Maria, 'What shall I take? Some bottle to toast their healths?' No, that was the father's duty.

'Perhaps a bunch of flowers?'

She looked at me aghast. 'That is for the dead, it would be terrible.' So I went, empty-handed, slowly round to their house. The frail mother had had no respite. She had produced the son and heir and all the neighbours were there celebrating the event. I was the last of a whole group of excited people. The mother, who had a weak heart, had had a long labour with no anaesthetic. She was lying, pale and exhausted, in a huge double bed which took up more than two-thirds of the room. The space around it was filled with laughing and drinking Sicilians all of whom kissed the baby loudly and fully on the mouth. The father, behaving as if he had done it all himself, was jumping across the corner of the bed, to and fro, to and fro, as he leapt to fill the glasses of his guests. It was his only way to move around. The mother winced, but did not protest at the joggling of the bed. A few days later the baby was named Michelangelo after the absent grandfather in the Bronx. A telegram was sent to him: 'Your namesake is born.' But still there was no answer. We assumed that he had made his bit in New York, founded a new family and that was that.

We were wrong. When the baby was about three, his grandfather suddenly came alive: he was returning! As for so many Sicilian emigrants to the United States, the paradise aimed at was not America but to return to his country enriched by an American pension. He had probably wearied of his American family and his thoughts had turned once more to Anna and her unknown family. He gave no date for his return and they waited with a mixture of fear and curiosity. What would he be like? How would he behave? Would she recognise him?

He arrived with no further warning. His train drew up at 2.30 one morning way down at the station below the town. There was no bus at that hour and not even a taxi. So, after thirty-five years, he climbed in the dark up the long, steep hill carrying two suitcases and resting every now and then on the winding path which snaked up the all but perpendicular slope. He had to ring the bell a long time before they answered . . .

Some months later some friends who could not afford to pay hotel prices asked me to find them a simple room near my house. I knew that they would enjoy being in a Sicilian household and one, moreover, that spoke some sort of English. So I went over to Donna Anna to ask for a double room. She had one free and was delighted that it should be let.

'Will they want a matrimonial bed, or will they wish to sleep *all'inglese?*' she asked me.

'*What* did you say?'

'Will they want one or two beds? Don't you know, Signorina, that's what we call it?' She stared at my amazed face and then watched in silence as I began laughing.

'But why do you call it that?'

'Well we all know that the English are cold, and so when people want two beds we call it the English way.'

To save our English pride, I said that doubtless they would like a matrimonial bed.

'Haven't you really heard that saying?' she asked me. 'We Sicilians are so different, we are hot-blooded. Why when my husband came back after all those years, I modestly prepared to sleep *all'inglese* and got ready two separate beds. You remember how late he came, after he had walked all the way up with those heavy suitcases? Well, at about five o'clock in the morning after we had drunk all our healths and after he had held the baby in his arms, I took him — and I felt shy — to our old room. But when he saw the beds he shouted, "I'm no cold-blooded Englishman. Make me a matrimonial bed!" And so I had to start all over again, Signorina: even at that hour he couldn't let it be!'

The Crucifix

He had hung high up on the kitchen wall since the house was first built in the early 1900s. For over fifty testing years he had been the chief protector of old Maria, the cook. Unlike the usual Spanish crucifixes with their hideously bleeding wounds, the papier-mâché figure was a simple one moulded in faith and devotion by some peasant artist and attached to a plain wooden cross. Over the years it had been completely blackened by wood smoke from the ancient stove, and this had even hidden the severe fractures in the limbs.

After Maria's death, the kitchen had to be repainted. Very carefully we took the crucifix down. Maria's successor, Beppe, never went to Mass and was outspokenly anti-clerical. I did not like to force the symbol upon him, and therefore tentatively suggested that it would be nice to put it once more in its old place if he had no objection.

'I don't mind at all — in fact I *like* to have him there.'

We carefully mended and re-hung it.

A few minutes later the old gardener, Buneri, came indoors. His face lit up like the flares at a *festa:* 'He's back. I'm glad he's back.'

'So am I,' I said. 'He reminds me of Maria; he was always in her kitchen.'

Buneri paid no attention to me. With growing excitement he addressed himself to Beppe: 'You remember, Don Beppe, that time we got eleven results right out of twelve in the football pools, we did it at his feet. I'm *glad* he's back.'

Years later, on the day when Buneri's grandfather was buried and the funeral had startled those of us unaccustomed to the hair-raising howls, screams and wails of the chief mourner, his uncle, I found four-year-old Antonio, alone in the kitchen, gazing with fury at the crucifix, shaking his fist at it and shouting: 'Wicked, wicked *Gesù* to take my grandfather away and make my uncle cry.' I calmed him as best I could, telling him that his poor old Nonno had been very tired and old and was now resting. He accepted the comforting, but remained thoughtful.

Ten days later, an old friend of eighty-eight, who had been adopted as a second grandfather, also died. Antonio was again shaken, although this time he was not involved in a funeral.

'Signorina,' he said, looking up again at

the frail figure on the cross, 'How can he keep them all up in the sky? Does he use feet as well as his arms — or will they all fall down on us?'

Our Local Venus

Only Sicily could have a Saint Venus, or Santa Venere. She is the protector of a beautiful baroque town on the east coast, while a nearby village has for a patron Santa Venerina, or Little Saint Venus. Because babies are often called after the patron saint, many are the Veneres and Venerinas to be found in the neighbourhood.

Donna Venere was a beautiful old lady when I first knew her. She would bring me the expensive bouquets that Sicilian friends feel it incumbent on them to send me before or after I invite them to a simple meal or, when I have done them some paltry favour. Her dress was semi-mourning, her hair was grey, her shoes were worn, but she walked with tremendous dignity carrying her beautiful flowers done up in cellophane. I suspected poverty, but never did she lament or beg. Her head was always held high. At Christmas and Easter whenever I met her, I would slip 2,000 lire into her hand hoping that I was not insulting her. She would receive it with dignity — her need was clearly too great to refuse.

With the years, her hair and teeth became scanty and her walk slower. As prices rose, her earnings sank. I enquired with as much delicacy as possible where she lived and with whom. With a sister older than she was.

'She can earn nothing, she has five ills, but she gets a small pension. *Tiriamo* — we drag along,' she said.

I asked had she any other family — any young able to earn?

'Yes I had two children. They were sent by the Holy Ghost so I got no allowance for them and they don't have much to do with us. I never married.'

In a flash I saw the picture of the beautiful girl she must have been; the seduction perhaps by the son of the house where she could have been a servant and therefore fair game; with no dowry and therefore no chance of buying herself a husband, despite her beauty and courage.

One Christmas I didn't see her. I made enquiries. She was in hospital. She had left by the time I visited. Transferred. Where? Perhaps Messina. Who knows?

But I would have liked her to have known of my concern and admiration. How much money she had made for others! Had the Holy Ghost helped at the end? I hope so. After all, he had a debt.

A Generous Aunt

Fifteen years after I had, in all but law, become mistress of Casa Cuseni, my aunt, then eighty-three, wrote that each one of us had a duty to think, as she put it, of our possible future or non-future. It would therefore be useful if I would let her have the name and address of *my* lawyer. She and her friend and companion led modest lives in Berkshire and unspent income had accumulated. She summoned a meeting there of her two executors, myself, then in England, my brother-in-law, the Kitson family lawyer and the adviser from her bank. We were hoping that she might realise the advantage to the next generations if she divested herself of some of her capital, to lessen death duties. The Lord Mayor thoroughly enjoyed taking the chair once more and was magisterial, as well as deaf. She signed nine £500 cheques, one for each of her nine great-nieces and nephews, or 'niblings', as she called them. At least it was a start.

At the end, the lawyer took me on one side and said, 'Please will you extract Miss

Kitson's will from her? She *won't* give it up and I *must* have it.'

Cautiously I approached my aunt, fully aware that, as she put it, she wouldn't have anyone 'playing ducks and drakes' with *her* money.

'Well,' she said, 'he can have it if he likes, but it won't be any use to him: I'm going to make a new one!'

'Is it really necessary?'

'Yes, I'm going to cut you out, as you will have Casa Cuseni.'

It was a serious blow, but it was her will, not mine. Skittishly she tapped the lawyer with the large, rolled document saying she was going to make a new one.

'But *this* is pretty new. Do you really need to?'

'Yes I'm going to cut Daphne out, she will have Casa Cuseni.'

Simultaneously, the lawyer and my brother-in-law daringly exclaimed: 'But you *can't* do that!' My dear brother-in-law pointed out that I had no husband to support me — and had given up my profession to try to save the house. Without some private income I might have to sell it. Mercifully they were listened to and, in compensation, she left my three siblings £5,000 extra each. The threat to Casa

Cuseni was averted.

But the house still wasn't legally mine. I was hoping that she was going to transfer it before it was too late. Again, the lawyer was listened to and I was asked to get my Sicilian lawyer to prepare the necessary documents. Typically, he insisted on two contradictory acts, one donating the property to me and the other a false act of sale (he would decide later which it would be best to use). Anxiously, I reminded him that my aunt had been a magistrate in England and she might not care for this very Sicilian subterfuge. He insisted, and I took the documents to Berkshire. Fortunately the old lady was amused and agreed to sign both when, in due course, all preliminaries had been completed.

I made appointments with notary, lawyer and witnesses and phoned her. No answer. All that day I phoned, growing steadily more frantic. She and her old friend, who seldom nowadays left their village, had vanished into thin air, leaving no message with dailies or neighbours. Like a detective, at last I achieved a slight clue from the family of the friend: 'Wisbech'. I seized an AA book and rang the more modest hotels in their area of England until I ran them to ground. They had gone off to help an old friend who had become senile and incompetent, and they had completely forgotten about the transfer of Casa Cuseni. They were returning on the Saturday. I was leaving for Sicily on the Tuesday — and Saturday was not a working day. At 11 a.m. they agreed to wait at the platform barrier in Liverpool Street station for me. Miraculously, the notary (from a firm with the Dickensian name Cheesewright and Murly) had agreed to work at the weekend once he knew how urgent it was.

The two octogenarians arrived on time, dressed in sober grey and carrying their suitcases. Porters — they existed in those days — would have been an extravagance. In the Great Eastern Hotel in that (then) least romantic and gloomiest of stations, Casa Cuseni became officially mine as we signed an Act of Donation and the Act of Sale. I felt that only whisky could be adequate to the occasion, though fearing my aunt's reaction to my extravagance. While the two sipped lemonade, we toasted Miss Kitson in Scotch. I relaxed.

I tried to call a taxi and asked them where they would like me to invite them to lunch. They knew a vegetarian restaurant to which a bus would take us — a taxi was *quite* unnecessary. She had just transferred to me a property of immense value and they seemed to be living like church mice. It reminded me of my uncle who, having paid me and my mother's fare to Venice and for our stay in a leading hotel, erupted alarmingly in the Piazza San Marco when I, a shy eighteen-year-old, asked for a *cappuccino* instead of an espresso: 'Don't you know how expensive it is?' he asked angrily.

I returned to Casa Cuseni feeling incredulous that all of it was now really and truly mine.

Angelo and his Women

We had just returned from Sara's annual joy-ride — to the cemetery. Three hundred and sixty-four days of the year she could be found in her tiny, dilapidated, one-roomed 'house', shaped like the prow of a ship between two roads. But on the anniversary of her beloved Angelo's death she dressed herself in her best black, now turning slowly green, and, with a black mantilla on her head, she waited for me to help her into my car to go down to the rows of graves, rising in shelves on the rocky hillside, below the town.

Hobbling with difficulty, hanging on to my arm, she would wait for me to tell her when we had arrived. Then, terrifyingly, she would insist on mounting the ladder to the third row of cemented-in corpses, each with the photograph of the departed beside his or her name and dates, to place the flowers I had brought in the tiny vase, which was all there was room for. Deaf, rheumatic, and with growing cataracts, she somehow found the strength. Once more on firm ground, she would intone prayers for her lamented, entrusting him to the care of the Madonna and all the saints.

'You were good, oh so good to me, *carissimo,* but why, why, my little brother, did you leave me so early? Why did you abandon me to the wicked uncaring others? Who could have known that such a disaster would befall me? The good go first and we are left.' Tears pouring down her face, she would turn slowly away, then ask me to lead her to other family graves. Earth-bound this time, she stood mouthing an almost silent prayer while I had to climb up and place a flower on each. Her duty done, she would then, more briskly, seek out her enemies and curse them:

'*Maledetto,* accursed one, you who promised to help me — on the very deathbed of my Angelo you promised to help me, but once he was gone, you looked the other way when we passed each other in the street. May you pay for this — may the blessed Virgin and all the saints make you suffer for this. And you who cheated me, a poor lonely woman who foolishly trusted you, may the good God see that you pay. Can I believe that he won't?'

And so on and on. She was a religious woman, certain, she thought, of a privileged place in the next world, and the chief comfort of her old age was the knowledge that, penniless as she was, she would have a splendid funeral, with all the Daughters of Mary following her coffin through the main street of the town. Her long membership and her payments in the past had assured her this honour, and in the endless, day dreaming, lonely hours she pictured with relish the funeral to come and the grave in a first-class site.

This year was different. We drove slowly back to her hovel and turned the corner into her street. With horror I saw what she could not. A heavy truck had crashed halfway through the rickety building demolishing her room and carrying with it her bed and the chair on which, every other day of the year, she would have been sitting. A crowd was shouting and gesticulating, entirely blocking the road. I pulled up a hundred metres away. Sara was still mumbling her prayers, happy that she had fulfilled her annual duty. Her neighbours, absorbed in the excitement of the disaster, had no time to spare a thought for the poor old tenant. A miracle had saved her — and that was that.

Slowly I broke the news to her. Dazed and bewildered, she needed the comfort of her own people and her own dialect. At last a kindly neighbour took her into her home and comforted her with fresh, fried sardines.

Gradually her numbed, shocked mind clutched at its only lifeline: 'It must have been St Anthony's work!' she exclaimed. 'Who else could have known those brakes would fail? Who else could have brought it about that only an empty chair and bed should be the victims? He is indeed a great saint, worthy of all our devotion.'

In a few days she was resigned to going into the Hostel for the Aged Poor.

Sara's brother was eighteen when, for the first time, he left the small Mediterranean town that had been his birthplace and his only home. He was ambitious and opportunities there were few, so he sailed for the US to try his luck. On his side in the coming struggle he had nothing but his youth and hopes, his outstanding good looks, his charm and his violin.

A few years later Angelo was established as a prosperous, Midwest American citizen. He taught the violin, he played in an orchestra and he had married a rich, elderly widow who, shortly afterwards, obligingly died. His second marriage was to an Illinois girl of Irish descent and both were deeply in love. He was no longer a practicing Catholic, and the wedding took place in the Protestant church which Mary Ellen regularly attended. Three daughters were in due course born to them and spoiled, as is the adoring Sicilian way. They were, however, brought up as pure Americans, and never showed any desire to explore their European background for which their father often, secretly, pined.

After the two eldest were grown up and married, and the youngest had died of some children's illness to their lasting heartbreak, Angelo, with some difficulty, persuaded his wife to visit his country and to leave the States for the first time in her life. By chance, she had seen a picture of snow-capped Etna rising over the Mediterranean on an Alitalia calendar. She was good advertisers' fodder and this had persuaded her where Angelo had failed. By now he was the 'Maestro': tall, slim, with clear-cut features and strong bone structure under a mane of brushed-back white hair, his distinguished looks underpinned by a loose black bow and surmounted by a broad-brimmed, black felt musician's hat. He soon became the conductor of the town's *orchestra al plettro.*

The family gave the rich uncle and aunt a great and noisy reception. Brother, nephews, nieces, cousins all gathered around and insisted, in turn, on being their hosts while they looked for a suitable flat or house. The only one who could not offer anything, but by far the most overjoyed at his coming home, was his widowed sister Sara. She had worshipped her brother all her life. He was the generous, good one of the family. Many years ago she had married, late in life, and had soon lost her husband. Since then she had never been out of widow's weeds, and never would be according to the then inexorable custom for Sicilian women. She had been left with a house and enough money to exist in respected and moderate comfort. However, ill-educated and gullible, and barely literate like most of her backward sex in the island, she had been persuaded by a greedy relation — a man, of course — to sign her name without reading the document. She then discovered, too late, that she had lost both income and property and was dependent upon charity. Three things sustained her: her unshaken faith in the Church and more particularly the Virgin and St Anthony; her membership of the Daughters of Mary; and last, but certainly not least, the remittances sent by her adored American brother. His return was the one worldly joy she had experienced for years, her only pleasures up to then being the religious festivals in which she regularly processed, thus earning merit in this world and the next.

Angelo found her in extreme poverty in one room with a leaking roof. The money that he had been sending regularly had often been deflected by the other brother, a hard, miserly, unmerciful man with a grasping wife and an equally avaricious son. All were willing to stoop to any petty deceit to advance in the world, even if their sister lived near starvation. Had she been rich, or even had a pittance to leave her relations, they would all have been fussing round her. But her total possessions were a few old bits of furniture, clothes given to her by nuns and charitable friends, and a small family of cats to whom she somehow managed to give the odd bit of spaghetti and now and then a drop of milk.

To their credit the 'Americans' took her into their house all day long, giving her an allowance in return for which she helped with the household chores. Her happiness was complete. And so was that of the couple. Angelo, said his wife, was rejuvenated in every way. It was like a second honeymoon. They managed to fit in with the unjustifiably snobbish, foreign group and at the same time to endure, with seemingly endless patience, the possessiveness, gossip and noise of their Sicilian relations.

So much did they both enjoy the place that they decided to build a house and to settle there for most of the year, only returning to the States to fit in with the conditions for Angelo's retaining his American citizenship. The brother, a builder, was delighted, and so was his draughtsman son: the pickings would be good. So good, in fact, did they turn out to be — owing to the innocence of the pair — that Angelo found his dollars running out and the house still only a shell. By the time he investigated, he found out that he had been steadily swindled in every direction. The paradise they had thought to have found turned sour. In disgust and pain, the two flew back to America. But his funds there had been diminished by his generosity to their two daughters. Before returning to Europe he had sold his Stradivarius and investments. and had given each daughter a house, one in the Middle West and the other in Louisiana. The understanding had been that each should provide a lodging for their parents should they ever need one in their old age. Their year would then be divided between the two.

Back in Sicily old Sara mourned, her happiness destroyed. However, this time she received the monthly allowance of dollars. Angelo, sadly now aware that he could not trust his relations blindly, saw to it that she got what he sent. It was small consolation for the absence of the companionship, devotion and reflected glory that had buoyed her up for so short a period. She had counted on its lasting for life — after all, he was her little brother, and Mary Ellen was several years younger than he. She prayed with all her fervent faith many times a day to that greatest of all miracle workers, St Anthony, that he would bring her dear ones back.

A year or so went by and still she prayed, her faith unshaken, certain that help would come. And suddenly, on St Anthony's Day in June, there they were once more. Her delight was unbounded. Not only did she have her brother and his good wife, but she also knew, beyond a doubt, that her saint would never let her down.

The pair were as expensively dressed as

before, but gradually it was seen that money was a good deal shorter. There was less entertaining than before, even of close relations and friends, with the exception of Sara who was treated exactly the same. The house they rented was smaller and less elegant than its predecessor.

Little by little the story of their American stay came out. They had gone to one daughter in the north, expecting to live with her for a few months in their own quarters, built with Angelo's money. But the daughter said that she was sorry, she was expecting another baby shortly and the rooms promised would be needed; to put up her parents was out of the question. Hurt and bruised, the pair had turned south, but that son-in-law had just started in business on his own and needed the extra rooms for his office. They both regretted it, of course, but they were certain their parents would understand the impossibility of their offering hospitality for more than a few days . . .

Shattered by this second blow, the couple moved around, finding expenses great and hating their rootlessness. Finally, one day in June, they decided to return to the place where at any rate there was *one* human being who adored them and would give them a heart-warming, reassuring welcome. They had gone to book tickets for the 15th. All seats were taken, but there were two free on the 13th. They seized this chance. They had forgotten that it was St Anthony's Day. He brought them safely back to the praying Sara.

Sadly, the miracle was not complete. Angelo, who did not believe much in doctors and had at one time flirted with Christian Science, had had a lump for years. There was some pain, but not enough to make him take it seriously. It affected his bladder but, as he was now well on in his late seventies, it grew slowly and he could blame it on old age. At first his happiness dulled the discomfort, but, little by little, inexorably, the pain made itself more felt. He often took to his bed. If he played his second violin it was out of tune and painfully sad to hear. Gradually, inevitably, he sank into despair. Meanwhile, their lack of money became ever more obvious.

A friend wrote to the elder daughter, now known over on this side as 'Goneril', telling her of the grim situation. Not only was there no money for drugs to dull the pain, but there was practically nothing for food. Not that Angelo needed much, but her aunt and mother had to have something more than Angelo's tiny income could provide. There was no answer. A letter to 'Regan' received the reply that she was sorry to hear of the situation, but she could do nothing as business was bad and babies numerous. 'Cordelia' was of course dead. Mary Ellen's world was shattered. Now she realised that treatment had been left too late. They were in a country where, especially if the patient had no money, pain was not much relieved by drugs.

Suddenly there was a moment of flickering hope. Angelo announced that he wanted to see the sea again, and to go fishing where he had so often been as a boy. A car was rented. He took his rod and sat on the lava rocks in a place of some danger from the threatening waves. His eyes sparkled once more. He caught no fish, but he felt hungry and ordered a dish of fried prawns and the good, local wine. To Mary Ellen it seemed a miracle as he scrambled back to eat and drink, but sadly the sickness returned and, after the first excited attempt to eat, he pushed the plate aside. The same with the wine. The gaiety faded, although he bravely went back to pretend to cast his line.

It was the last time he left his bed. In the

gloomy, oak-panelled bedroom (furnished in imitation of the Victorian style which had been the fashion when the first foreigners had settled in the town) old Sara sat like a bedraggled black crow, but firm as a rock in her bigoted faith, murmuring her prayers for his soul which she knew was in danger of everlasting damnation. She hardly ate or slept, and day and night was at her brother's side.

Mary Ellen, shattered by the rapid deterioration of her husband, lacked the courage even to enter the death chamber. She remained outside, imploring me to keep the noisy relations away. Of the lot she could only stand the devoted, and almost silent, Sara. Hardly knowing what she was doing, she sat in the garden scandalously dressed in trousers and the briefest of blouses, with her bare and elderly midriff displayed to all who came by. This in a world then only slowly freeing itself from Arab ideas as to what could be exposed. In her circumstances she should have been decently covered from head to foot and at the bed-head. At last I persuaded her that, for Sara's sake, the priest should be called.

At first she exclaimed angrily, 'He has no need of their ticket, he's *a good* man.'

Then, in order to diminish Sara's terrified concern, she agreed.

What none of us non-Catholics had realised were the necessary preliminaries.

Indignantly she greeted me one morning: 'The priest's been here. *Now* what do you think? They want to marry us! We *are* married, and have been for forty years. And more!'

She had refused.

An hour or so later the priest returned with two small boys dressed in surplices and carrying incense. The three went straight into the house.

In a few minutes out came one of the boys: 'Would the Signora please put on a skirt? And a decent blouse?'

Mary Ellen reeled with shock and indignation. I calmed her and said that I would explain to the priest that the wife was too distressed and would remain in the garden.

The peremptory answer came back: 'The bride must be present.'

Making a supreme effort for Sara's sake, Mary Ellen staggered inside, dressed herself as required and the ceremony began. The bridegroom was pulled up and supported with difficulty in a sitting position. Throughout, wild-eyed and worlds away, with his white and withered arms he was conducting a fantasy orchestra. The ring was taken off the finger where it had been for over forty years and then replaced. No responses were heard. The only sounds were the grunts of the bridegroom and the rapid murmuring of the priest with the final, breathless, 'Amen-a-thousand-lire.' The fee was paid and the three left.

Sara rose to her feet, clasped her hands, smiled for the first time in all those terrible weeks and cried: 'Aren't you glad your children are no longer *bastardi?* Now perhaps a miracle will happen and he will get better.'

But this time St Anthony failed her. That night, in the early hours of his seventy-ninth birthday, Angelo died.

He was dressed by an old Gamp in his white tie and tails, and lay in state in the gloomy, panelled hall, looking in death the distinguished conductor he had never been in life. At last the relations were allowed in. They sat in a circle performing their mourning duties, moaning, wailing and shocked at the absence of the so recently married widow. She was lying in a state of shock on the matrimonial bed, allowing only calmer friends to come near her.

We were now aware, to our dismay, that we had been left with two destitute women on our hands. Angelo, improvident and doubtful of the morrow as are so many Sicilians — perhaps owing to centuries of being conquered and exploited and with the fear of earthquakes and eruptions — had lived for the day, dressing and entertaining well and putting nothing on one side for any uncertain future. His good clothes, a pension that died with him and a few bits of furniture were all that was left after the daughters had had their share. And the funeral had to be paid for. It had to take place by law within twenty-four hours. The family didn't want to lose face, but even less did they want to shell out money. There was the second violin. We examined it carefully. Made in Warsaw in the eighteenth century, the maker's name was on it. Could it be of value? We none of us knew. A bargain was struck: the nephew would pay for the funeral and the violin would be handed over to him as a pledge. He was not to sell until we had obtained at least two expert valuations. There might, after all, be enough money for a good, respectful funeral and a balance left to help the poverty-stricken women. The pact agreed, the nephew returned to the family group and the corpse while we tried to sustain the widow with tea.

Suddenly she broke into hysterical shrieks. We feared the threatened collapse was happening, but she got control and sobbed out: 'I *have* something left. I now remember Angelo told me that if anything happened to him, in the bank in Minnesota he had put my return fare home!'

Some relief, but not much.

The funeral took place next day. Ominous grey clouds soon fulfilled their threat of heavy rain, and the nephew's intention to economise by having the men of the family carry the coffin on their shoulders down to the distant cemetery — the traditional way of showing respect for the dead — gave way to his opposing desire of saving his strength and sparing his smart clothes and of maintaining his dignity by ordering the very first motor hearse in the neighbourhood, a resplendent violet and black affair with four chubby cherubs in silver at the corners of the roof. Slowly the procession, with the priest ahead, the hearse next and the mourners following on foot, moved down the central street with the shops on either side pulling down their shutters as it passed. At the main gate of the walled town the majority turned back, their respect shown and their duty fulfilled. The small group of chief mourners, and the foreign friends supporting the widow in her borrowed black, continued to the end of the road.

No funeral feast followed, nor was there any will to be read, there being nothing to leave; Angelo had not made one. We took Mary Ellen back to Casa Cuseni and fortified her — and ourselves — with 'Irish coffee'. The whiskey was generous and spirits lightened. Some mail had just arrived from the States. Mary Ellen opened the first letter. Out fell, wrapped inside a vulgar, garish birthday card from 'Regan' wishing her father the happiest day of his life, a five dollar bill. We added still further whiskey to the coffee . . .

The violin was of no great value. After the funeral, and the purchase of the grave in the third row of cement shelves, there was nothing over and the nephew was left in sole charge of the violin. To protect himself against still more loss, he made off with Angelo's expensive American shoes and clothes, together with the cooking stove, all of which the widow had intended should go to Sara for her to sell.

'*Pazienza, pazienza!*' exclaimed Sara, clasping her hands in an attitude of prayer. 'It is the will of God.'

Not for the first time, I asked myself

what kind of a God was this.

Mary Ellen, after three weeks negotiating for the money left by Angelo in Minnesota, bought an air ticket for the States and flew off, to suffer a nervous breakdown. However, with the resilience of her Irish forebears, she recovered to become once more an occupational therapist, this time in the hospital which had helped her recovery. Years later, when I last heard of her, at an advanced age she was still working as director of the department.

Less often than I should, I visit Sara in a hostel kept by devoted nuns. She is probably living in more comfort than she had known in all her previous years, but, as a fellow inmate says, 'If that one found herself in Paradise, she'd still be complaining.'

She hugs and kisses me. She weeps with pleasure mingled with distress that her Angelo is no longer with us. And then, eyes ablaze with bigotry, she clasps her hands together: '*I* made them man and wife,' she cries. 'Owing to *me* she has the right to bear his name.' And once more she praises St Anthony and his miracles, in one of which she had been allowed to play her not so humble part.

Henry Faulkner

I am still surprised at myself for having done it. I cannot think what made me. For me, an on the whole cautious Anglo-Saxon, to have invited (on only a second en-counter) a strikingly eccentric American painter born at Egypt, Kentucky, to come and live, rent-free for as long as he liked, in the small flat in my garden which was then empty in the absence of a gardener, was in-deed astonishing. Henry jumped at the op-portunity and came up at once to see it. It had two rooms and was barely furnished, but it had a view between tangerine trees over to Mount Etna. Henry was enchanted. I told him that he could have it in return for painting the outside front of the cottage: 'Yes, any colour you like.' I had learned from my uncle's example to ask for some re-turn, however small, when giving a special favour. It was good, he felt, for the self-respect of the recipient and more than one person had told me how, when there was real poverty and unemployment and they had asked him for help, he had said, 'Yes, but you must do something for me.' He would give them some brief, morning job for which he paid them a month's wages. 'He respected us,' they said; 'he did not treat us as beggars.' It took Henry less than a day to produce and apply a beautiful blue wash, with warm, pinkish orange surrounds to the three deeply inset windows, a décor which still gives me pleasure many years later.

In his mid-thirties, Henry was a small, sprite-like figure who sprang and danced rather than walked along; he had striking, very alert, green eyes and a mop of medium-long, generally uncontrolled, blond hair. He had a puckish laugh, but underlying was a steel-like quality produced, one sensed, by a hard, hard struggle in the past that was possibly even now not over. He had, as a friend put it, 'a used face'. His clothes were just Henry's, and no one else's, with no attention paid to fashion or custom: striped trousers, almost pyjama-like, and pale-coloured shirts were his usual wear, but he also possessed a funereal black suit in which he would dress up if he decided that the occasion demanded it. We could never guess when he would choose to do so.

He was in Sicily, it turned out, because

Alice Delamarr of Florida, a patroness of young painters and friend of Bernard Berenson, had spotted him and decided to help. He was the second young painter she had sent to Sicily, with enough money for the fare and to support himself for several months. Henry hoped to repeat the considerable success of the first.

Day and night he worked. His material needs were few. He didn't want more furniture, it would get in the way, but might he paint a frieze on the wall? This was carried out in a strong, unhesitating design in black, gold and blue with a fleur-de-lys motif; lovely but quite out of proportion to the height of the room. Following in famous footsteps, Henry persuaded the owner of the best restaurant in town to give him one large meal a day in return for paintings. The owner, won over by Henry's charm, took a risk. Henry was quite unknown, but the bright oil colours, the dreamlike buildings, the flowers, the stylised animals which every now and then popped up between them, appealed tremendously to Sicilian eyes.

By now he was living and eating without paying anything; he had his whole allowance to spend. He rooted round all the antique shops buying antique frames, pottery with patterns that took his fancy, old prints, wooden statuettes, gilded candlesticks and so on. Those were the days when exciting treasures were still to be found by anyone with an eye and some leisure, and Henry was an inexhaustible searcher. With shrewd, Kentucky-peasant determination, he bargained and beat down prices, obviously loving the battles which amused the vendors as much as Henry himself. I think that it would have bored him to buy without a 'beating of beaks' as it is called. And Henry was generally the winner. Sometimes his opponent would yield, simply to get rid of the persistent magpie. His possessions increased at such a rate that the flat was not big enough to hold them. After a time, he had to get a carpenter to make thirteen packing-cases of such a size that I wondered how on earth we were going to get them, when reassembled and full, down the several terraces to the road. As each was filled Henry hammered on the lid with the largest of nails. He did not intend to have them opened until he reached the States. I wondered about Italian Customs, which does not like any unexamined pictures to leave the country.

After a week or so of this strenuous work

Henry suddenly collapsed. We found him lying on his bed fully dressed, breathing heavily and unconscious. We could not rouse him when, after some hours, we tried. This was alarming. Had it anything to do with his once-fractured skull about which he had told me? I felt that local doctors, even if competent in such matters, would have difficulty in dealing with him. Fortunately an English friend, then working in an up-to-date Department of Neurology and Psychiatry, was prepared, with me, to take the risk of holding a watching brief. Thankfully, after several anxious hours, Henry woke up. He was a bit dazed and didn't know where he was, but soon he was on his feet again and hungry.

'Henry, you've been unconscious. You frightened us. Have you ever been like this before?'

'Oh yes, I think so — I get blackouts. It's lucky I was here.' He did not seem deeply concerned. Suddenly he rummaged among a pile of papers and pulled out a handful of sheets, saying: 'Here are my poems. I'd like you to see them.'

I sat beside his bed to read. They were like his pictures, painted in strong colours, full of fantasy and surprising images, with undertones of deep sadness.

'You never told me you were a poet as well as a painter. Henry, these are lovely — at least I think so. Has any serious critic ever seen them?'

'Oh yes.'

'What did they say?'

'That they should be published.'

'Well, I agree. Was it anyone I would have heard of?'

'Oh yes,' he said doubtfully, 'I think so.'

'Who?'

'Tennessee Williams and Ezra Pound.'

'Yes, I've heard of them!'

Wherever had these three met? Could it have been in a mental hospital? It seemed likely.

A few days after the alarming coma, Henry wandered into my drawing room and with joy began eyeing some Persian vases and their lovely rare colours — deep blues and emerald greens. One particularly took his fancy: 'Oh Ma'am, how *beautiful*. Look at that pattern. It's like a Klee. Oh, I wish I'd seen it before. I'd have put it in a picture. Now it's too late. I'm off to Agrigento in the morning. I must see the temples before I leave, and time is getting on.'

'How long are you going for?'

'A week or ten days, I expect.' And off he

went to the much wilder and violent part of this astonishing land.

A day or two after he had gone off, I saw that the Persian vase he had been so taken by was missing. This really shocked me. It was a rare, medieval piece of great interest and beauty. I hated to think that Henry had taken it but, in the absence of any trace of breakage, the case against him looked black. I asked the daily who came in for an hour or so: no, she knew nothing and she convinced me of this. The loss was really serious. What should I do? It seemed almost certain that the vase was in one of those thirteen huge packing-cases.

Henry had made no fixed plans — he would take train, bus or lift just as they turned up. After a fortnight I began to worry. No sign or sound of Henry. He might just have forgotten passing time, he might have gone into a coma, or been beaten up by Sicilians less used to the strangeness and eccentricities of foreigners than those of this, more tourist-ridden, side of the island. Another week passed. I reluctantly decided that the next day I must report his absence to the police. Anything might have happened, and who could start a search but me?

That night I was in my bath when there was a tap at the door, and a laconic 'That lunatic's back', from an old English friend who hid with difficulty his wonder at my affection for Henry.

'Thank goodness! Please tell him I can't see him tonight but must in the morning. I urgently need to talk with him.'

But in the morning there was no sign of Henry except a parcel, exquisitely wrapped in white tissue paper with pale green ribbon and a spray of tiny pink roses, lying on the doorstep of the french window in the drawing room and addressed: 'To Daphney, with love.' (He never learned to spell my name.) It contained a dress length of white organdie with a bewitching pattern of tiny emerald green stars. I was much touched, but it was hardly suitable for one of my age so I gave it to a six-year-old friend, who was enchanted. Henry was alive. That was a relief, but the vase problem had still to be tackled.

When at last he returned, there was no explanation of where he had been this time.

As soon as I saw him I started: 'Henry, you remember that vase, the blue one with the lovely Klee-like pattern, the one you loved so much? Well, it's disappeared. What do you think could have happened to it?'

'That's bad.'

'Yes, *very* bad.' Pause, then: 'You know you're a bit of a magpie, you had that blackout?' Trying to give him an excuse if he *had* taken it. 'You could have taken it perhaps while you were still a bit odd? It really took your fancy. Do you think that it could be in one of those packing-cases?'

He calmly considered the idea: 'Could be,' he finally admitted.

'Well, what are we going to do about it?'

Another long pause, several moments' silence. Then, 'Ma'am, will you trust me?'

I took a deep breath. This time it was I who was silent: I minded so much about the vase, but how could I insist on opening and searching through all those cases? Finally, I gasped and said 'Yes, Henry.'

He looked at me with relief and surprise. Perhaps it was the first time in his life that anyone in such a situation had trusted him. How much did I, I asked myself? I hardly knew, but I felt that the only hope lay in his friendship for me. I think his lifelong devotion to me began at that moment.

'Well,' he said, 'I'll go off and when I get to New York the Customs will go through everything I've got. They never leave anything alone.'

I thought this was only too likely in view of Henry's appearance and behaviour, and the crates of antiques and canvases.

'Oh Ma'am, I do so hope we find your vase!'

Off he went and I wondered whether I should ever hear from him again.

Two months later a letter arrived, beginning: 'Daphney, with stars in your mind and daisies in your eyes. We didn't find your vase. I am so sad. I would have done anything to make you happy, but it wasn't there.' Suddenly, intuitively, I knew, beyond a shadow of a doubt, that this was indeed the truth. It must have been broken by the daily and all traces carefully vacuumed away. As compensation I had gained Henry's undying loyalty and trust.

Gradually, over the months he stayed with me, I had heard something of his history. He told me that he was the twelfth child, a twin, of a family of small farmers in the remotest mountains of Kentucky. This, I subsequently learned, is a part of the world where Shakespeare would have felt at home with the language. So remote and self-contained is it that the dialect had remained unaltered for centuries. When Henry was two, his mother died in childbirth. All he could remember of her was crawling into her coffin to try to make her wake up and talk to him, 'but she wouldn't'. His father put several of the children into an institution; Henry thus lost his second mother, his oldest sister. He was lonely and in desperate need of affection. A social worker found him a foster home, but he was soon sent back to the institution; needing something to love, he had cuddled too hard the only soft, fluffy thing he could find and suddenly found it went limp in his hands. The chicken had been killed by too much love. A beating and expulsion was the penalty. His protectoress found him other families, but he was always sent back to the institution in disgrace for one reason or another.

At long last he was settled in Clay County where a foster family could tolerate, even if they could not understand, his strange behaviour. When he should have been working in the fields with the others, he was always making patterns in the clay. These he would decorate with flowers, shells, feathers, berries, stones — anything that he could find. He had never heard of painters or paintbrushes, but he had this compulsion to make patterns. One day his foster father was drawn to look at what Henry was doing and, surprisingly, he stopped scolding and threatening and instead joined in, producing pebbles that had taken his fancy. Slowly a relationship developed between them. Henry also became attached to his foster mother and this time he stayed with them until he was twelve, although they continued to beat him for not pulling his weight in the general work. (Years later, long after his journey to Sicily, he supported his last foster mother, to the end of her life, with both money and affection.)

Although he had put down some roots, the urge to make patterns, and to see something of the rest of the world, was too strong. One fine day he decided to run away. He just started walking; he walked and walked with only a small piece of bread to eat all day. He had no map, no idea of distances or any notion of where he was making for. Darkness came. He lay down in a ditch to try to sleep, but soon he heard the terrible roar of a wild animal. It came nearer and nearer. Summoning all his courage he raised his head and looked towards the noise. He saw two huge luminous eyes. So strong was their light that he was almost blinded. Helplessly he waited for whatever was to come, but the car passed him by without stopping. It was the first he had ever heard or seen. It seems difficult to believe that in the United States in 1936 this could have been possible but I am assured that, in the remote mountains of Kentucky, it could well have been true.

He found a job as a bell-boy in a Californian hotel. How he got there, I don't think I ever learned. Years later he got to an art school, working his passage, though I don't think he was there for long. How he got to Key West in Florida and met Alice Delamarr and Tennessee Williams, again I don't know.

I was far from being the only person fascinated by Henry's strange personality: his extraordinary impishness, his charm, his courage, his dedication to his painting, and his childlike capacity for living for the moment. Because of all this, we overlooked his crazily promiscuous sex life (this was before AIDS) which every so often brought him lots of trouble.

Three years or so passed, with strange and devoted letters from Henry coming at long intervals. Then one day a Sicilian, not known to me, came to my house asking if I had any Henry Faulkners for sale.

'Why do you ask?'

'Because a man has come from America

and bought all the pictures that he left with the restaurant. He gave a good price.'

I hadn't any to sell. Henry had generously given me two: one an enchanting small oil of a white house, with three doors of strange shapes, one in emerald green, the next in apple green and the third in grey mauve; in the background, floating away into the distance across a delicate iron railing, was a golden haze of flowers. The other one was of the leaning tower of Pisa with the flowers of Casa Cuseni bursting out of its windows. I was certainly not going to sell these gifts of Henry's.

It was clear that Henry was fulfilling Alice's hopes for him. A year or so later came the notice of Henry's first show in New York. Astonished, I read that among the collectors of Henry Faulkner's paintings were Bette Davis, Marion Brando, Mrs Ernest Hemingway, Daphne Phelps, Tennessee Williams, Bertolt Brecht and one or two Blue Grass country millionaires. I could hardly be called a collector, but it was impressive all the same.

Henry's second eruption into my life happened about six years after the first. Written on pale green paper, a letter arrived, saying that he was on a liner, terribly excited because the very next day he would land again in Italy. He would go straight to Perugia in the hope that they would teach him some Italian; then he would buy a car (the idea of Henry *buying* a car, still more be capable of *driving* it, was indeed astounding) and make at once for my house. It ended: 'much, much love, Henry'. Then 'PS. I have three dogs and six cats with me, but don't worry.'

Already I had two dogs who, properly Sicilian, were very possessive of their territory. Whatever would happen? But I told myself that 'Sufficient unto the day . . .' He might not turn up. But at 9.40 p.m. on Christmas Eve, when to say the least I was not exactly idle, there he was, certain of my wholehearted welcome. He got it! But he was not alone. With him was an American *capellone*, or hairy one, with a bushy beard and a huge fuzzy hair-do. Mercifully Henry had not attempted to drive the car — he had had enough to do controlling the animals. He was helped in this by Gentry, a magnificent pedigree collie. Tied to Henry's wrist by a piece of white plastic cord was Esquire, a superb pedigree Siamese. He was tied because he was *cattivo*, or wicked, because, as Henry delicately put it, unlike the other cats he was 'unchanged' and would fight to kill the ones that had been changed. These were Black Rastus (a black Persian), Gerolomo (a white Persian with one green and one blue eye) and Black Sister (a half-Siamese black cat) that was expecting Esquire's kittens. Two tabbies completed the troupe. Henry had saved them from cruel fates. To all these, except Esquire, I still had to be introduced. What was I to do? I drove the car out of my garage and the *capellone* drove theirs in. None of the dogs was small: Gentry was a big collie; Lady was his wife and rather bigger. She was not a pedigree Alsatian, explained Henry; she had got run over in front of his house in Lexington and 'of course' he had to take her in. Onassis was their son and the largest dog I had ever seen.

'Henry, why Onassis?'

'Because he *thinks* he's big.'

'But he *is*, he really is.'

He was still a huge, lolloping puppy, falling about and occupying most of the available space.

Sitting in the passenger seat, from which it never moved for the next two days and nights, silent and scared, sat what Henry called a white duck.

'You never mentioned this — you surely haven't brought it across the Atlantic?'

'I only got her yesterday.'

'But how? Where?'

'She was in the Christmas market in Perugia; she spoke to me, I loved her and I call her Daphne!'

'Not Daphne, but Daphnis!' Like most Sicilians, curiously enough Henry did not know the difference between a duck and a drake.

I told the two that they must look after, exercise and feed all the animals — that I would not have a moment to think what we should do with them until Christmas was well and truly over. I gave them the key.

'But what about him and me?' nodding toward the *capellone*.

'Well, I'll just be able to fit you two into the house, and of course I can feed you.'

'Esquire will have to come too: I can't leave him with the others, he would kill the neuters.'

'All right, but you must see that he doesn't kill or maim my dogs.'

Just before Christmas lunch, Henry announced that he must go shopping. I told him that nearly all the shops would be closed, but he said he must get some presents.

'But none of us will expect them, it's really not necessary.' However, go he must.

'Well, we shan't wait for you.'

We began the traditional feast of turkey and plum pudding which, despite the Sicilian December warmth, we all still seemed to want and expect. Henry turned up when we were halfway through, carrying an exquisite arrangement, with a passion flower placed on a series of coloured papers on a majolica plate. When I lifted the flower there was a silver dollar — his last. Most shops had of course been closed, but by sheer perseverance and the exercise of his not inconsiderable charm, he had managed to collect a special Christmas treat for the menagerie in the garage.

Two days later, the burden of Christmas over, I had time to think about what was to be done with the animals. Henry had disappeared and there was silence in the garage. But in the garden I found a very sorry-for-itself drake with two long white rags tied, one to each foot, to stop him from flying away — or even walking very far. He was still dazed after three days and nights in the passenger seat of what turned out to be a hired car. (The later argument in Perugia as to who should pay what, for the damage, was a long one. I never knew the result, but I believe that the *capellone*, when he drove the car back to Perugia, had been deputed to settle matters. He had yielded to the demands of the owners and had reimbursed himself by selling all Henry's collection of carefully gathered antique frames. Henry did not seem particularly surprised. He just started to search for more.)

I housed the lot of them — Henry and animals, with the exception of the drake whom we put on a pond — in a four-roomed flat in the garden which I had, in any case, intended to redecorate before the next tenants.

Henry told the troupe that they were all to stay away from my dogs' territory and, surprisingly, they obeyed. One day, however, when my old Nico was around, the cats began fighting. Henry didn't see him, and shouted 'Go get 'em, Gentry!', supposing that Gentry had seen the cats and would rush to fulfil his main duty which was to separate them. But Gentry had seen Nico, and in one moment he had the poor old thing by the scruff of the neck, and was shaking him till he rattled. 'That's *ma* baby!' yelled Henry. Immediately Gentry released him, barely the worse. Gentry never touched him after that.

After three weeks of hard work, painting and selling pictures, Henry turned up one evening just at dusk, very excited and carrying something in his arms: 'He's a new member of the family!'

'Whatever is it?'

'He's Massimo, he's three weeks old. I was painting up in the hills and a wicked woman was going to cut his throat, so I bought him.'

'What are you going to do with him?'

'Paint him.'

'But where'll you keep him?'

'In the bath.'

It was late. I was weary and not anxious for a discussion which would doubtless be long and inevitably lost by me. I also had no better solution, so off the two went to my flat.

'He'll never be able to rear him,' said Concetta, a countrywoman. 'You can raise a lamb by hand at that age, but never a kid.'

Henry introduced what must have been a very scared Massimo to the troupe and went off to buy a baby's bottle. Every now and then we heard a feeble bleating from the bathroom, but I was never able to catch Henry when I had a free moment.

The following morning Concetta said the words I dread to hear: they always signify disaster around the corner: 'Signorina, you must do something.'

'Why? What's happened?'

'We had a *notte di grande confusione*. No one could sleep. All the neighbours will complain.'

'What kind of confusion?'

'Doors banging, dogs barking, Massimo crying, men shouting.'

Whatever could have happened? She could explain nothing and only repeated that things couldn't go on like that. The shutters of the flat were closed and for a wonder silence reigned. They were all clearly tired after the night. I kept the door in sight, determined that Henry should not escape me.

Suddenly he dashed in to my kitchen, agitated and almost in tears: 'You've *got* to help me, you must all help me or my *bambino* will be dead.'

'But what's happened?'

'He's got pneumonia. Last night he had a high fever. He couldn't keep anything down — not even milk.' (I could picture Henry shoving a thermometer up one end and a bottle down the other.)

'But why all the noise and confusion?'

'Oh, it was terrible; it was three o'clock, and I knew that I *must* have a doctor. I didn't want to disturb you. Then I remembered that you had said the Mayor was a doctor, so I phoned him.'

'But you can't mean that the Mayor came out at night?'

'Of *course* he did.'

'But he never goes out at night except before elections.' (The poor man had severe sciatica and had to wear a *busto,* or surgical jacket, so one sympathised with him.) 'What did you say to make him come?'

'I was frightened so I was almost crying. I said that I was an *Americano* in the house of the Signorina Kitsoni and my *bambino* is dying. Of *course* he came.'

Later I heard from the Mayor's wife that she had urged a most reluctant Mayor to dress, *busto* and all, and go. They could hear down the telephone the weak bleatings of Massimo, just like those of a baby. 'Think of the scandal, Giuseppe, if an American baby dies and it gets out that you refused to go.'

So the poor man got up, dressed and took out his car. It says much for Sicilian humanity and patience with mad foreigners that instead of throwing Massimo at Henry's head, slamming the door and going back to bed, he recognised who the patient was and soothed Henry by giving

Massimo a shot. Whatever it was, it calmed both of them down. Then he had said: 'But this isn't really my profession, you know. I think we should call my friend the vet.'

And at 4.15 a.m. with all the doors banging, dogs barking and cats whining, along came the vet. He had not liked to refuse the Mayor!

The vet agreed with Concetta: Massimo needed a Mamma. He couldn't be raised by hand.

'And now,' said Henry, 'you've all got to help me to find one.'

He was confident that we should put everything on one side to help him, and we did just that. I knew we had to. Henry had told me that when Alice, his adored goat, died he had not been able to paint for a year. If he didn't paint there would be no money either to pay me rent or to feed the menagerie.

After three hours searching the countryside, we found a man with a nanny goat with lots of milk. Neither kid had been kept because milk was needed for the owner's children. Henry went down on his knees and embraced her; he never thought to ask where her two kids had gone. I had to make the bargain for him: Massimo should have all the milk from one *mammella* and the children should have that from the other. The cost? Four hundred lire a day. Henry, restored to happiness, brought Massimo wrapped up, despite the heat, in two wool blankets.

'Take those damn things off!' growled his new foster father.

Henry protested: 'But he's got pneumonia.'

'They'll make him worse.'

A blanketless Massimo was put to suckle and began sucking vigorously at once. He never looked back.

One evening three weeks later, Henry hunted me out and announced that he had to go back to Kentucky on business. 'It'll be only for three weeks. I've consulted my astrologer and she says I must travel on a Tuesday.'

The idea of Henry having 'business' of any kind except buying antiques and selling pictures was a new one.

'It's to do with my property,' he explained, 'Bad tenants — must go and sort things out. Next week would be a good time to journey.'

'What about the animals?'

'I'll leave them here.'

'But I can't look after all of them.'

'No, I'll find somebody.'

'But this is Sicily. People who are good with animals and ready to take the trouble are few and far between.'

'I'll manage.'

And he did. I felt that I should keep the three most difficult ones: Gentry who would grieve deeply at Henry's absence, Esquire who, uncontrolled, would murder, and Black Sister who was still expecting.

'Before I go I need a pen and paper — have you got some?'

I produced them and prepared to leave the room.

With an imperative gesture he commanded me to stay. 'I need you. Do you know how to make a will?'

'I know a bit about how to make an Italian one and I've made one in England, but I know nothing about how you do an American one.'

'Well, we'll have to work it out together. How do you spell your name?'

Taken by surprise, I said that I didn't think that I was in any way suitable to appear in Henry's will: 'I'm thirteen years older than you!'

He made a peremptory gesture, almost Sicilian in its utter rejection of my protest, and went on: 'Now I'm going to leave you two houses in Lexington, Kentucky. One is very valuable, only three blocks away from the university and with columns. It's full of antiques, but there are 1,000 dollars still owing on it. So I'm going to leave you another smaller one, where my foster mother is now living. You'll have to sell that in order to pay the debt and the death duties — do I need to write that down?'

'No I don't think so but —'

'And you shall have my poems,' he interrupted. 'Now to Alice Delamarr I'm leaving my house in Key West and my pictures.' He was writing hard. I felt that it would be ungracious if I asked if Alice could give me a picture and I could give her a poem, but it would have been nice. 'And to Stephan Brecht my two farms in Kentucky. I think that's all.' He paused a moment, then, 'Oh, I've forgotten darling Tennessee. Well, he's rich, he doesn't need it. Alice must give him two pictures. Now I think that's really all. You must keep the will in case you need it while I'm gone. Oh, but of course I must write down all the particulars that you might need.' And he rattled off the number of three bank accounts, his social service number, the name and address of his lawyers, one in Florida, two in Kentucky with telephone numbers of the lot — all from memory. 'There, I think that's all. Now we must find two witnesses — better if they're American, I think.'

Off he went down the Corso to find some. He returned with two interesting young hippies who were making a documentary film about Sicily. It was the early days of beards and hair, long dresses and hanging beads, and they made an exotic pair. They were highly intrigued by the roles in which Henry had cast them. He didn't look, from the point of view of either age or possessions, someone likely to be making a will. They signed: one from Vermont and one from Chicago.

As an afterthought Henry added, still further stimulating the curiosity of his witnesses, 'Love and blessings to Tennessee. Love also to Marion Vacarro of Miami with three paintings, and George Black of Brickle Ave. Miami, Fla.'

And that was that — except that I repeated once more that I was in no way suitable as his heiress, only to be waved down again.

'But why have you chosen us three?'

'Because you were the ones who helped me when I was nobody and had nothing.'

'I know what Alice did for you, but

Stephan Brecht? What did he do?'

'He found me one day painting under a railway bridge. I was also sleeping under it and was cold. Stephan looked at my pictures, said he liked them. Then he said, "You look as if you could do with a good meal." And he invited me home. I ate and ate. He then said, "I think you could do with a bed." So I stayed with them for nine months.'

'He certainly earned his share. I did very little by comparison. By the way, how old is Alice?'

'Oh, perhaps she's eighty-three.'

'Henry dear, she's even more unsuitable than I am to be in your will.'

He wouldn't listen.

But I persisted: 'Henry you told me that when you were small, and nearly always in trouble, you were helped by a psychiatric social worker.' She always accompanied him to court and managed, with her reports, to sway the magistrate in his favour. She would declare that sending him to another institution would not help, and would turn him into a chronic delinquent. It was essential for her to keep in close touch with him. She did so for years. 'Henry, you shouldn't be leaving *me* houses, she has done *far* more for you. You must think of her.'

'Yes of course I should. But it's no use, honey, I've lost her.'

'But if she's really a trained PSW, I could help you to trace her through our professional association.'

'Oh no you can't. You see she eloped with a married patient and they struck her off the register.'

So for the time being I remained a protesting beneficiary.

Two days later off he went, soberly dressed and carrying a dispatch case full of documents.

'It's only for three weeks, I promise you.'

I was sure that his absence would be more than that. Gentry mourned. His fur lost its sheen and he was heard sadly moaning to himself at night. It was difficult to persuade him to eat. Esquire was unpleasant and a problem to control, but at least there were no changed cats around to bully. Black Sister produced six kittens looking as if they were three-quarters Siamese, with Concetta acting as midwife. Now and then I went to enquire about Onassis and the others, and I kept an eye on Massimo, who grew and grew. The drake was, meanwhile, lonely but seemed happy enough on my pool.

Six weeks went by. No word from Henry. I even began to fear that I might be left with all the animals. But halfway through one morning Gentry suddenly perked up. He sprang on to the terrace wall whence he could survey the whole front garden, gazing towards the sea right down below, and he refused to move.

He sat there till ten o'clock in the evening when, without any warning, Henry came rushing up the garden and embraced first the wildly excited dog and then me.

'Henry, it's incredible, but this morning Gentry knew you were coming.'

'Of course he did, I was telling him,' said Henry matter-of-factly. In the air, hundreds of miles away over the Atlantic, he thought it unremarkable that he should get a message through to the dog. He was surprised at my surprise . . .

Life with Henry around was never without interest. One day he turned up with a bundle of table legs under his arm. 'Look, look, Ma'am,' he called out. 'Just see these wonderful patterns all carved out by worms — it's better than lace! How Klee would have loved it!'

I looked with some distaste at what I felt sure was about to be taken into my flat, where the worms would probably spread from there to my priceless antiques. 'Henry, yes, the patterns are lovely, but would you mind painting them outside, not *in* my house?'

He paid no attention; his thoughts had moved on. 'Ma'am, there's a whole dining room suite down there for you.'

'Whatever are you talking about?'

'It's all in a cave with lots of things thrown away. We can go and collect it with your car.'

'But I *have* a dining suite, and I don't need another.'

'Oh well, that's a pity. Are you sure you don't want it?' Then after a second, casually: 'I also found these.' He put his hand in his pocket and pulled out a handful of broken terracotta.

This time I was excited. 'Where did you get these? These are Greek, no doubt about it. Some are from Asia Minor, some I think, but I'm no expert, are local, but all must be over 2,000 years old. Wherever did you go? Are there any more?'

He answered calmly, surprised at my excitement at something of so little interest or beauty to him: 'It's in a cave, on a hill just near here. We can go there if you like — but I do think you should take the table at least.'

I wanted to arouse no suspicion on the part of bystanders or the people in the neighbouring houses, so I waited until a nearby hotel shut for the end of the season. The cave was deep and damp, with beautiful mosses on the wall, but Henry had eyes only for the suite. *My* eyes were searching the walls for shards. I dug one or two out of the wall; they were undoubtedly Greek, but someone must have got there before us. With difficulty I detached a disappointed Henry from the suite, which was as worm-eaten as its legs, and we climbed up the hill behind. Suddenly we came upon a huge mound of shards. Someone had clearly been there first and taken whatever vases, lamps or figures there had once been. Who can tell what they may have destroyed? That it had been a sanctuary dedicated to a Greek god or goddess was later confirmed by the archaeologists whom I told about the site. Henry remained far more impressed by the handiwork of the worms . . .

Then there was the episode of the glitzy prostitute, a very sham blonde in gold sandals whom I saw one day opening Henry's door with a key she took from her purse. She disappeared inside. When I caught Henry and asked how come, he declared that he'd met this poor girl, a German, in the town and someone had stolen all her money. She was destitute so of course he had to help. She would soon earn enough money to pay her fare back to Germany.

'But I don't really care to have her earning it in my house. It might cause great trouble with the police. I might even lose my licence. I can't risk it, it would be really disastrous.'

'Honey, it won't be long, I promise you.'

Further protest was useless.

It wasn't long. The very next day a disconsolate blonde dragging a shoddy suitcase, still in gold sandals, went down the garden steps clanging the gate angrily behind her.

'I threw her out,' Henry explained. 'I *had* to.' (Had even he found her clients too much?) 'I had told her she mustn't let any of the animals out of the rooms I had left them in, and she went and let Esquire in with the dogs. *Anything* might have happened.'

His family, to my relief, came before helping a poor tart, however destitute.

A few weeks later Henry began planning his return to the States. He found he could get a boat direct from Naples to Fort Lauderdale in Florida — one actually willing to take the animals. The kittens were now eleven in all. He did realise that there wasn't room for Massimo, who by now was a huge, horned billy goat, and I persuaded him that it would not be fair to subject the drake to such a journey. He would be happier on my pool. But he could find no possible Sicilian owner whose care of cats was likely to measure up to his standards. I wanted none of them.

'Well,' he said, 'they'll have to come too.'

The animals had all to be inoculated before entry into the US. Henry didn't agree with it. He would find a way round. In return for a picture, he found a doctor willing to sign all the false certificates. Not an unusual Sicilian occurrence — only generally the price is higher . . .

But how was he to get the crowd to Naples? No train or taxi would take them. He must buy a car.

'You'll never be able to find one big enough to take them and everything.'

By now the picture frames were many and his paintings innumerable. He was planning for another show in the US where now his works were selling as fast as he could turn them out. Incredibly he found and bought a huge American station wagon. It was easy to persuade the owner to sell. He was a diminutive Sicilian barber who had spent nine years in New York before returning with his savings. In order to save face, and I suspect to cover up comparative failure in the New World, he had brought this huge car over the Atlantic. He discovered how crazy this was when he got here: it drank petrol, the licence fee was huge and there was little room for it in narrow Sicilian streets. It was providential for him that Henry turned up.

Months later a woebegone little man was to come to me; Henry's cheque had bounced and he was desperate for the cash. I don't know whether Henry had just got muddled between his three bank accounts, or whether he had hoped to gain time until he sold some pictures. I wrote him a severe, no-nonsense letter and a valid cheque arrived by return of post. Still more months later, Henry was to offer me a second cheque 'to pay for the car'. He didn't want to leave any bad debts. He was relieved to hear that he *had* paid — I'd made him. He had just got muddled.

To my relief, Henry had no intention of driving the huge car to Naples himself. He found a driver willing to take the job on for a good price, then spent a whole day getting all his possessions into it. The animals, led by Gentry, hopped in first. They were determined not to be left behind. Suitcases, rugs — many of them valuable — pictures, frames were all piled up around them. Halfway through the day Henry suddenly decided that he must have a second car. Miraculously at such short notice, and in his magical way, he found a driver willing. There were no motorways then, and the drive through the mountains of Calabria was tough at the best of times.

The two cars at last set off. It seemed only too probable that they might not make Naples in time to stop the boat sailing without them. But they just did. I was to hear the story later. Henry was urging, 'Faster, faster', when one of the drivers, deciding that he hadn't made a good enough bargain, stopped the car and refused to go any further until the promised sum was raised. A furious Henry had no choice. All the money he had on him was needed. He pulled out a picture from the luggage and angrily shoved it at the villain who, knowing the story of the restaurateur, was only too pleased with the bargain. And on they went. They got to the port through the chaos of Naples with a few minutes in hand.

To the Captain's displeasure, the ship was held up while Henry's odd possessions were unloaded, tickets and certificates checked, the animals encaged, and the empty station wagon craned first on to the deck and then into a lift down to the hold. When this had been firmly bolted and secured for the journey, Henry discovered that a kitten was missing. Hysterically, he demanded that the car must be searched. The Captain refused. Henry threatened to throw an epileptic fit. The Captain still refused. It was too late to return to port to dump the lunatic and of course he did not want to be left with the animals, unaccompanied, for the rest of the trip. Nor to have Henry as a raving passenger for the whole week — he was clearly capable of keeping up his crazy screaming and threats. His only option was to yield and open the hold. The kitten was found and Henry calmed.

The show was a success. The list of buyers grew ever more numerous and distinguished. Henry still insisted that I should figure in his will. While continually protesting my unsuitability, I felt such curiosity that I yielded to one of his pressing invitations to stay 'for a summer, for a year', and flew to Kentucky.

Henry was there on the airfield with arms outstretched to greet me, on a lovely summer day when the grass was nearly blue. He led me to the famous station wagon bought in Taormina.

'People keep running into me,' he said, to explain its state.

'But what has happened to the windscreen, Henry?'

'Oh, a shot.'

'Do you mean that it's *that* dangerous to drive in Kentucky?'

The windscreen had a large round hole in the centre, the plastic foundation was flapping round it and there were cracks radiating across my vision.

'No, dear love, don't worry. It was when it was parked at night three months ago!'

I got out my dark glasses to protect my eyes and struggled to adjust the safety belt, to be told that it was dirty and so didn't work. But I *made* it. We drove along with him blowing kisses to all and sundry including the toughest-looking policemen and with me saying: 'Henry, look, the light's red!'

'Lovely people!' he said as two rows of cars waited kindly for him to drive right across their bows because he had got into the wrong lane. 'Now, honey, don't go putting the brakes on all the time — there aren't any on that side anyway!'

The house, part of my inheritance — and I was thinking that it was only too likely soon to be mine — was a lovely Southern, colonial mansion with white wood columns at the front door. It stood in a good deal of ground on a very valuable site. It was filled with antiques of all kinds and stank of cats ('unchanged' male cat — and there is nothing worse). Henry had been scrubbing it until 4 a.m. with the help of two characters, Larry and Kenny. The former had PROPERTY OF THE UNIVERSITY OF KENTUCKY written over his chest. The other was introduced as a 'mountaineer', that is he came from somewhere near Egypt, Kentucky, Henry's birthplace. His hands were delicately clean and it looked as if he had never done anything useful with them in his life.

My room was gorgeous. It had a huge mahogany bed, but no mattress. Someone had left the door open and the cat had gone in and had her kittens on it. ('We'll fix that later,' said Henry.) There were three vast oval, gold-framed mirrors, a hideous Tiffany lampshade hanging over a bowl with hart's-tongue ferns, great bunches of unknown white flowers, a trumpet, a violin, a cot with Victorian dolls in it, a great gold and white column, gold putti flying on the walls between festoons of necklaces and exquisite bead bags, a tiny Paul Klee picture bought from Clifford Odets, a gold medallion with a goat's head, a whip — I *think* for decorative purposes only — antique chemists' jars and a great gold baroque wall piece with INDULGENZA PLENARIA on it. The floor was covered with beautiful little oriental rugs, which Henry shamefacedly told me he had tried to protect from the animals before I could reprove him as before. The wallpaper on two sides was a sumptuous green with great gold patterns on it. The windows were barred by enchantingly delicate, but quite unfunctional, iron railings. In due course a mattress was produced with one dubiously clean sheet — the next one turned up the day after — and two dirty pillows with spotlessly clean slips. I slept in my dressing gown.

The four of us rushed off to a cafeteria lunch: 'No time to have a good one; giving a party for you at five.' He paid by cheque, which seemed to surprise no one but me. The University of Kentucky one was then sent to the liquor store to collect six bottles of Scotch, four of gin, etc. etc. that Henry said he would now order by phone. He had to go next door as his phone had been cut off for non-payment of bills. I queried the quantity and asked the number of guests. Henry, who neither drank nor smoked, said: 'Oh, about twelve, but you never know!'

While I rested after my journey, a massive table covered with an enormous, clean white damask cloth was prepared. In front of it was a huge merry-go-round wooden goat, a magnificent animal embellished by the addition of two dangerously sharp and twisted horns. The guests began to arrive long before five, to the loudly voiced disgust of Henry, who wasn't dressed. Though they must have heard, they were not disturbed and began to settle in and sit on the chairs left vacant by the dogs, four of whom, the moment the doors were opened, took up the sofas. First came a troupe of hippies with two guitars; had I not heard Joan Baez the night before I might have been impressed by their music. They occupied all the delicate little gold Regency chairs in the centre, almost oblivious to the rest of the party and hardly drinking. Henry thoughtfully went up to my room to see that my bag was safely hidden: 'With the hippies you never know.'

There followed a couple straight out of Picasso's blue period, only he was in dark green, lanky, cadaverous and felt-hatted. She, in black, had a pallid baby curled in the crook of her arm. Next, a couple of exquisite homosexuals, a hairdresser and a beautician, with perfectly cut and creased suits and satin stocks. They were led in by a black, miniature poodle and all three seemed only willing to mix with me. Then a girl in a crimson maxi — it was sultry and warm — with a buckle the size of a soup plate at her waist. She said she *worshipped* Henry's poems, and she brought her father with her, an elderly lawyer. A be-pearled and metallically smart woman journalist asked me how I could bear Henry's driving. I said I couldn't. She promised kindly that she would take us round the Blue Grass country and stables the next day. And then there appeared the really respectables: the accountants who fielded his bouncing cheques, the lawyers who kept him more or less unharmed in his many skirmishes. They brought their elderly wives, typical American club-women who found Henry just 'too cute', most of whom had invested in his paintings. Also, a pleasant, elderly social worker, the Professor of Psychology, and his deceptively innocent-looking wife who offered me a bath in her house if I wanted one. She knew that the seventy-eight-year-old plumber had failed, at the last minute, to get the hot water system functioning. In fact, his men were still digging near the front door as the hippies began to arrive. This was the incongruous collection of people, all of whom seemed to agree that Henry gave the best parties in Lexington.

Punctually, at seven o'clock, Henry clapped his hands and shouted: 'The party's over now. Go away!' And with no sign of surprise they all got up and filed out.

It was a fantastic and enjoyable three days, but that was enough. I could never have endured a summer or a year.

Back in Sicily Massimo grew and grew. The drake settled down on my pool, a poor lonely thing until he made a strange friendship with my dog.

Some months after his departure, Henry had phoned in the middle of the night: 'Honey, you must get Massimo on a plane to Lexington.'

'Whatever do you mean? I can't drag him all the way to Catania.' It was a good sixty-five kilometres away, and no car or bus would take him.

'Get that man to do it.'

'But Henry, even if he could, or would, the fare would cost a fortune. You forget, Massimo is no longer a gentle little kid, he's a whacking great billy goat, fierce and accustomed only to one master. He's having a lovely time up in the hills.'

Slowly he saw reason. Sadly he said: 'Well, all right. I did so want to see him. Please, please see that he's in a lovely valley with a lovely stream and lots of beautiful nanny goats around him.'

I promised once more to do my best, but valleys with streams are rare in East Sicily, and he remained up in the mountains, as happy I expect as most Sicilian goats.

The next sign of Henry's existence was a telegram: 'Mr Tennessee Williams is at the San Domenico Hotel. Go call on him, love Henry.' He never learned to be concise even on a transatlantic cable!

I was intrigued, but hesitated. How could I miss the chance of meeting him? But his world was hardly mine. He probably had a circle of flatterers around him and would be bored by someone who had never seen any of his plays — they don't put them on within reach of me. And I knew very little about him except his international reputation and his questionable morals. But I summoned up courage and phoned the luxury hotel. A charming Southern voice answered me.

Nervously I began, 'Henry wanted us to meet. Perhaps he told you?'

'Yes, but I'm leaving for London the day after tomorrow. The hotel staff is going on strike and I'm not paying these prices to make my own bed and to carry my own luggage.'

'Is there time for you to come up here for a drink?' I boldly asked, wondering whether that was the right thing to offer.

'It'll have to be tonight or tomorrow.'

Daringly I suggested that very evening and asked if he'd be on his own, or had he a friend he'd like to bring?

'I have my secretary.'

'I'd be delighted to see them too,' I said, doubtful as to which sex it would be.

He turned out to be a tall, handsome footballer of little brain, but he made Tennessee laugh with his naivety. They were both immaculate in their light summer suits.

I had not realised how very short-sighted Tennessee was. Etna was in spectacular eruption, but he seemed not to notice it.

Nor did he comment on the beauty of my house and its treasures, as most do. I offered the drinks; he wanted a dry martini.

'I'm afraid that I never mix them for Americans. Can one of you do it?'

The secretary did. I was the only one to have a second. I needed it. The conversation never got off the ground. We were all polite but bored. I walked with Tennessee across the terrace, sad and disappointed, but at least I would have pleased Henry.

Suddenly Tennessee said, 'Would you care to dine with me tomorrow night?'

His only remaining one! How was it possible?

'I'd love to.'

'Where shall we go? I want the best. Da Carmelo's?'

'That used to be in Henry's day, but it isn't now.' I asked if he would let me arrange it. 'I know somewhere they'd be thrilled to have you. There is a waiter who is an artist to his fingertips — you'd enjoy him.'

I went to the restaurant and arranged for us to have their very best, leaving the decoration of the table to Nino. I knew that he would put all his skill and pride into it.

The next night the two men arrived in

the huge hotel car, not wise in the narrow, overcrowded streets. It would have been simpler to walk. I sat in the back with Tennessee and prepared myself for a slow, sad evening. Why on earth had he asked me? Embarrassing silence once more.

Then suddenly: 'How's your sleep?'

Startled, I asked what he meant. How? When? Where? Then: 'Actually it's the *first* thing that gets upset whenever I'm troubled or worried. I can lie awake for hours with my mind going round and round and nothing helps.'

'Just the same here. Ghastly! In the snake pit they took all my drugs away.'

The floodgates were opened. No more silences. He talked and talked, and listened and listened. He spoke about his sister, about the cruel brother who put him in the snake pit, about his successes and his recent failures. And then we got on to Henry.

'The trouble with him is he *will* telephone, sending cables and doing long foreign calls, and as he hasn't paid his bills for ages, he comes round to my place to do it.'

I changed the subject, telling him about Henry and the Mayor and the animals. He, too, had been often embroiled with the menagerie and had mixed feelings about Henry — deep affection, fascination, irritation and admiration for the maverick who had made his own rules in life, and dazzlingly succeeded despite his desperate background.

While the secretary and I ate the delicious food heartily, Tennessee toyed with the first course, his attention distracted by Henry's adventures and Nino's charms. The latter's obviously new wedding ring must have been a disappointment . . . Gradually his appetite improved as one dish after another appeared, all of them decorated exquisitely by the proud Nino, and to his expressed surprise he enjoyed his appetite.

The next day he left for London. The striking staff at the hotel got a message to me: Signor Williams had left a parcel for me: would I like to fetch it? It was heavy. In it were several books, the largest, Ezra Pound's *Cantos*, and the smallest paperback *The Night of the Iguana* simply inscribed 'To Daphne Phelps from Tennessee Williams'. And the most moving, *The Glass Menagerie*, 'To Daphne, who shares forgiveness of Henry, from Tennessee 1971'. Strange that insomnia had been our link.

★ ★ ★

Again a gap of a few years and then Henry returned with Tennessee. He said that he was now Tennessee's 'manager'. He was organising Tennessee's life and trying to help him to achieve the fresh triumph that he was desperately, and unsuccessfully, striving for.

'He's spending and spending, he'll soon have nothing left if he goes on like this. He insisted — I couldn't stop him — on coming on Concorde and paid for both of us. It's a *loathsome* plane. I knew it would be, but he wouldn't listen. Our teeth were chattering all the way with that hateful air conditioning. Would you like a blanket? A good one? I *had* to get it for the journey or I'd have died of pneumonia. It's a good double one, the best wool. I'm sure you'd like it. And some paper? I've got stacks.'

They invited me to dinner. Our table at the San Domenico, with the morgue-like luxury and ageing, rich clientele, was the only one that sparkled — almost indecently — with talk and laughter. Perhaps the others had eaten themselves into silence and boredom? Tennessee was his charming, exquisitely mannered, Southern gentleman self.

Next day Henry came laden. The

blanket was, as he said, a splendid one. The writing paper was headed 'The Berkeley Hotel, London'. I began to suspect that the blanket as well had been lifted. He had travelled wrapped in it like a cocoon throughout the journey.

A day or two later, Henry came up in despair. His 'management' had failed: Tennessee was drinking and drinking. He didn't leave his room and there was no hope of his starting to write again. Henry would have to earn the money quickly with his paintings.

'I'm glad I've got a good public here — they'll take anything.'

So pot-boilers were turned out and sold to a local shop willing to take the lot, and even pay for them.

I never saw either Tennessee or Henry again. The next news came from a Lexington lawyer who enclosed Henry's last will. In it I was the first-named beneficiary. He left 'My house in Taormina to Daphney Phelps'. He had got the Phelps right, although he stumbled over my address. He had ignored my plea to be left out. I had had no wish to be burdened with two houses in Kentucky with the all but certainty of legal disputes lasting years, with his family from Egypt, about Henry's competence to make a will. My property in Sicily provided anxieties enough. But perhaps a house in Taormina that I could sell or let might help to solve some of those very problems?

The lawyer made no mention of the manner of Henry's early death and I had to wait weeks before I heard. He had been driving the huge, rickety station wagon he had bought in Taormina, at night. At a major crossing the lights were in his favour. A nineteen-year-old girl, who had already caused a minor accident that evening, came at full speed across the road and hit Henry. He was killed instantly. She was stone drunk.

Tennessee was shattered. His own lonely death happened soon afterwards in a hotel room after he swallowed and choked on the top of a medicine bottle. I had guessed that he wouldn't last long after the death of his 'manager'. It was the final blow.

I never discovered whether or not Henry had ever had a house in Taormina. He had never mentioned it to me. My guess is that he had signed the first deed and put down a deposit. Then the accident prevented him from paying the next instalments. In all foreigners' dealings in Sicilian property there must be a go-between, especially when there are language difficulties, and Henry had doubtless had one. If any other than the seller had benefited from the deposit, it must have been the go-between. I never bothered to waste time in the Messina Land Registry office pursuing the contract that Henry may, or may not, have made. What mattered was his thoughtfulness. He had hoped to lessen the burden of living in a house which took so much of what little money I had. Dear Henry.

One day, years later, Concetta came in with my post saying excitedly 'Enrico! Enrico!' And there on top of the pile was a huge postcard with a Faulkner painting of flowers and animals. A friend, visiting the Ernest Hemingway museum in Key West, Florida, had recognised Henry's unmistakable style from having seen the pictures at Casa Cuseni. The card was of a picture in the place of honour over Hemingway's bed. Clearly he had shared Concetta's and my admiration of Henry.

Dogs and Ducks

A high-up official from Washington, DC returning from the Corso one day exclaimed: 'These people are wonderful. They're all individuals, alert and with such expressive faces. In Washington they're all deadpan. It's a lovely change.'

I was surprised. Didn't Washington draw people from all over America, in all their variety?

'They're all bureaucrats,' she answered.

I think that Sicilian dogs are just as full of personality as the humans, and as varied. And both have very mixed ancestors adding to the interest.

The first dog I owned in Sicily, and I hadn't wanted one as my future was uncertain, was Frilla, a pretty little mongrel with some golden cocker in her ancestry and some . . . who knows? Her master, my near neighbour Pancrazio, had come to me saying: 'My father is dead, the donkey too. I cannot earn here so I am going to Switzerland to seek my fortune. But Signorina, what can I do with Frilla?

Please will you have her?'

I owed Pancrazio a debt. My nine-year-old nephew had been staying with me; he was an active child who awoke with the dawn around 4.30 a.m. His mother was in a nervous state recovering from a tough war. Every minute she would warn Christopher, as he played on the terraces, 'Don't go too near the edge. Don't get sunstroke.' After a bit of this he solemnly asked me how many precipices up was my friend's house. These were the small terraces made over the centuries by peasants striving to stop the ceaseless erosion of soil caused by the reckless felling of trees from Roman times onward.

To my relief, Pancrazio had made friends with the boy through his donkey and his Frilla. He would invite him to go off for the day to 'help' till his land, to ride the donkey and to play with the dog. Christopher loved animals. Before he left he spent all his pocket money — the tourist allowance was only £35 for an adult so his part was very small — on a carved cigarette holder for Pancrazio and a carved pipe for his old blind father. Pancrazio, deeply touched, gave what I later realised was the only treasure that he could do without: his military bracelet. It was one from when, after being a prisoner of the Germans, he had become a 'co-belligerent' of the British. Christopher had left for England in tears.

'Cheer up,' I said, 'you'll soon be back.'

'But I shan't see the donkey again, or the old man, they're *really* old.'

I went round to thank Pancrazio and I saw for the first time the utter poverty in which the two men lived. It was a two-roomed house with a mud floor. They had, it seemed, two knives and forks, two glasses, and a plate or so. And yet on Sundays and *festas* Pancrazio was as elegantly dressed as any rich Taorminese. When, after his father's death, he asked me to take Frilla I felt I had to say yes, leaving him free to go to Switzerland in search of work.

Frilla was rechristened Brilla. A Swedish friend said that Frilla was a rude word in her language and I couldn't possibly go round calling her that in view of the many Swedish tourists that might be in the town.

Mischineddu was my next dog.

One day as I was walking down the Corso, Madame Rosa, the firm friend and admirer of the British, called out, 'Signorina, Signorina! Come here! You *must* give this poor little dog a home.'

Afraid of yielding if I saw the dog, I walked on.

'An Englishwoman deserting a dog in distress!' she called after me.

I turned back.

'Rosa you old blackmailer, where is he?'

She led me into her shop and there, more bruise than dog, was a poor little, long-haired, white puppy rather like those in Carpaccio's paintings of San Girolamo. He was held by one of the toughest, degraded men of Taormina. I saw at once that I had no choice. I picked him up and his captor demanded 1,000 lire.

'What do you mean?'

'That's his price.'

'A thousand lire for *this?* I'll be paying the vet a thousand to put him down tomorrow. Rosa, you're my witness, I did *not* steal this dog.'

I carried him up to the house where some friends exclaimed, 'That's the puppy we saw yesterday! Boys were teasing him, tying a tin can to his tail. We were just going to do something when a policeman came up and drove them off.'

When a Sicilian policeman intervenes to save a mongrel against bullying boys things must indeed be bad. I gave him a cushion and some milk with bread in it and left him in peace, which I felt was his greatest need. In the morning he looked as if he meant to survive. Within days he was my watchdog, bravely barking at strangers. Within a week he was my shadow. We called him 'Mischineddu' — in pure Sicilian 'little misery'. If ever I went out without him he would lie on his back, paws in the air, looking as if I had beaten him for ten minutes. I weakly gave in and whenever possible took him with me. He was a perfect guard for the car; he behaved beautifully in restaurants and hotels; he was never carsick. When people saw him riding beside me they would say, 'Mischineddu? Maybe once, but now a *gran' signore*. He rides while *we* walk!'

The tax on dogs was heavy, especially when it was considered to be a 'luxury dog', as Mischineddu evidently was. I protested that even his name showed he wasn't.

'Well, what is he? He isn't a hunting dog' (tax much reduced).

'No, he's a watchdog.'

'Not allowed to have one in a built-up area.'

I paid.

The next year he was assessed as a *cane de affetto*. I couldn't deny it. They won again.

In Catania one day, Mischineddu and I went to lunch in a restaurant. All the tables were occupied except the one right by the door. I sat down and Mischineddu curled himself up, as usual, under my chair and went to sleep. Suddenly he woke up as the door opened and an unsavoury-looking lay brother, in a faded, dirty cassock, came in shaking a money box and in a whining voice asked for alms for the orphans. The usually gentle Mischineddu began growling and snarling in a clear warning that he wished the man out of the place.

We *pagani,* as we were considered in the days before Pope John XXIII, were tired of receiving post-free appeals to support Catholic orphanages all over Italy. I thought that there were enough rich Catholics in Catania to support their own orphanages while we looked after ours in Taormina. The man tried to insist, above the increasing rage of Mischineddu. Had I not had some wine I don't think I would ever have behaved as I did, but my hackles were also up and I refused to budge.

'*Ma Signora, i bambini . . .*'

'My dog will really bite. I would take care if I were you!'

Muttering what were probably curses he moved on from table to table and most, grudgingly, put in a pittance. Only when he passed our table on the way out did Mischineddu once again start snarling. The man scuttled out and the dog went back to sleep.

I felt terribly ashamed. I was, after all, a guest of Sicily and I should not have let the dog's feelings influence mine to that extent. I blushed and busied myself with my spaghetti, hoping that the incident would soon be forgotten. Not a bit of it. I heard a buzz of comment going from one table to another: '*He's* lucky, he can say what he thinks. We can't, we just have to shut up and give.' 'He's a fortunate one, he is! Wouldn't we like to bark like that?' 'Those ones, always asking and asking. And what do they do with it we'd like to know? Not to feed the orphans better, of *that* we're sure.'

Then, 'Where do you come from, Signora? *Inghilterra?* Well did you know that the football match between our two countries is on today? It's just about to start. Let's all watch it together. Is he safe, that one?' looking doubtfully at Mischineddu.

Owner, clients, waiters and kitchen staff all gathered together with the friendly dog around the '*TVu.*' I was the only woman.

The two national anthems opened the broadcast: 'God Save the Queen' and, to our astonished ears, the music to which Mussolini's Fascists used to march. We looked at each other in amazement. Some Englishman had slipped up and made this monstrous mistake. In Rome, there was a minor diplomatic incident. However, in the Catania group there was nothing but friendliness. Fortunately the players added to the general contentment: the result was a draw and no patriotic feelings were hurt.

The idea of going to a lost dogs' home had always alarmed me but when, after several years, I had to find a successor to Mischineddu I braced myself to face it. I feared that too many pathetic eyes would be appealing to me to rescue them. A Sicilian home would surely be even more upsetting. I needed a dog as an essential guard and I had always been used to their uncritical companionship. As a child, when I hated the world and felt that the world hated me, it was my dog in whom I confided — and he told me I was wonderful and unique.

After several fruitless enquiries I was directed to the house of an aged German, the widow of a Sicilian *barone*. The house, on the outskirts of the town, was surrounded by a high wall with a solid, iron gate. I rang the bell beside it and soon a manservant was peering at me through a small peephole he opened in the formidable barrier. Deciding that I was not a danger, he let me in. In the large garden surrounding the house I saw about sixteen of the oldest, illest, most pathetic creatures — apparently dogs. One had three legs, one was blind, one half paralyzed, one covered in mange, and so on.

'But I don't want a dog like these!' I exclaimed in horror. 'I wanted a young and healthy one.'

'You wouldn't be allowed one of these, these are the Baronessa's special pets. The young ones are away in the country. You'll have to come back tomorrow.' These are the words heard endlessly in every Sicilian office, hospital or any organization dealing with the long-suffering public. 'Before you will be allowed a dog, Signora, the Baronessa will have to interview you.'

Surprised and even pleased that such care should be taken in an island with its near Arab ways with animals, I requested that it should be done today. He went into the house and returned saying that I could be received at once. Outside, the sun was shining, the garden was a lovely spring green. Inside all was dark and Teutonic: a huge hall with heavy, purple velvet curtains; a wide staircase carpeted in deepest brown; huge chandeliers dimly lit; heavy Victorian furniture totally out of place in this land of light.

The Baronessa appeared as old as some of her pets but, unlike them, she seemed in robust health. She received me graciously then, seating herself behind a vast oak desk and speaking in Italian with a heavy German accent, she put me through my paces as a dog owner. How would I feed it? How would I exercise it? Had I a garden? Would it be tied up? Or have a muzzle? I was thinking that I was doing rather well when in the midst of the interview the vet was announced and I was led out of the room while the invalids were discussed. After a time a message was brought by the manservant: I need wait no longer, I had passed the test and could pick a dog any time I wanted.

The next week I set off again. This time I went straight to the kennels. There were about fifty huts in a straight row. Each had a small cemented space in front of it. All were occupied, and in some there were two, or even three, dogs. I passed quickly down the line. The noise was shattering. Poor things . . . they were mostly unattractive and, shamefully, I found that I felt no compulsion to rescue several, or even two. There were pedigree Alsatians, boxers, poodles, spaniels, all adding to the pandemonium. I was firm. I wanted a medium-sized dog, a Sicilian mongrel for preference as they are more disease-resistant and generally more intelligent and interesting. Several were let out and leapt at me, barking madly. They reminded me of children in an orphanage who would snatch and grope at visitors, starved, as they were, of human contact. And then I saw one I liked. He was silent and treated with dignified detachment the horrid little yapper at his heels. He was medium sized, his coat was light-coloured cream and he had large, dark brown eyes. His cage was clean. When he was let out he went straight to a tree, lifted his leg and made an enormous puddle. Only then did he come to me wagging his tail. His history was unknown, he was a stray. The choice was made.

We called him Nicuzzu, a name chosen by the fishermen at Acitrezza where I and a friend lunched that day. I said I wanted a Sicilian name to follow Mischineddu, what did they suggest? In dialect Nicuzzu suggests someone in need of protection. It was a splendid choice. For the next fifteen years Nicu was a devoted guard and watchdog, generally gentle, but ferociously courageous when necessary. He never made a mistake. He would sit bolt upright like a Queen's Beastie on my wall, keeping the whole front garden under his eye and giving tongue the moment anyone so much as approached the gate. No one ever had a more reliable doorbell. Generously he accepted the next dog I had to adopt, but refused to play with him.

Morgie had been given to a group of young English tourists. He was threatened with blindness and the group paid for a vet who saved his sight. They named him after *Morgan, a Suitable Case for Treatment*, a popular film of the time. In Sicily this rapidly became Morgie. Despite, or perhaps because of, his mixed ancestry he was a dog of intelligence and elegance. Medium sized, with chocolate brown, smooth hair, a white shirt front and a small white tuft on the end of his tail, he could run like a greyhound and his hunting ancestry was evident. If a ball was thrown he was incapable of not returning it to the thrower; it might have been tied to him by a piece of elastic.

But Morgie became bored. He missed the group and the life of the town. He consented to eat and sleep at Casa Cuseni, but spent all his days away. I decided that he would be much happier in the country. We heard of two hunters who wanted him and would treat him well. They promised that he would not be tied up, except until he had settled. They seemed kind as far as I could tell. With his towel, his lead and collar, I saw him leave in their car to drive thirty-eight kilometres away.

I worried about him the next three days: this is Sicily. On the fourth day, the moment the house was opened, there he was. He rushed straight up to my room, jumped on to my bed, round my back and down again. He did this three times. He had never before shown he was in any way attached to me. Of course he had earned the right to stay. A very happy dog, he spent all his days away. Expensively I had the garden wired to keep him in. By now cars had increased and there was a dog catcher for strays. But Morgie defeated us. He never let us see where he got out and always seemed to know when we were spying on him, so he never attempted to escape when we were.

He stayed at home after he developed

severe distemper. I had been told he'd been inoculated against it. Again more expense, but the vet pulled him through. He was rapidly becoming my 'luxury dog'. But, after his illness, either he decided that we had won the battle, or he had become attached to the house. However, once he became a reformed character he was bored. One walk a day with me didn't satisfy him.

There was another bored creature on the pool above — Daphnis, the drake left by Henry. Most dogs seeing it would have barked and scared it. Not so Morgie. He danced and pranced around it, advancing, retiring, returning, growling, and the drake loved it. As soon as he heard the dog he would come out of the pool and try to attract his attention. Sometimes Morgie would play hard to get, paying no attention, or even looking provocatively up at the sky, or anywhere but at the drake. Then suddenly he would rush towards it, chasing it back to the water, and the game would start, the drake quacking and swimming alongside the dog as he moved along the edge. Then Morgie would gently pull the bird out of the water by his head. The dancing, chasing, quacking and growling would begin again. Often they would embrace, Morgie with one front paw round the drake's back with the latter stretching up to nuzzle the dog's neck with a kind of nibbling. The dog would gently detach himself and nibble at the other's head. Never did he try to mount him. Never, in the autumn and winter, did either do the other harm, but with the spring the drake really attacked, hanging on to the dog's lip and refusing to let go. Morgie became scared and the games ceased. The summer was too hot, but with the autumn they started up again.

By this time Morgie had been identified as a Pharaoh hound by Danish friends, who were devoted to him. They sent me photos of what appeared to be him, but was in fact their Queen's new dog. Every detail seemed identical — his colouring, with his white chest and paws and the white tip on the end of his tail, the way he sat and the way he appeared while walking past the Royal Guard. I had known that Sicilian cats had come from Egypt, but had had no idea that dogs too had been imported. In Sicily the hunters' favourite dog was a *Cernecco dell'Etna,* which was descended from Pharaoh hounds. Both Morgie and the royal dog were much darker in colour than the Cernecco, but this seemed the only difference. No wonder the two hunters had wanted Morgie.

Ever since Henry had left I had tried to find a wife for Daphnis, but it seemed that white ducks didn't exist in east Sicily. On three occasions friends brought me what they thought was a duck. I saw at once that it was a drake, but decided to try them together. The result was a battle royal and twice the so-called duck had to be sent back. But the third time, the new drake was younger; he still had some yellow down showing through his white. We introduced them and this time they made friends. Soon they were an inseparable, homosexual couple with the younger — now bigger — mounting the old one. Morgie went on playing with the first one, but never attempted to with the second, who became jealous of the games and would try to drive the dog away, without succeeding. Daphnis wanted games to go on.

After some years Henry's drake was found dead of old age. The games ended. Once again I had a lonely bird. One day, however, a Sicilian neighbour asked me if I'd give a home to a goose. Her husband had found a little gosling beside the road and he had taken it to her to rear. But she had only a roof terrace; the goose was now full grown and suffering under the hot sun without a pond. The last thing I wanted was a goose but I felt I must go and see the poor creature. To my surprise, I saw a mongrel, brown and white duck. Was she the companion we were looking for? I had really wanted a white wife and found that I was a bit of a racist in the matter, but she was the best we could provide.

I took the scared bird and introduced her to the pool while the homosexual drake was held apart. The duck swam off happily. Then, not knowing what to expect, we carefully introduced them. There was a moment's suspense, then they swam off amicably together. It was the beginning of a long and happy marriage. Both behaved normally. Morgie never played with either of them, but at times when they strayed down the terraces which he considered too close to the house, he would drive them playfully back up to their pool. She made several nests over the years but, although she was a surprisingly faithful sitter, only a few eggs were fertile and sadly they didn't hatch out.

Then the aged husband died, and once again we had a lonely bird on our hands.

But over the garden wall was a splendid pedigree drake with iridescent feathers. His companions were a group of unappealing hens and he had no pool. Concetta, with whom he flirted every morning, flying on to the wall to talk as soon as he heard her voice, said that his owner, ten-year-old Giovanni, just *might* be persuaded to let him come over to us to marry our lonely duck. When asked, Giovanni said, 'Yes, he'll be much happier there, but you must promise never to kill or eat him.' It was not difficult to give my word. In any case he was much too beautiful for that.

Another successful partnership developed; she nested in the agapanthus each year, but no egg hatched out. As soon as they heard Concetta or me they would fly to catch us up and chat, even when we gave them no food.

One morning our neighbour phoned. He begged me not to go up the garden alone — something terrible had happened and the ducks were dead. He was in a hurry and said no more. Picturing a scene of carnage, probably caused by stray dogs, I waited for an hour or so for Concetta to come with me. We found the duck dead and the beautiful drake just alive. There was no sign of blood or violent injury, but each had four pin holes in their breasts and had been sucked dry of blood. A weasel was the murderer. Clearly the drake had put up a fight in defence of his wife before being attacked himself. I gave him water, dropping it into his beak, and soon he drank avidly himself. It seemed he couldn't have enough and slowly he regained some strength. I tended him for the whole day, but he had suffered too much and that evening he just gave up. We buried them under the grapefruit tree. I have not got involved with ducks since, but I have another dog, Zittu, chosen by Concetta.

Roald Dahl

One day, a phone call from the San Domenico: would I wait? I did, for what seemed a long time and I was busy. Then, at last: 'I'm Felicity Crosland, my friend Beak Adams has given me an introduction to you. May we come up for drinks? I expect you know of my companion? He's Roald Dahl.'

It is an indication of my total immersion in the problems and joys of Sicily that, when Dahl was at the height of his international fame, I had never heard of him. I was truthfully able to answer, 'No.'

She was surprised. 'Where is your house? Can we walk or should we take a taxi?'

'If you walk at all, I'd think you can manage it. It's only ten minutes, but it's uphill.' I gave her detailed instructions.

Usually people give me a chance to invite them up. I was miffed, but Beak is a good friend so I fixed a date a few days ahead. I took no trouble with eats and put the plainest Scotch and gin on the table —

not my usual way.

My other guest was a professor of philosophy at the University of Toronto who had written his *magnum opus* on Leibniz in Casa Cuseni. He, too, had never heard of Dahl, his children being grown up. We sat on the terrace for ten, then twenty minutes past the invited time. At thirty minutes we began to drink. A short time later up on to the terrace, against the dramatic backdrop of Etna, came a gigantic figure with a vast straw hat, a cerise shirt and the brightest of scarlet trousers — altogether an eyeful. He was mopping his brow and holding his back.

'Christ! We've been halfway up to fucking Castelmola!'

An anxious Felicity followed him: 'Poor, *poor* Roald, he's absolutely whacked. We lost our way and overshot your gate and went on and on up the hill. He's got steel in his back and hips, due to his plane crash, poor man.'

I sat them down and offered my meagre hospitality.

When recovered, she said, 'I must tell you why we particularly wanted to come and see your house. I'm adapting a mews flat in Battersea and Beak Adams is my architect. I always look out in *Vogue*, and so on, for designs that could give me ideas. One day, on top of a small pile of cut-outs, I showed him one of a room with three, huge, french windows looking out through pillars on to a large terrace. I said "I don't know where this is, it doesn't say, but I love it." Beak looked at it and said, "I can tell you, it's Casa Cuseni. I stayed there last September." So that's why I was determined to see your house.'

I felt she could have explained on the phone before inviting themselves up. While I showed her the ground floor, the philosopher, a small man who had spent three years as a prisoner of war in Germany, offered to show Roald some of the garden. They went off affably together, but Bob was more than a little surprised when this stranger, describing someone else, said, 'He's a stringy little bugger, like you!' I learned later that Dahl enjoyed upsetting smart dinner tables by making utterly outrageous remarks and watching the effect. Bob took it philosophically and shortly after that they left, telling me that they were at the San Domenico while hammering out a contract with RAI, the Italian state television, for the showing of *Tales of the Unexpected*.

'By the way, the food at the hotel is

rotten. Can you tell us of some good places to eat?'

This was surprising. If it is known in the hotel that you are important and rich, and they like you, they can put on as good a meal as anywhere in the world. Somehow he must have got on the wrong side of them.

I gave two names, one in the mountains behind Taormina, and the other down on the beach. Then I said, looking at him doubtfully, 'If you wouldn't mind being bullied by mine host, you could get the very best meal and a value in Taormina at U Bossu — but you *would* be bullied. You'd have to be there no later than 7.50 p.m. If he doesn't like your face, he'll probably refuse to serve you and you'd be wise to take his advice about the menu.' Mine host is a prima donna, a manic depressive, and he has even been known to throw plates over his clients' heads at the chef — his Spanish wife — while in a manic phase.

Ten days later, Bob and I were invited for drinks at the San Domenico. We found Roald and Felicity in the Royal Suite once occupied by Edward VII and the Kaiser. The manager was humming around them, and there were about twelve bottles of the most exquisite Scotch, none less than ten years old, and a good supply of other drinks.

Roald sat on the arm of my chair, not comfortable for either of us. 'Your advice about restaurants was absolutely rotten!' he began.

'Really? How come?'

'We went down to the fish one on the beach. The waiters were all in striped fishermen's jerseys — they lounged around. The risotto was swimming in water and the main course was tepid.'

'How disastrous. I guess the chef must have had a night off.'

'Then we went to U Bossu.'

'We were terribly good,' said Felicity quickly. 'We arrived early and Roald asked for his wine list. Mine host snapped: "This is a trattoria. If you want wine lists, you remain at the San Domenico." So we took his local wine. I must say it was good.'

I expect U Bossu was angry and didn't give them the best, or serve them with the respect they wanted. There was some quarrel over the zabaglione and Roald refused to eat it. Then there was a row during which Roald called him a prick. Whereat an English spinster at a nearby table turned to Roald and in haughty tones exclaimed: 'You're disgusting! I'm ashamed to belong to the same nation as you!' The bill was paid and they left hastily.

The philosopher Bob's comment as we left: 'Can't you just imagine the battles that go on in *that* bedroom!'

In Somma

This is the expression meaning, roughly, to sum up, that foreigners not too sure of their Italian are apt to use to gain time while thinking of the next word or phrase.

It is difficult to sum up my half-century of Sicilian life. The experience has been so rich and varied. 'Casa Cuseni is like a river,' once exclaimed a teenage guest as she saw numbers arriving and leaving. They have come from twenty-six countries all over the world, with friends introducing their friends. Around Brangwyn's round table I have mixed people who in normal life would be unlikely to meet, or if they did so would be unlikely to fraternize: highbrow and lowbrow, left and right, U and non-U, black and white, British and American (divided by a common language). I have even tried to persuade northern Italians to appreciate their, quite wrongly, despised fellow citizens from the south. Only once or twice has the magic not worked. 'Nice bunch of Communists *you've* got there,' once declared an ignorant American. There wasn't a Communist among them, but there was a diplomat aptly described by an Australian historian as 'an American who in fair weather and foul was always honest about China'. In Chungking he had made friends with Chou En-Lai and Teilhard de Chardin. He was just one of the friends from whom I have learned so much.

During my fifty years in Sicily I have seen a major revolution slowly take place. Above all it affects women. Not only do women now wear trousers, but more importantly, women now drive cars to the great convenience of their menfolk. I am no longer the only one.

The progress of women in the professions is perhaps the most striking development. There are now women physicians, surgeons, architects, lawyers, judges, ministers and courageous fighters against the Mafia. But they are still given the male title of *medico, architetto,* etc. when it would be so simple to substitute a final 'a' in place of the 'o'. Perhaps men have not yet fundamentally accepted the liberation of women brought about principally by improving education, the car, television but, above all, by contraception, which has released them from constant childbearing. In early years I would see swarms of ill-fed and ill-clad children — not in Taormina where the presence and example of foreigners has influenced the birth rate, but elsewhere in the island. Despite the Pope, Italy now has the lowest birth rate in Europe and this is clearly seen as one journeys about the island.

Modern problems are different: unemployment and drugs. The Mafia takes rich pickings from both, offering a tariff of rewards to the workless — so much for a murder, so much for trafficking and so on. Also sad is teenage pregnancy among the less chaperoned girls; even in Taormina girls of fourteen, no longer rigidly controlled, become pregnant. It is distressing to see so much smoking among the young of both sexes; despite all the warnings the girls are as addicted to smoking as the boys, showing their liberation from the past. Their behaviour on the innumerable *motorini* with no helmets, despite the Road Code, passing to right and to left at high speed, seems to indicaate that they still live for the present moment of pleasure with no thought for the future. Perhaps in an island of sudden and great disasters — earthquakes, eruptions, tidal waves and abrupt destructive winds — this is understandable.

Meanwhile, problems have left me continually on my toes. They haven't swamped me all at once but have revealed themselves one by one so that I've usually had time to consider and then cope.

I have missed England, where I go for two months every year to escape excessive Sicilian heat and for theatres, cinemas, concerts and the far, far superior broadcasting. But my family and friends I have not missed. Sooner or later they all come to stay; generations have mixed, cousins have met. I see far more of them than I would at single meals, the ration of most aunts and great-aunts. At Casa Cuseni we have days or weeks together.

I think two traits in my character have led me to a life in Sicily; first, I am a bit of a maverick and should have hated a regular existence, with each tomorrow predictable. Secondly, I have always had a strong feeling for place. One of my earliest memories is of myself sitting on a sunk fence, legs dangling over the side in a posture of utter misery. My grandmother had just told me that she was no longer able to live in the house in Yorkshire I so adored. It had to be sold. Never again would I play in that vast rookery, pick peaches in the peachery or grapes in the vinery, or sleep in that romantic tower. Later it was to become a dream that perhaps one day I should live in a place I should love as much. Casa Cuseni improbably became that place.

Never have I tired of the ever-changing beauty of the garden, or of the dignity and perfect proportions of the house built in golden stone. And that view . . . To live opposite Etna, the highest, most active volcano in Europe, is indeed a privilege. A queen and a spitfire, I feel she is essentially feminine. I can watch her from my bed without lifting my head from my pillow and have come to know her in all her moods. The exquisite, snow-covered mountain rising out of the clouds, seemingly so remote and unearthly, can suddenly be transformed into a menacing monster, hurling fire and rocks thousands of metres into the sky, followed by a great river of molten, flaming lava, kilometres long, slashing the mountain in two. All accompanied by a continuous rumble interrupted by booming explosions that have been likened to an enraged bull imprisoned deep in the earth. If the wind is our way this can be heard in Casa Cuseni over fifteen kilometres away as the crow flies. But the house is never in danger, there are too many hills and valleys in between. Lava cannot flow uphill, although on its way down, when it meets an obstacle — a house, a hillock, a road — it will slowly pile up and up, then, having devoured it, will fall precipitously on the farther side, continuing its merciless destruction of orchards, villages and livelihoods. Fortunately efforts can now be made to deflect the flow from villages and our anxiety for the victims is somewhat lessened.

I have been up to the central crater, but was not allowed to peer over the edge — Etna can be unpredictable in her rages. 'She once ate eleven people who took liberties,' Turiddu had warned me. In a Dantesque scene I have seen eight black-cassocked and shovel-hatted priests outlined against a gigantic Niagara of fire.

But it has been the warmth of Sicilian affection and the beauty of Casa Cuseni that have bound me to the place just as, nearly a century ago, they bound my uncle.

The employees of Thorndike Press hope you have enjoyed this Large Print book. All our Large Print titles are designed for easy reading, and all our books are made to last. Other Thorndike Press Large Print books are available at your library, through selected bookstores, or directly from us.

For information about titles, please call:

(800) 257-5157

To share your comments, please write:

Publisher
Thorndike Press
P.O. Box 159
Thorndike, Maine 04986